CW00518576

14·12·84

Reading Gronow is like drinking champagne—effervescent and mildly addictive.

PREMIÈRES DANSEUSES AND THEIR ADMIRERS―THE GREEN ROOM OF THE OPERA HOUSE (KINGS THEATRE) 1822.

EARL OF FIFE.
BALL HUGHES.   MDLLE. MERCANDOTTI   MDLLE NOBLET.   LORD PETERSHAM.
                                                 PRINCE V. ESTERHAZY.   MDLLE. HULLIN.

THE REMINISCENCES OF CAPTAIN GRONOW, II.

In this final volume of Gronow's Reminiscences we meet again many old friends—Byron and Brummel, the Duke, the outrageous Dan Mackinnon, the habitués of Almacks and the army of the Peninsula. There are amusing descriptions of life in Paris, French manners and French cooking ("It suits the French; but it would never do in England.") and he gives a first hand account of the coup d'état of 1851. He returns often to his favourite themes of the Napoleonic wars and Regency London and there is a full supporting cast, drawn both from the beau monde and the demi-monde, of emperors, actresses, dandies, lunatics, etc, including some "shocking bad hats".

Repeat the prescription—a Gronow anecdote after lunch, two before dinner and not more than six or seven at bed-time.

The R.S. Surtees Society intends to publish in a single volume Gronow's "Celebrities of London and Paris" and "Last Recollections".

The second volume will also be based on the limited edition of 1889 and will be uniform in size and format with the present volume. It will include the 12 full-page coloured plates of the 1889 edition.

The Society's edition will be available by the end of September, 1985.

Pre-publication prices

For those who subscribe **before 31st May, 1985,** the prices will be:

(a) **£11.50** per copy for books which are collected from J.A. Allen & Co., 1 Grosvenor Place, Buckingham Palace Road, London S.W.1 (subscribers collecting their books will be notified when they are available), and

(b) **£13.50** per copy for books which are posted, the price including packing and postage.

The post-publication price will be substantially higher.

A list of those subscribing before 31st May, 1985, will be printed at the end of the book.

Minimum of pre-publication subscribers and ordering

A minimum of 1500 subscribers must be obtained by 31st May, 1985. All cheques will be acknowledged. All pre-publication money will be kept in a separate *Gronow* bank account and will be returned in the event of publication not going ahead.

A leaflet, which includes an order form, has been enclosed. If no order form is available, write to **the Hon. Mrs. Robert Pomeroy, R.S. Surtees Society, Rockfield House, Nunney, Nr. Frome, Somerset.** Your order should be accompanied by a cheque for the appropriate amount, made payable to the R.S. Surtees Society. Please show your name and address clearly.

Illustrations

Complete sets of the full-page illustrations mentioned above will be available at the end of November, 1985. These are offered at £5 a set, packing and postage included.

"Ecce iterum Crispinus"
Here's old Jorrocks again!
—Free Translation

HILLINGDON HALL

OR

THE COCKNEY SQUIRE

"IT'S SIR ROBERT PEEL'S GRAND BOOLE!"

Jorrocks becomes a squire, a scientific farmer and a Justice of the Peace. He tells his tenants and neighbours they are "a long way behind the intelligence o' the day".

Hillingdon Hall is the last of the Jorrocks books. It deserves to be much better known. Surtees mocks pseudo-scientific farming, his fellow J.P.s, complacent Whig noblemen (the then Duke of Northumberland, according to John Welcome, instantly struck the Surtees family off his invitation list), the wearing of the kilt ("jest one of Walter Scott's wagaries") and an unintended *double-entendre* in Sir Robert Peel's Agricultural Speech at Tamworth.

James Pigg rescues Jorrocks from his farming difficulties and William Bowker, now an unscrupulous agent of the Anti-Corn Law League, betrays a confidence from the Duke of Donkeyton so that a contested election at Sellborough is inevitable. Jorrocks, a Whig when he arrived at Hillingdon Hall, becomes the farmer's friend and the Anti-Repeal candidate.

With his triumph at the poll Jorrocks leaves us. Surtees, alas, did not record his subsequent career.

The R.S. Surtees Society's edition will be available by the end of March, 1985. It will contain 13 full-page coloured plates, including reproductions of the 7 plates by Wildrake and Heath which accompanied the serialisation in *The New Sporting Magazine* in 1843–44. The text will be a facsimile of the 1888 edition, known as "the first octavo illustrated edition".

The cover will have the same pictorial stampings as the 1888 edition. In size and format *Hillingdon Hall* will be similar to the Society's earlier Surtees publications. **Lord Blake,** Provost of the Queen's College, Oxford, has written an Introduction.

Pre-Publication Prices
For those who subscribe **before 28th February, 1985.**

(a) **£10.75** per copy for books which are collected from J.A. Allen & Co., 1 Grosvenor Place, London, S.W.1 (subscribers collecting books will be notified when they are available), and

(b) **£12.70** per copy for books which are posted, the price including packaging and postage.

The post-publication price will be substantially higher.

Members of the Society are entitled to a discount of £1 per copy from whichever of the prices mentioned above is applicable.

Subscribers may choose cut or uncut pages, the price in either case being the same.

Ordering
All cheques will be acknowledged. All pre-publication money will be kept in a separate *Hillingdon* bank account and will be returned in the event of publication not going ahead.

A leaflet, which includes an order form, has been enclosed. If no order form is available, write to **the Hon. Mrs. Robert Pomeroy, R.S. Surtees Society, Rockfield House, Nunney, Nr. Frome, Somerset.** Your order should be accompanied by a cheque for the appropriate amount, made payable to the R.S. Surtees Society. Please show your name and address clearly.

Hillingdon Hall illustrations
Complete sets of the 13 full-page illustrations mentioned above will be available at the end of March, 1985. These are offered at £5 a set, packing and postage included.

Other R.S. Surtees novels
Mr. Sponge's Sporting Tour, Mr. Facey Romford's Hounds, "Ask Mamma", Handley Cross and Jorrocks' Jaunts and Jollities are still available. See the Advertisements at the end of this book.

REMINISCENCES

OF

CAPTAIN GRONOW

VOLUME THE FIRST

Engraved by J. C. Armytage from a Miniature

THE

Reminiscences and Recollections

OF

CAPTAIN GRONOW

BEING

"Anecdotes of the Camp, the Court and the

Clubs at the close of the last war with France"

and

"Recollections and Anecdotes"

THE R.S. SURTEES SOCIETY

First published in this edition in 1984
by The R.S. Surtees Society
Rockfield House
Nunney
Nr. Frome, Somerset.
© This edition and compilation, The R.S. Surtees
Society 1984.

ISBN 0 9507697 7 0

Printed and bound in Great Britain by
Butler & Tanner Ltd, Frome and London

CONTENTS.

—⊷—

CONTENTS.

CONTENTS.

LIST OF ILLUSTRATIONS,

NEWLY ETCHED FROM ORIGINAL AND CONTEMPORARY DESIGNS BY JOSEPH GREGO.

VOLUME THE FIRST.

PUBLISHER'S PREFACE
TO THE 1889 EDITION

——+——

THE four portrait-groups of notabilities familiarly recognised at the date of the author's early career —which appeared in Captain Gronow's First Series of " Reminiscences," were welcomed as greatly increasing the interest of his social sketches, and the publisher of the present volumes felt that an edition illustrated throughout would be acceptable to the public. The four engravings on wood executed for the initial series have been retained, and the fifth, from a contemporary study in the possession of Captain Gronow, has been re-engraved. The portrait of the author is from a miniature by J. C. Armytage.

The task of illustrating this new edition has been entrusted to Joseph Grego, and, while no attempt has been made to produce what might be entitled original designs, the plan adopted in the above five original illustrations has been carried out on a more comprehensive scale, and all the new subjects are drawn from authentic contemporary sources, and

from pictures which have a direct reference to
the text.

As Captain Gronow's "Reminiscences" deal largely
with eccentric personages, odd celebrities and incidents somewhat out of the common order, it has
been considered in keeping to select portraits and
subjects which are strongly characterised, though
not precisely caricatures.

The larger portion of these illustrations refer to
the early part of the century, and, as an endeavour
to preserve consistency, the twenty additional plates
etched by Joseph Grego throughout, are finished in
aquatint, an art which flourished at the period in
question, and was much in favour for book illustrations.

The art of aquatinting, described by the French
as " the washed manner," once esteemed a felicitous
method of imitating shaded drawings — has now
become almost extinct as originally practised ; Mr.
Grego has been fortunate in securing the assistance
of an artist who for more than half a century has
devoted himself to the development of this branch
of art.

Captain Gronow's " Reminiscences " have become
standard authorities, but owing to the absence of
indices to the original series, it has been found a
difficult and inconvenient labour to readily alight
upon passages or names required for immediate
reference or quotation ; to remedy this manifest

defect, an exhaustive index, containing several thousand references, has been supplied to each volume.

As regards the text, beyond the correction of French passages and phrases which were incorrectly printed in the earlier editions, no attempt has been made to re-edit the work ; it was considered judicious that the author should be left to speak for himself, it being evident to the reader that the later references—to events then current, and to personages then in the flesh but since deceased —apply to the years 1862 to 1866, when the four successive volumes were first introduced to the public.

INTRODUCTORY CHAPTER.

CONCERNING CAPTAIN GRONOW AND HIS RECOLLECTIONS.

O friends regretted, scenes for ever dear !
Remembrance hails you with her warmest tear !
Drooping she bends o'er pensive fancy's urn,
To trace the hours which never can return.

THESE lines, which appear on the title-page of Captain Gronow's first series of "Reminiscences and Anecdotes," epitomise the sentimental aspect of his recollections. For half a century it was the fortune of the narrator to be thrown into contact with the notabilities and notabilia of London and Paris. A pronounced taste for fashionable society, an early introduction to the best circles, the advantage of possessing an extensive acquaintanceship with the most conspicuous celebrities of his day, an omnivorous appetite for racy anecdotes, a retentive memory, which, without effort, gathered and stored up the literary waifs and strays—the conversational "small change" which passed current in his generation — were in themselves elements sufficient to qualify the gallant captain as an exceptionally entertaining *raconteur*. After detailing his piquant store of anecdotes to his contemporaries for a couple of generations, Captain Gronow was

induced to take up his pen, and commit to
print an experimental instalment of the incidents with which he had hitherto regaled his
friends *vivâ voce*, with light rapid touch, and in
a brisk unaffected style which preserves the point
of lively converse. The brilliant traditions of the
town, the superficial characteristics of a period
which presented salient traits of individuality—
when manners and morals were less restricted
than in our day—are dexterously handled, and the
ready easy flowing record is directed by the instinct
of a fine gentleman. " How these estimable pro-
genitors of ours dressed, drank, swore, fought,
gambled and beggared their unhappy descendants,"
an oft-told tale, acquires a fresh interest in these
varied glimpses of a once bustling and motley
Vanity Fair—the booths of which have long since
departed, and many of the actors therein seem
almost as distant from our time as those described
by John Bunyan himself.

Captain Gronow modestly observes his "Reminiscences" are merely fragmental and miniature illustrations of contemporary history, and, in the eyes
of posterity, it is this circumstance which gives
value to his anecdotes ; the subjects recorded by
his pen are, of necessity, for the most part outside
the province of graver historians or more serious
biographers, and are precisely those familiar sketches
which fill in realistic details, and supply the essen-
tials of local colour.

The First Series appeared in 1862, and met with a flattering reception. The writer, as he averred, was able to recall, with all their original vividness, scenes which occurred in his early days, nature having endowed him with the retentive faculty of "distinctly recollecting the face, walk, and voice, as well as the dress and general manner of every one whom he had known."

It had been the lot of Captain Gronow, as he informed his readers, "to have lived through the greater part of one of the most eventful centuries of England's history; to be thrown amongst most of the remarkable men of his day, whether soldiers, statesmen, men of letters, theatrical people, or those whose birth and fortune—rather, perhaps, than their virtues and talents, have caused them to be conspicuous at home and abroad." The writer, from motives of delicacy, omitted much which,—though lively and interesting even beyond what he has left us, —he thought it expedient to withhold from publication, no less from respect to the memory of the dead, than out of consideration for the sensibilities of the living. In the pictures which hung in the long gallery of his memory, Captain Gronow thought proper to "confine himself to facts and characteristics which were familiar to the circles in which he lived, and perhaps are as much public property as the painted portraits of celebrities." The reviewers pronounced the writer's manner possessed "the merit of a sensible man of the world's freedom from egotism." Captain Gronow was deferentially apologetic as to possible defects of style, due to inexperience, merely claiming to have jotted down the anecdotes "in the best way he could." He wrote, "Soldiers are not generally famous for literary excellence, and when I was young, the military man was, perhaps, much less a scholar than he is at the present day."

The initial Series,—"Anecdotes of the Camp, the Court, and the Clubs, at the close of the last war with France"—was indulgently received beyond the expectations of the writer, and Captain Gronow was encouraged to redeem a conditional promise that, if his work met with the approbation of the public, he hoped to publish, from the materials stored in his memory, a further repertory of similar nature. A Second Series of Reminiscences appeared in 1863, particularly dealing with the events of 1815, and that momentous struggle of which the writer was not only an eye-witness, but also bore the dangers of the day with his comrades of the Guards: "Though the battle of Waterloo is almost a hackneyed subject, yet it has been latterly so frequently brought forward by French writers of celebrity, that I have thought some further observations might not prove altogether without interest." This paragraph refers more immediately to the works of M. Thiers, Colonel Charras, Quinet's Defence of Marshal Ney, and Victor Hugo's romance of "Les Miserables."

In his brief preface to the Second Series of "Recollections and Anecdotes," Captain Gronow, with excellent taste, begs the indulgence of his readers for the occasional introduction of sentences in foreign idioms, unavoidable under the circumstances, where no English equivalents are available, and the spirit of the original would be sacrificed by a vernacular rendering. "I must conclude with an apology for having introduced French and Italian words and phrases into an English book; but the fact is, that though our language is a far richer one than at least the French, there are certain words that cannot be rendered into their exact corresponding meaning by translation, and consequently the point of many jokes and clever sayings would be entirely lost."

The third series of Captain Gronow's "Recollections," which appeared in 1865, was devoted to "Celebrities of London and Paris," and, amongst the special features, the writer, as an eye-witness, detailed his experiences of the "Coup d'État," which, according to his convictions, restored prosperity and power to France; the imperial dynasty had his sympathy, and as he did not live to see the defects of the third Empire and the sudden downfall of Napoleon III., his reminiscences naturally refer to that sovereign as the ruler of the French nation. Concerning his notes upon the high-handed movement which placed Napoleon III. upon the throne, the writer assures his readers that the accuracy of his statements may be relied upon, since he had not entirely trusted to his own memory, but had taken the precaution of verifying every circumstance by reference to contemporary living authorities.

The unpretentious preface to the Third Series is characteristic of the author—"As in conversational groups one story suggests another, some modest anecdotes may become the parents of a numerous progeny, though the offspring may not prove equally interesting or amusing, and some may even be born lame ; so this Third volume of my 'Recollections' is to be attributed to the conversational philoprogenitiveness of friendly gossip. I cannot help feeling that, amongst my numerous anecdotal progeny, there may be some abortions ; for it often happens that what is interesting or amusing to ourselves from association, fails to amuse others, and I may have noted down reminiscences unworthy of record. But it appears to me that I am very much in the position of some *raconteur* in society whom a friendly party is bent upon making talk on."

Captain Gronow lived to prepare a Fourth and concluding Series of "Reminiscences and Anecdotes," and, while the proofs of the volume were in the hands of the writer for final revision, there came the unexpected news of his death, which occurred in Paris, 20th November 1865 ; the work was issued in 1866 as "Captain Gronow's Last Recollections." As with the premonition of his own approaching end, the author mournfully wrote :—

"I have lived long enough to have lost all my

dearest and best friends. The great laws of humanity have left me on a high and dry elevation, from which I am doomed to look over a sort of Necropolis, whence it is my delight to call forth choice spirits of the past."

The professional career and subsequent life of Captain Gronow are fairly and sufficiently chronicled incidentally in the pages of his personal recollections. "Nothing extenuate nor set down aught in malice," the principle he meted out to others, should justly be his right. He was apparently a favoured child of fortune, was presented with a commission in the Grenadier Guards on leaving Eton—in the stirring days of the Peninsular war the youth of England early received its "baptism of fire"—and from the age of sixteen, Gronow mixed freely with that select community emphatically described as "the world"—otherwise the favoured portion of society. He joyfully accepted and with keen enjoyment took his part in fashionable life with characteristic complacency and nonchalance; from early days appreciating to the full all that life could offer to a "dandy guardsman"—the excitement of campaigning, a well-filled purse, social gaiety, congenial associates— "fair women and brave men," with, for a season, a seat in the first Reformed Parliament. It may be interesting to note that,— to account for certain mysterious but unauthenticated rumours of distinguished and even royal patronage—characteristic of the young guardsman's generation,—the family of Captain Gronow claimed royal descent. He was the son of William Gronow of Court Herbert. On the authority of Sir Bernard Burke ("Landed Gentry"), the Gronows were a very ancient family originally seated in North Wales, where they had large landed possessions.

In the reign of Edward III., Sir Tudor ap Gronow, an ancestor of the regal house of Tudor, claimed the honour of knighthood, for by the laws and constitution of King Arthur, he deemed himself entitled to that distinction upon the ground of possessing the following threefold qualifications— birth, estate, and valour. King Edward III., being pleased with the bold and lordly mien of Sir Tudor ap Gronow, was induced to confer the honour upon him. Owen Tudor, the grandson of this bold knight, married the widow of Henry V., and their son Jasper Tudor, Earl of Richmond, was the father of Henry VII.

Being thus regally connected, the family 'scutcheon bears in its quarterings the lions of England.

In the choir of St. David's Cathedral there remain two recumbent effigies in armour, representing two members of this family. On the breast and back of each figure is sculptured a lion rampant, that in one of them being differenced by a label.

The writer passed so much of his life in Paris, and has drawn such animated pictures of French society, that it is amusing,—as a contrast to his own impressions of Parisian celebrities,—to learn the opinions of a foreign contemporary upon Captain Gronow, and this we are enabled to do from the pages of M. H. de Villemessant's "Memoirs of a Journalist," * published in 1872.

"Mr. Gronow, when I knew him, was small, spare, and about fifty years of age ; his hair was thinning, and he wore a small moustache, of which the edge was daily shaved, which did not disguise the circumstance that the Captain's latent vanity had recourse to a brown dye. He always wore a blue tight-fitting coat, closely buttoned, just allowing a narrow line of white waistcoat to be visible.

"It was customary, in certain circles, to lay wagers that he slept with the top of his gold-headed cane between his lips. This action was characteristic. With the head of his well-known stick pressed to his lips, the Captain spent his days, seated at the window, watching every one he knew in Paris pass the 'Petit Cercle,' of which he was one of the founders, and where the latter part of his life was spent. This 'Cercle' was a small and select Club, occupying a suite of rooms in the 'Café de Paris' on the boulevard des Italiens.

"He was very 'good form,' had a great respect for everything that was proper and convenient, and a strong propensity to become eccentric. He committed the greatest follies, without in the slightest disturbing the points of his shirt collar. He had married a lady of the 'corps de ballet,'

---

* H. de Villemessant, "*Memoires d'un Journaliste.* 1ere *Série,* ch. ix. 1872.

and would rather have blown out his brains than have gone to the opera in morning costume.

"This little man, with his hair well arranged, scented, cold, and phlegmatic, knew the best people in Paris, visited all the diplomats, and was evidently intimate with everybody of note in Europe."

A natural reserve, which prevented Gronow from enlarging, amongst comparative strangers, upon his family connections, led, in the minds of slight acquaintances who had no better information on the subject, to vague and romantic surmises as to his origin; opinion wavered between the assumption that the Captain was the descendant of a race of wealthy retired brewers, and the more popular hypothesis, that he was the illegitimate son of an exalted personage. It was rumoured that his mother had been very intimate with Mrs. Jordan, and that it was due to this influence that young Gronow had obtained a company in the Grenadier Guards at the outset of his career. These imaginary antecedents must be dismissed as the fabrications of ignorant gossip; the French writer merely recorded the irresponsible tittle-tattle floating on the surface, and he moreover seems to have confused his remembrances of the Captain with certain episodes related in Gronow's own "Recollections;" a certain Captain Hesse, a putative son of the Duke of York, was probably the actual hero of the following apocryphal anecdote M. de Villemessant relates :—

" Gronow was one of the prettiest dandy officers of proud Albion, and for years his miniature portrait was secretly carried about by a great princess who was madly in love with him, and sometimes, when a fashionable beauty was passing, he was observed carelessly opening the red morocco case in which he found again the souvenirs of his youth and his successes; then he sighed and shut it again. This was the only proof of sensibility he ever gave." On the same authority, ' classical ' and ' thorough-bred ' were the two words with which the subject of these curious revelations expressed his admiration for female beauty. "The princess must have spent some very happy moments," writes the journalist. " Gronow belonged to the school of ' silent diplomatists,' which implies that he said a great deal, and spoke diffusely whenever he made up his mind to unburden himself."

The " Memoirs " continue: "He was fond of English literature, and though he had not much sympathy with the character and politics of Lord Byron, Gronow greatly valued him as a poet. This little man, who had a face like marble, felt very deeply, a contrast not altogether exceptional.

"Perhaps he had been obliged to conceal his feelings, the better to baffle prying looks when he was not kneeling at the feet of his princess (still that fair personage of Fairyland!) and he had never been able to throw off the mask. But when he was extolling the sombre and impressive creations of

Byron no one could doubt that passion had formerly dwelt in the heart of this man of past experiences.

"With genuine enthusiasm he analysed the tempests which must have raged in the souls of the heroes of his favourite poet, of *The Giaour*, *The Corsair*, and above all of *Lara*, whom he claimed to have known, for, if Gronow may be credited, *Lara* and *Manfred* really existed, and their living prototype was the once well-known Captain Trelawney, who became very intimate with Lord Byron in Greece. Gronow related certain of Trelawney's adventures without hesitation—sometimes in an impassioned tone of voice, but (according to habit) without ever ceasing to rub his chin with the handle of his stick. And when his auditors inquired 'what subsequently became of this hero of romance?' he replied: 'I don't know. Trelawney now eats pudding in England, and does not care for us!'" Much has been written elsewhere upon the subject of Trelawney as a Byronic hero, but according to Gronow's own recollections, "the noble bard could never write a poem or drama without making himself its hero."

The above description of our author is given on its merits; in any case it is somewhat entertaining. In conclusion, it is interesting to learn from authoritative sources that, while Captain Gronow's latter years were occupied in recording these reminiscences, they were cheered by the society of his wife and family.

CAPTAIN GRONOW'S
RECOLLECTIONS AND ANECDOTES.

My Entrance into the Army.—After leaving
Eton, I received an Ensign's commission in the
First Guards, during the month of December 1812.
Though many years have elapsed, I still remember
my boyish delight at being named to so distinguished
a regiment, and at the prospect of soon taking a
part in the glorious deeds of our army in Spain. I
joined in February 1813, and cannot but recollect
with astonishment how limited and imperfect was
the instruction which an officer received at that
time; he absolutely entered the army without any
military education whatever. We were so defective
in our drill, even after we had passed out of the
hands of the sergeant, that the excellence of our
non-commissioned officers alone prevented us from
meeting with the most fatal disasters in the face of
the enemy. Physical force and our bull-dog energy
carried many a hard-fought field. Luckily, *nous
avons changé tout cela,* and our officers may now
vie with those of any other army in an age when
the great improvements in musketry, in artillery
practice, and in the greater rapidity of manœuvring,

have entirely changed the art of war, and rendered the individual education of those in every grade of command an absolute necessity.

After passing through the hands of the drill sergeant with my friends Dashwood, Batty, Browne, Lascelles, Hume, and Master, and mounting guard at St. James's for a few months, we were hurried off, one fine morning, in charge of a splendid detachment of five hundred men to join Lord Wellington in Spain. Macadam had just begun to do for England what Marshal Wade did in Scotland seventy years before; and we were able to march twenty miles a day with ease until we reached Portsmouth. There we found transports ready to convey a large reinforcement, of which we formed part, to Lord Wellington, who was now making his arrangements, after taking St. Sebastian, for a yet more important event in the history of the Peninsular War—the invasion of France.

DEPARTURE FOR AND ARRIVAL IN SPAIN.—We sailed under convoy of the *Madagascar* frigate, commanded by Captain Curtis; and, after a favourable voyage, we arrived at Passages. Our stay there was short, for we were ordered to join the army without loss of time. In three hours we got fairly into camp, where we were received with loud cheers by our brothers in arms.

The whole British army was here under canvas; our allies, the Spaniards and Portuguese, being in the rear. About the middle of October, to our great delight, the army received orders to cross the Bidassoa. At three o'clock on the morning of the 15th our regiment advanced through a difficult country, and, after a harassing march, reached the top of a hill as the grey light of morning began to dawn. We marched in profound silence, but with a pleasurable feeling of excitement amongst all ranks at the thought of meeting the enemy, and perhaps with not an equally agreeable idea that we might be in the next world before the day was over.

As we ascended the rugged side of the hill, I saw, for the first time, the immortal Wellington. He was accompanied by the Spanish General, Alava, Lord Fitzroy Somerset, and Major, afterwards Colonel Freemantle. He was very stern and grave-looking; he was in deep meditation, so long as I kept him in view, and spoke to no one. His features were bold, and I saw much decision of character in his expression. He rode a knowing-looking, thorough-bred horse, and wore a grey overcoat, Hessian boots, and a large cocked hat.

We commenced the passage of the Bidassoa about five in the morning, and in a short time infantry, cavalry, and artillery found themselves upon French ground. The stream at the point we forded was nearly four feet deep, and had Soult been aware of what we were about, we should have found the passage of the river a very arduous undertaking.

Three miles above, we discovered the French army, and ere long found ourselves under fire. The sensation of being made a target to a large body of men is at first not particularly pleasant, but, " in a trice, the ear becomes more Irish, and less nice." The first man I ever saw killed was a Spanish soldier, who was cut in two by a cannon ball. The French army, not long after we began to return their fire, was in full retreat; and after a little sharp, but desultory fighting, in which our Division met with some loss, we took possession of the camp and strong position of Soult's army. We found the soldiers' huts very comfortable; they were built of branches of trees and furze, and formed squares and streets, which had names placarded up, such as Rue de Paris, Rue de Versailles, &c. We were not sorry to find ourselves in such commodious quarters, as well as being well housed. The scenery surrounding the camp was picturesque and grand. From our elevated position, immediately in front, we commanded a wide and extensive plain, intersected by two important rivers, the Nive and the Nivelle. On the right, the lofty Pyrenees, with their grand and varied outline, stood forth conspicuously in a blue, cloudless sky; on our left was the Bay of Biscay, with our cruisers perpetually on the move.

We witnessed from the camp, one night about twelve o'clock, a fight at sea, between an English brig and a French corvette, which was leaving the Adour with provisions and ammunition. She was chased by the brig, and brought to action. The night was sufficiently clear to enable us to discover distinctly the position of the vessels and the measured flash of their guns. They were at close quarters; and in less than half an hour we discovered the crew of the corvette taking to their boats. Shortly afterwards the vessel blew up, with a loud explosion. We came to the conclusion that sea-fighting was more agreeable than land-fighting, as the crews of the vessels engaged without previous heavy marching, and with loose light clothing; there was no manœuvring, or standing for hours on the defensive; the wounded were immediately

taken below and attended to ; and the whole affair
was over in a pleasingly brief period.

THE UNIFORM AND BEARING OF THE FRENCH
SOLDIER.—The French infantry soldier averaged
about five feet five or six in height ; in build they
were much about what they are now, perhaps a
little broader over the shoulder. They were smart,
active, handy fellows, and much more able to look
after their personal comforts than British soldiers,
as their camps indicated. The uniform of those
days consisted in a shako, which spread out at the
top ; a short-waisted, swallow-tailed coat ; and large,
baggy trousers and gaiters. The clothing of the
French soldier was roomy, and enabled him to
march and move about at ease : no pipeclay acces-
sories occupied their attention ; in a word, their
uniforms and accoutrements were infinitely superior to our own, taking into consideration the practical necessities of warfare. Their muskets were
inferior to ours, and their firing less deadly. The
French cavalry we thought badly horsed ; but their
uniforms, though showy, were, like those of the
infantry, comfortably large and roomy.

I have frequently remarked that firearms are of
little use to the mounted soldier, and often an in-
cumbrance to man and horse. Cavalry want only
one arm—the sabre. Let the men be well mounted,
and at home in the saddle. It requires great knowledge in a Commander-in-Chief to know when and
how to use his cavalry. It has been my misfortune
to witness oft-repeated blunders in the employment
of the best-mounted regiments in the world. I consider the French generals had more knowledge of

the use of cavalry than our own when a great battle
was to be fought.

MAJOR-GENERAL STEWART AND LORD WELLING-
TON.—If the present generation of Englishmen
would take the trouble of looking at the newspaper which fifty years ago informed the British
public of passing events both at home and abroad,
they would, doubtless, marvel at the very limited
and imperfect amount of intelligence which the
best journals were enabled to place before their
readers. The progress of the Peninsular campaign
was very imperfectly chronicled; it will, therefore, be easily imagined what interest was attached
to certain letters that appeared in the *Morning
Chronicle* which criticised with much severity,
and frequently with considerable injustice, the
military movements of Lord Wellington's Spanish
campaigns.

The attention of the Commander-in-Chief being
drawn to these periodical and personal comments
on his conduct of the war, his lordship at once perceived, from the information which they contained,
that they must have been written by an officer holding a high command under him. Determined to
ascertain the author—who, in addressing a public
journal, was violating the Articles of War, and, it
might be, assisting the enemy—means were employed in London to identify the writer. The result
was that Lord Wellington discovered the author of
the letters to be no other than Sir Charles Stewart,
the late Lord Londonderry. As soon as Lord Wellington had made himself master of this fact, he
summoned Sir Charles Stewart to headquarters at

Torres Vedras; and, on his appearance, he, without the least preface, addressed him thus :—

"Charles Stewart, I have ascertained with deep regret that you are the author of the letters which appeared in the *Morning Chronicle*, abusing me and finding fault with my military plans."

Lord Wellington here paused for a moment, and then continued :—

"Now, Stewart, you know your brother Castlereagh is my best friend, to whom I owe everything; nevertheless, if you continue to write letters to the *Chronicle*, or any other newspaper, by God, I will send you home."

Sir Charles Stewart was so affected at this rebuke that he shed tears, and expressed himself deeply penitent for the breach of confidence and want of respect for the Articles of War. They immediately shook hands and parted friends. It happened, however, that Sir Charles Stewart did not remain long in the cavalry, of which he was Adjutant-General. Within a few weeks he was named one of the Commissioners deputed to proceed to the Allied Armies, where the Sovereigns were then completing their plans to crush Napoleon.

ST. JEAN DE LUZ.—During the winter of 1813, the Guards were stationed with headquarters at St. Jean de Luz, and most comfortable we managed to make them. For some short time previously we had been on scanty commons, and had undergone considerable privation: indeed we might have said, like the Colonel to Johnny Newcome on his arrival to join his regiment, "We sons of Mars have long been fed on brandy and cigars." I had no cause to complain personally; for my servant, a Sicilian, was one of the most accomplished foragers (ill-natured persons might give him a worse name) in the whole army; and when others were nearly starving, he always managed to provide meat or poultry. He rode on his mule sometimes from twenty to thirty miles, often running the greatest dangers, to procure me a good meal; of which he took care to have, very justly, a large share for himself.

At St. Jean de Luz, we were more attentive to our devotions than we had been for some time. Divine service was performed punctually every Sunday on the sand-hills near the town; Lord Wellington and his numerous Staff placed themselves in the midst of our square, and his lordship's chaplain read the service, to which Lord Wellington always appeared to listen with great attention.

The mayor of the town, thinking to please "the great English lord," gave a ball at the Hôtel de Ville : our Commander-in-Chief did not go, but was represented by Waters. I was there, and expected to see some of the young ladies of the country, so famed for their beauty; they were, however, far too patriotic to appear, and the only lady present was Lady Waldegrave, then living with her husband at headquarters. What was one partner among so many? The ball was a dead failure, in spite of the efforts of the mayor, who danced, to our intense amusement, an English hornpipe, which he had learnt in not a very agreeable manner, viz., when a prisoner of war in the hulks at Plymouth.

There were two packs of hounds at St. Jean de Luz; one kept by Lord Wellington, the other by Marsden, of the Commissariat: our officers went uncommonly straight. Perhaps our best man across country (though sometimes somewhat against his will) was the late Colonel Lascelles of my regiment, then, like myself, a mere lad. He rode a horse seventeen hands high, called Bucephalus, which invariably ran away with him, and more than once had nearly capsized Lord Wellington. The good living at St. Jean de Luz agreed so well with my friend that he waxed fat, and from that period to his death was known to the world by the jovial appellation of Bacchus Lascelles.

Shortly before we left St. Jean de Luz, we took our turn of outposts in the neighbourhood of Bidart, a large village, about ten miles from Bayonne. Early one frosty morning in December, an order came, that if we saw the enemy advancing, we were not to fire or give the alarm. About five, we perceived two battalions wearing grenadier caps coming on. They turned out to belong to a Nassau regiment which had occupied the advanced post of the enemy, and hearing that Napoleon had met with great reverses in Germany, signified to us their intention to desert. They were a fine-looking body of men, and appeared, I thought, rather ashamed of the step they had taken. On the same day, we were relieved, and on our way back met Lord Wellington with his hounds. He was dressed in a light-blue frock-coat (the colour of the Hatfield hunt) which had been sent out to him as a present from Lady Salisbury, then one of the leaders of the fashionable world, and an enthusiastic admirer of his lordship.

Here I remember seeing for the first time a very remarkable character, the Hon. W. Dawson, of my regiment. He was surrounded by muleteers, with

whom he was bargaining to provide carriage for innumerable hampers of wine, liqueurs, hams, potted
meat, and other good things which he had brought
from England. He was a particularly gentlemanly
and amiable man, much beloved by the regiment :
no one was so hospitable or lived so magnificently.
His cooks were the best in the army, and he, besides
had a host of servants of all nations—Spaniards,
French, Portuguese, Italians—who were employed
in scouring the country for provisions. Lord Wellington once honoured him with his company ; and on
entering the ensign's tent, found him alone at table,
with a dinner fit for a king, his plate and linen in
good keeping, and his wines perfect. Lord Wellington was accompanied on this occasion by Sir Edward
Pakenham and Colonel du Burgh, afterwards Lord
Downes. It fell to my lot to partake of his princely
hospitality, and dine with him at his quarters, a
farmhouse in a village on the Bidassoa, and I never
saw a better dinner put upon table. The career of
this amiable Amphitryon, to our great regret, was
cut short, after exercising for about a year a splendid
but not very wise hospitality. He had only a younger
brother's fortune ; his debts became very considerable, and he was obliged to quit the Guards. He
and his friends had literally eaten up his little
fortune.

FOOLHARDINESS.—I may here recount an instance
of the folly and foolhardiness of youth, and the
recklessness to which a long course of exposure to
danger produces. When Bayonne was invested, I
was one night on duty on the outer picket. The
ground inside the breastwork which had been thrown

up for our protection by Burgoyne was in a most disagreeable state for any one who wished to repose after the fatigues of the day, being knee-deep in mud of a remarkably plastic nature. I was dead tired, and determined to get a little rest in some more agreeable spot; so calling my sergeant, I told him to give me his knapsack for a pillow; I would make a comfortable night of it on the top of the breast-work, as it was an invitingly dry place. "For heaven's sake, take care, sir," said he; "you'll have fifty bullets in you: you will be killed to a certainty." "Pooh, nonsense," said I, and climbing up, I wrapt myself in my cloak, laid my head on the knapsack, and soon fell into a sound sleep.

By the mercy of Providence I remained in a whole skin, either from the French immediately underneath not perceiving me or not thinking me worth a shot; but when General Stopford came up with Lord James Hay (who not long since reminded me of this youthful escapade), I received a severe wigging, and was told to consider myself lucky that I was not put under arrest for exposing my life in so foolish a manner.

Among the many officers of the Guards who were taken prisoners in the unfortunate sortie from Bayonne, was the Hon. H. Townshend, commonly called Bull Townshend. He was celebrated as a *bon vivant*, and in consequence of his too great indulgence in the pleasures of the table, had become very unwieldy, and could not move quick enough to please his nimble captors, so he received many prods in the back from a sharp bayonet. After repeated threats, however, he was dismissed with what our American friends would be pleased to designate "a severe booting." The late Sir Willoughby Cotton was also a prisoner. It really seemed as if the enemy had made choice of our fattest officers. Sir Willoughby escaped by giving up his watch and all the money which he had in his pockets ; but this consisting of a Spanish dollar only, the smallness of the sum subjected him to the same ignominious treatment as had been experienced by Townshend.

Among the numerous bad characters in our ranks, several were coiners, or utterers of bad money. In the second brigade of Guards, just before we arrived at St. Jean de Luz, a soldier was convicted of this offence, and was sentenced to receive 800 lashes. This man made sham Spanish dollars out of the pewter spoons of the regiment. As he had before been convicted and flogged, he received this terrible sentence, and died under the lash. Would it not have been better to have condemned him to be shot ?—It would have been more humane, certainly more military, and far less brutal.

DISCIPLINE.—When the headquarters of the army were at St. Jean de Luz, Soult made a movement in front of our right centre, which the English general took for a reconnaissance. As the French general perceived that we had ordered preparations to receive him, he sent a flag of truce to demand a cessation of hostilities, saying that he wanted to shoot an officer and several men for acts of robbery committed by them, with every sort of atrocity, on the farmers and peasantry of the country. The execution took place in view of both armies, and a terrible lesson it was. I cannot specify the date of this event, but think it must have been the latter end of November 1813. About the same time General Harispe, who commanded a corps of Basques, issued a proclamation forbidding the peasantry to supply the English with provisions or forage, on pain of death ; it stated that we were savages, and, as a proof of this, our horses were born with short tails. I saw this absurd proclamation, which was published in French and in the Basque languages, and distributed all over the country.

Before we left the neighbourhood of Bayonne for Bordeaux, a soldier was hanged for robbery, on the sands of the Adour. This sort of punishment astonished the French almost as much as it did the soldier. On a march we were very severe ; and if any of our men were caught committing an act of violence or brigandage, the offender was tried by a drum-head court-martial, and hanged in a very short time.

I knew an officer of the 18th Hussars, W. R., young, rich, and a fine-looking fellow, who joined the army not far from St. Sebastian. His stud of horses was remarkable for their blood ; his grooms were English, and three in number. He brought with him a light cart to carry forage, and a fourgon for his own baggage. All went on well till he came to go on outpost duty ; but not finding there any of the comforts to which he had been accustomed, he quietly mounted his charger, told his astonished sergeant that campaigning was not intended for a gentleman, and instantly galloped off to his quarters, ordering his servants to pack up everything immediately, as he had hired a transport to take him off to England. He left us before any one had

time to stop him; and though despatches were sent
off to the Commander-in-Chief, requesting that a
court-martial might sit to try the young deserter,
he arrived home long enough before the despatches
to enable him to sell out of his regiment. He
deserved to have been shot.

Sir John Hope, who commanded our *corps d'armée*
at Bayonne, had his quarters at a village on the
Adour, called Beaucauld. He was good enough to
name me to the command of the village; which
honour I did not hold many days, for the famous
sortie from Bayonne took place soon after, and the
general was made prisoner.

SIR JOHN WATERS.—Amongst the distinguished
men in the Peninsular war whom my memory brings
occasionally before me, is the well-known and highly
popular Quartermaster-General Sir John Waters,
who was born at Margam, a Welsh village in Glamorganshire. He was one of those extraordinary
persons that seem created by kind nature for particular purposes; and without using the word in an
offensive sense, he was the most admirable spy that
was ever attached to an army. One would almost
have thought that the Spanish war was entered
upon and carried on in order to display his remarkable qualities. He could assume the character of
Spaniards of every degree and station, so as to
deceive the most acute of those whom he delighted
to imitate. In the posada of the village he was
hailed by the contrabandist or the muleteer as one
of their own race; in the gay assemblies he was an
accomplished hidalgo; at the bull-fight the torreador
received his congratulations as from one who had

encountered the toro in the arena; in the church he would converse with the friar upon the number of Ave Marias and Paternosters which could lay a ghost, or tell him the history of every one who had perished by the flame of the Inquisition, relating his crime, whether carnal or anti-Catholic; and he could join in the seguadilla or in the guaracha.

But what rendered him more efficient than all was his wonderful power of observation and accurate description, which made the information he gave so reliable and valuable to the Duke of Wellington. Nothing escaped him. When amidst a group of persons, he would minutely watch the movement, attitude, and expression of every individual that composed it; in the scenery by which he was surrounded he would carefully mark every object:—not a tree, not a bush, not a large stone, escaped his observation; and it was said that in a cottage he noted every piece of crockery on the shelf, every domestic utensil, and even the number of knives and forks that were got ready for use at dinner.

His acquaintance with the Spanish language was marvellous; from the finest works of Calderon to the ballads in the *patois* of every province he could quote, to the infinite delight of those with whom he associated. He could assume any character that he pleased: he could be the Castilian, haughty and reserved; the Asturian, stupid and plodding; the Catalonian, intriguing and cunning; the Andalusian, laughing and merry;—in short, he was all things to all men. Nor was he incapable of passing off, when occasion required, for a Frenchman; but as he spoke the language with a strong German accent, he called himself an Alsatian. He maintained that character with the utmost nicety; and as there is a strong feeling of fellowship, almost equal to that which exists in Scotland, amongst all those who are born in the departments of France bordering on the Rhine, and who maintain their Teutonic originality, he always found friends and supporters in every regiment in the French service.

He was on one occasion intrusted with a very difficult mission by the Duke of Wellington, which he undertook effectually to perform, and to return on a particular day with the information that was required.

Great was the disappointment when it was ascertained beyond a doubt that just after leaving the camp he had been taken prisoner, before he had time to exchange his uniform. Such, however, was the case: a troop of dragoons had intercepted him, and carried him off; and the commanding officer desired two soldiers to keep a strict watch over him and carry him to headquarters. He was of course disarmed, and being placed on a horse, was, after a short time, galloped off by his guards. He slept one night under durance vile at a small inn, where he was allowed to remain in the kitchen; conversation flowed on very glibly, and as he appeared a stupid Englishman, who could not understand a word of French or Spanish, he was allowed to listen, and thus obtained precisely the intelligence that he was in search of. The following morning, being again mounted, he overheard a conversation between his guards, who deliberately agreed to rob him, and to shoot him at a mill where they were to stop, and to report to their officer that they had been compelled to fire at him in consequence of his attempt to escape.

Shortly before they arrived at the mill, for fear that they might meet with some one who would insist on having a portion of the spoil, the dragoons took from their prisoner his watch and his purse, which he surrendered with a good grace. On their arrival at the mill they dismounted, and in order to give some appearance of truth to their story, they went into the house, leaving their prisoner outside, in the hope that he would make some attempt to escape. In an instant Waters threw his cloak upon a neighbouring olive bush, and mounted his cocked hat on the top. Some empty flour sacks lay upon the ground, and a horse laden with well-filled flour sacks stood at the door. Sir John contrived to enter one of the empty sacks and throw himself across the horse. When the soldiers came out of the house they fired their carbines at the supposed prisoner, and galloped off at the utmost speed.

A short time after the miller came out and mounted his steed; the general contrived to rid himself of the encumbrance of the sack, and sat up, riding behind the man, who, suddenly turning round, saw a ghost, as he believed, for the flour that still remained in the sack had completely whitened his fellow-traveller and given him a most unearthly appearance. The frightened miller was " putrified," as Mrs. Malaprop would say, at the sight, and a push from the white spectre brought the unfortunate man to the ground, when away rode the gallant quartermaster with his sacks of flour, which, at length bursting, made a ludicrous spectacle of man and horse.

On reaching the English camp, where Lord Wellington was anxiously deploring his fate, a sudden shout from the soldiers made his lordship turn round, when a figure, resembling the statue in "Don Juan," galloped up to him. The duke, affectionately shaking him by the hand, said—

"Waters, you never yet deceived me; and though you have come in a most questionable shape, I must congratulate you and myself."

When this story was told at the clubs, one of those listeners, who always want something more, called out, "Well, and what did Waters say?" to which Alvanley replied—

"Oh, Waters made a very *flowery* speech, like a well-bred man."

THE BATTLE OF THE NIVELLE.—We expected to remain quietly in our winter quarters at St. Jean de Luz; but, to our surprise, early one morning, we were aroused from sleep by the beating of the drum calling us to arms. We were soon in marching order. It appeared that our outposts had been severely pushed by the French, and we were called upon to support our companions in arms.

The whole of the British army, as well as the division of the Guards, had commenced a forward movement. Soult, seeing this, entirely changed his tactics, and from that time—viz., the 9th of December—a series of engagements took place. The fighting on the 9th was comparatively insignificant. When we were attacked on the 10th, the Guards held the mayor's house and the grounds and orchards attached: this was an important station.

Large bodies of the enemy's infantry approached, and, after desultory fighting, succeeded in penetrat-

ing our position, when many hand-to-hand combats
ensued.   Towards the afternoon, officers and men
having displayed great gallantry, we drove the
enemy from the ground which they courageously
disputed with us, and from which they eventually
retreated to Bayonne.   Every day there was constant
fighting along the whole of our line, which extended
from the sea to the Lower Pyrenees—a distance
probably not less than thirty miles.

On the 11th we only exchanged a few shots, but
on the 12th Soult brought into action from fifteen
to twenty thousand men, and attacked our left with
a view of breaking our line.   One of the most remarkable incidents of the 12th was the fact of an
English battalion being surrounded by a division of
French in the neighbourhood of the mayor's house,
which, as before observed, was one of our principal strategical positions.   The French commanding
officer, believing that no attempt would be made to
resist, galloped up to the officer of the British regiment and demanded his sword.   Upon this, without
the least hesitation, the British officer shouted out,
" This fellow wants us to surrender : charge, my
boys ! and show them what stuff we are made of."
Instantaneously a hearty cheer rang out, and our men
rushed forward impetuously, drove off the enemy at
the point of the bayonet, and soon disposed of the
surrounding masses.   In a few minutes, they had
taken prisoners, or killed, the whole of the infantry
regiment opposed to them.

On the 13th was fought the bloody battle of
the Nivelle.   Soult had determined to make a
gigantic effort to drive us back into Spain.   During
the night of the 12th, he rapidly concentrated about

sixty thousand troops in front of Sir Rowland Hill's *corps d'armée*, consisting of 15,000 men, who occupied a very strong position, which was defended by some of the best artillery in the world. At daybreak Sir Rowland Hill was astonished to find himself threatened by masses of infantry advancing over a country luckily intersected by rivulets, hedges, and woods, which prevented the enemy from making a rapid advance; whilst, at the same time, it was impossible on such ground to employ cavalry. Sir Rowland, availing himself of an elevated position, hurriedly surveyed his ground, and concentrated his men at such points as he knew the nature of the field would induce the enemy to attack. The French, confident of success from their superior numbers, came gallantly up, using the bayonet for the first time in a premeditated attack. Our men stood their ground, and for hours acted purely on the defensive; being sustained by the admirable practice of our artillery, whose movements no difficulty of ground could, on this occasion, impede, so efficiently were the guns horsed, and so perfect was the training of the officers. It was not until mid-day that the enemy became discouraged at finding that they were unable to make any serious impression on our position; they then retired in good order, Sir Rowland Hill not daring to follow them.

Lord Wellington arrived just in time to witness the end of the battle; and while going over the field with Sir Rowland Hill, he remarked that he had never seen so many men *hors de combat* in so small a space.

I must not omit to mention a circumstance which

occurred during this great fight, alike illustrative of cowardice and of courage. The colonel of an infantry regiment, who shall be nameless, being hard pressed, showed a disposition not only to run away himself, but to order his regiment to retire. In fact, a retrograde movement had commenced, when my gallant and dear friend Lord Charles Churchill, aide-de-camp to Sir William Stewart, dashed forward, and, seizing the colours of the regiment, exclaimed, "If your colonel will not lead you, follow me, my boys!" The gallantry of this youth, then only eighteen years of age, so animated the regiment, and restored their confidence, that they rallied and shared in the glory of the day.

THE PASSAGE OF THE ADOUR.—Immediately after the battle of Nivelle, Lord Wellington determined to advance his whole line on to French ground. The right, under his own command, pushed on towards Orthes, whilst the left, under the command of Sir John Hope, proceeded in the direction of Bayonne. We (the Guards) were incorporated in the latter *corps d'armée.*

Whilst these operations were going on, Soult was organising his discouraged army, in order to make, as early as possible, another convenient stand. The enemy fell back on Orthes, and there took up a strong position; Soult was, nevertheless, destined to be beaten again at Orthes. It so happened that, for the first time since the battle of Vittoria, our cavalry were engaged: the nature of the ground at Nive and Nivelle was such as to prevent the possibility of employing the mounted soldier.

I must here record an incident which created a

considerable sensation in military circles in connection with the battle of Orthes. The 10th Hussars,
officered exclusively by men belonging to the noblest
families of Great Britain, showed a desire to take a
more active part in the contest than their colonel
(Quintin) thought prudent. They pressed hard to
be permitted to charge the French cavalry on more
than one occasion, but in vain. This so disgusted
every officer in the regiment, that they eventually
signed a *round robin*, by which they agreed never
again to speak to their colonel. When the regiment
returned to England, a court of inquiry was held,
which resulted, through the protection of the Prince
Regent, in the colonel's exoneration from all blame,
and at the same time the exchange of the rebellious
officers into other regiments.

It was at the battle of Orthes that the late Duke
of Richmond was shot through the body, gallantly
fighting with the 7th Fusiliers.

Lord Wellington had determined to cross the
Adour, and Sir John Hope was intrusted with a
corps d'armée, which was the first to perform this
difficult operation. It was necessary to provide Sir
John Hope with a number of small boats; these
were accordingly brought on the backs of mules from
various Spanish ports, it being impossible, on account
of the surf at the entrance of the Adour, as well as
the command which the French held of that river,
for Lord Wellington to avail himself of water carriage. Soult had given orders for the forces under
General Thevenot to dispute the passage.

The first operations of our corps were to throw
over the 3d Guards, under the command of the
gallant Colonel Stopford; this was not accom-

plished without much difficulty: but it was imperatively necessary, in order to protect the point where the construction of the bridge of boats would terminate. They had not been long on the French side of the river before a considerable body of men were seen issuing from Bayonne. Sir John Hope ordered our artillery, and rockets, then for the first time employed, to support our small band. Three or four regiments of French infantry were approaching rapidly, when a well-directed fire of rockets fell amongst them. The consternation of the Frenchmen was such, when these hissing, serpent-like projectiles descended, that a panic ensued, and they retreated upon Bayonne. The next day the bridge of boats was completed, and the whole army crossed.

Bayonne was eventually invested after a contest, in which it was supposed our loss exceeded 500 or 600 men. Here we remained in camp about six weeks, expecting to besiege the citadel; but this event never came off: we, however, met with a severe disaster and a reverse. The enemy made an unexpected sortie, and surrounded General Sir John Hope, when he and the whole of his staff were taken prisoners. The French killed and wounded about 1000 men on this occasion.

The hardly-contested battle of Toulouse was fought about this period, but the Guards were not present to share the honours of a contest which closed the eventful war of the Spanish Peninsula.

ARRIVAL OF THE GUARDS AT BORDEAUX.—When we reached Bordeaux, which had now become a stronghold of the Royalists, we were received by the inhabitants with a welcome which resembled what would be shown to friends and deliverers, rather than to a foreign soldiery. Nothing could be more gratifying and more acceptable to our feelings, since it was the first time after our arrival on the Continent that we met with cordiality and an apparent desire to make our quarters as comfortable as possible. The Duc d'Angoulême had reached Bordeaux before us, and no doubt his presence had prepared the way for all the friends of the Bourbons. Everywhere some description of white rag was doing duty for a Royalist banner. I lived at M. Devigné's, a rich wine-merchant, who had a family of two sons and two beautiful daughters; the latter, as I thought, taken remarkable care of by their maternal parent. Here I had evidently fallen upon my legs, for not only was the family a most agreeable one, but their hospitality was of the most generous kind. Sir Stapylton Cotton was our frequent visitor, together with M. Martignac, afterwards Minister of Charles the Tenth.

Here I had an opportunity of meeting some of the prettiest women of a city famed all over Europe for its female beauty. The young ladies were remarkable for their taste in dress, which in those days consisted of a mantilla *à l'Espagnole*, and silken shawls of varied hues, so admirably blended, that the eye was charmed with their richness of colour. The *grisettes*, who were as much admired by the soldiers as were the high dames by the officers, were remarkable for a coquettish species of apron of a red dye, which was only to be obtained from the neighbourhood.

Of course we were all very anxious to taste the Bordeaux wines; but our palates, accustomed to the stronger vintages of Spain, I suspect were not in a condition to appreciate the more delicate and refined bouquets which ought to characterise claret. A *vin ordinaire*, which now at a restaurateur's would cost three francs, was then furnished at the hotels for fifteen sous : a Larose, Lafitte, Margaux, such as we are now paying eight or ten francs a bottle for, did not cost a third. I must not, however, forget that greater attention and care is now employed in the preparation of French wines. The exportation to England of the light red wines of France was not sufficiently profitable, as I learnt from my host, at that time to attract the cupidity of commerce.

In the Guards, Bordeaux was more affectionately remembered in connection with its women than its wine. We left it with regret, and the more youthful and imaginative amongst us said that we were wafted across the Channel by the gentle sighs of " the girls we left behind us."

MRS. MARY ANNE CLARKE.—Our army, despite its defects, was nevertheless infinitely better administered at home when I joined than it had been a few years before, owing principally to the inquiry that had taken place in the House of Commons, relative to the bribery and corruption which had crept in, and which had been laid open by the confessions of a female, who created no small sensation in those days, and who eventually terminated her extraordinary career, not very long since, in Paris.

The squibs fired off by Mrs. Mary Anne Clarke had a much greater influence, and produced more effect upon the English army, than all the artillery

of the enemy directed against the Duke of York
when commanding in Holland. This lady was remarkable for her beauty and her fascinations; and
few came within the circle over which she presided
who did not acknowledge her superior power. Her
wit, which kept the House of Commons during her
examination in a continued state of merriment, was
piquant and saucy. Her answers on that occasion
have been so often brought before the public, that I
need not repeat them; but, in private life, her quick
repartee, and her brilliant sallies, rendered her a
lively, though not always an agreeable companion.
As for prudence, she had none; her dearest friend,
if she had any, was just as likely to be made the
object of her ridicule as the most obnoxious person
of her acquaintance.

Her narrative of her first introduction to the Duke
of York has often been repeated; but, as all her
stories were considered apocryphal, it is difficult to
arrive at a real history of her career. Certain, however, is it that, about the age of sixteen, she was
residing at Blackheath—a sweet, pretty, lively girl
—when, in her daily walk across the heath, she was
passed, on two or three occasions, by a handsome,
well-dressed cavalier, who, finding that she recognised his salute, dismounted; pleased with her manner and wit, he begged to be allowed to introduce
a friend. Accordingly, on her consenting, a person
to whom the cavalier appeared to pay every sort of
deference was presented to her, and the acquaintance
ripened into something more than friendship. Not
the slightest idea had the young lady of the position
in society of her lover, until she accompanied him,
on his invitation, to the theatre, where she occupied

a private box, when she was surprised at the ceremony with which she was treated, and at observing
that every eye and every lorgnette in the house were
directed towards her in the course of the evening.
She accepted this as a tribute to her beauty. Finding that she could go again to the theatre when she
pleased, and occupy the same box, she availed herself of this opportunity with a female friend, and
was not a little astonished at being addressed as her
Royal Highness. She then discovered that the individual into whose affections she had insinuated
herself was the son of the King, the Duke of York,
who had not long before united himself to a lady,
for whom she had been mistaken.

Mrs. Mary Anne Clarke was soon reconciled to the
thought of being the wife of a prince by the left
hand, particularly as she found herself assiduously
courted by persons of the highest rank, and more
especially by military men. A large house in a
fashionable street was taken for her, and an establishment on a magnificent scale gave her an opportunity of surrounding herself with persons of
a sphere far beyond anything she could in her
younger days have dreamt of; her father having
been in an honourable trade, and her husband
being only a captain in a marching regiment. The
duke, delighted to see his fair friend so well received, constantly honoured her dinner-table with
his presence, and willingly gratified any wish that
she expressed; and he must have known (and for
this he was afterwards highly censured) that her
style of living was upon a scale of great expense,
and that he himself contributed little towards it.
The consequence was that the hospitable lady even-

tually became embarrassed, and knew not which way to turn to meet her outlay. It was suggested to her that she might obtain from the duke commissions in the army, which she could easily dispose of at a good price. Individuals quickly came forward, ready to purchase anything that came within her grasp, which she extended not only to the army, but, as it afterwards appeared, to the Church; for there were reverend personages who availed themselves of her assistance, and thus obtained patronage, by which they advanced their worldly interests very rapidly.

MRS. MARY ANNE CLARKE AND COL. WARDLE.— Amongst those who paid great attention to Mrs. Mary Anne Clarke was Colonel Wardle, at that time a remarkable member of the House of Commons, and a bold leader of the Radical Opposition. He got intimately acquainted with her, and was so great a personal favourite that it was believed he wormed out all her secret history, of which he availed himself to obtain a fleeting popularity.

Having obtained the names of some of the parties who had been fortunate enough, as they imagined, to secure the lady's favour, he loudly demanded an inquiry in the House of Commons as to the management of the army by the Commander-in-Chief, the Duke of York. The nation and the army were fond of his Royal Highness, and every attempt to screen him was made; but in vain. The House undertook the task of investigating the conduct of the duke, and witnesses were produced, amongst whom was the fair lady herself, who by no means attempted to screen her imprudent admirer. Her responses to the questions put to her were cleverly and archly given, and the whole mystery of her various intrigues came to light. The duke consequently resigned his place in the Horse-Guards, and at the same time repudiated the beautiful and dangerous cause of his humiliation. The lady, incensed at the desertion of her royal swain, announced her intention of publishing his love-letters, which were likely to expose the whole of the royal family to ridicule, as they formed the frequent themes of his correspondence. Sir Herbert Taylor was therefore commissioned to enter into a negotiation for the purchase of the letters; this he effected at an enormous price, obtaining a written document at the same time by which Mrs. Clarke was subjected to heavy penalties if she, by word or deed, implicated the honour of any of the branches of the royal family. A pension was secured to her, on condition that she should quit England, and reside wherever she chose on the Continent. To all this she consented, and, in the first instance, went to Brussels, where her previous history being scarcely known, she was well received; and she married her daughters without any inquiry as to the fathers to whom she might ascribe them.

Mrs. Clarke afterwards settled quietly and comfortably in Paris, receiving occasionally visits from members of the aristocracy who had known her when mingling in a certain circle in London. The Marquis of Londonderry never failed to pay his respects to her, entertaining a very high opinion of her talents. Her manners were exceedingly agreeable, and to the latest day she retained pleasing traces of past beauty. She was lively, sprightly,

and full of fun, and indulged in innumerable anecdotes of the members of the royal family of England—some of them much too scandalous to be
repeated. She regarded the Duke of York as a big
baby, not out of his leading strings, and the Prince
of Wales as an idle sensualist, with just enough
of brains to be guided by any laughing, well-bred
individual who would listen to stale jokes and
impudent ribaldry. Of Queen Charlotte she used to
speak with the utmost disrespect, attributing to her
a love of domination and a hatred of every one who
would not bow down before any idol that she chose
to set up ; and as being envious of the Princess
Caroline and her daughter the Princess Charlotte
of Wales, and jealous of their acquiring too much
influence over the Prince of Wales. In short, Mary
Anne Clarke had been so intimately let into every
secret of the life of the royal family that, had she
not been tied down, her revelations would have
astonished the world, however willing people might
have been to believe that they were tinged with
scandal and exaggeration.

The way in which Colonel Wardle first obtained
information of the sale of commissions was singular
enough. He was paying a clandestine visit to Mrs.
Clarke, when a carriage with the royal livery drove
up to the door, and the gallant officer was compelled to take refuge under the sofa ; but instead of
the royal duke, there appeared one of his aide-de-
camps, who entered into conversation in so mysterious a manner as to excite the attention of the
gentleman under the sofa, and led him to believe
that the sale of a commission was authorised by
the Commander - in - Chief ; though it afterwards

appeared that it was a private arrangement of the
unwelcome visitor. At the Horse-Guards, it had
often been suspected that there was a mystery connected with commissions that could not be fathomed ;
as it frequently happened that the list of promo-
tions agreed on was surreptitiously increased by
the addition of new names. This was the crafty
handiwork of the accomplished dame ; the duke
having employed her as his amanuensis, and being
accustomed to sign her autograph lists without
examination.

SOCIETY IN LONDON IN 1814.—In the year 1814,
my battalion of the Guards was once more in its old
quarters in Portman Street barracks, enjoying the
fame of our Spanish campaign. Good society at the
period to which I refer was, to use a familiar expression, wonderfully " select." At the present time
one can hardly conceive the importance which was
attached to getting admission to Almack's, the seventh
heaven of the fashionable world. Of the three hundred officers of the Foot Guards, not more than half-
a-dozen were honoured with vouchers of admission
to this exclusive temple of the *beau monde ;* the
gates of which were guarded by lady patronesses,
whose smiles or frowns consigned men and women
to happiness or despair. These lady patronesses
were the Ladies Castlereagh, Jersey, Cowper, and
Sefton, Mrs. Drummond Burrell, now Lady Willoughby, the Princess Esterhazy, and the Countess
Lieven.

The most popular amongst these *grandes dames*
was unquestionably Lady Cowper, now Lady Palmerston. Lady Jersey's bearing, on the contrary,

was that of a theatrical tragedy queen; and whilst
attempting the sublime, she frequently made herself
simply ridiculous, being inconceivably rude, and in
her manner often ill-bred. Lady Sefton was kind
and amiable, Madame de Lieven haughty and exclusive, Princess Esterhazy was a *bon enfant*, Lady
Castlereagh and Mrs. Burrell *de très grandes dames*.

Many diplomatic arts, much finesse, and a host of
intrigues, were set in motion to get an invitation
to Almack's. Very often persons whose rank and
fortunes entitled them to the *entrée* anywhere, were
excluded by the cliqueism of the lady patronesses;
for the female government of Almack's was a pure
despotism, and subject to all the caprices of despotic
rule: it is needless to add that, like every other
despotism, it was not innocent of abuses. The fair
ladies who ruled supreme over this little dancing
and gossiping world, issued a solemn proclamation
that no gentleman should appear at the assemblies
without being dressed in knee-breeches, white cravat,
and *chapeau bras*. On one occasion, the Duke of
Wellington was about to ascend the staircase of the
ball-room, dressed in black trousers, when the vigi-
lant Mr. Willis, the guardian of the establishment,
stepped forward and said, "Your Grace cannot be
admitted in trousers," whereupon the Duke, who
had a great respect for orders and regulations, quietly
walked away.

In 1814, the dances at Almack's were Scotch
reels and the old English country-dance; and the
orchestra, being from Edinburgh, was conducted by
the then celebrated Neil Gow. It was not until
1815 that Lady Jersey introduced from Paris the
favourite quadrille, which has so long remained

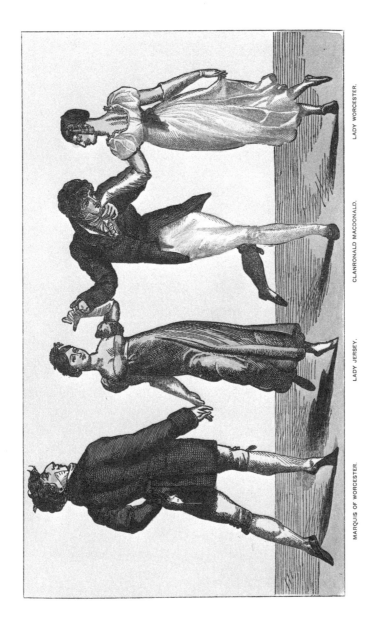

MARQUIS OF WORCESTER.   LADY JERSEY.   CLANRONALD MACDONALD.   LADY WORCESTER.

THE FIRST QUADRILLE AT ALMACK'S.

popular. I recollect the persons who formed the very
first quadrille that was ever danced at Almack's:
they were Lady Jersey, Lady Harriett Butler, Lady
Susan Ryde, and Miss Montgomery; the men being
the Count St. Aldegonde, Mr. Montgomery, Mr.
Montague, and Charles Standish. The " mazy waltz "
was also brought to us about this time; but there
were comparatively few who at first ventured to
whirl round the *salons* of Almack's; in course of
time Lord Palmerston might, however, have been
seen describing an infinite number of circles with
Madame de Lieven. Baron de Neumann was frequently seen perpetually turning with the Princess
Esterhazy; and, in course of time, the waltzing
mania, having turned the heads of society generally,
descended to their feet, and the waltz was practised
in the morning in certain noble mansions in London
with unparalleled assiduity.

The dandies of society were Beau Brummell (of
whom I shall have to say something on another
occasion), the Duke of Argyle, the Lords Worcester,
Alvanley, and Foley, Henry Pierrepoint, John Mills,
Bradshaw, Henry de Ros, Charles Standish, Edward
Montagu, Hervey Aston, Dan Mackinnon, George
Dawson Damer, Lloyd (commonly known as Rufus
Lloyd), and others who have escaped my memory.
They were great frequenters of White's Club, in St.
James's Street, where, in the famous bay window,
they mustered in force.

Drinking and play were more universally indulged
in then than at the present time, and many men
still living must remember the couple of bottles of
port at least which accompanied his dinner in those
days. Indeed, female society amongst the upper

VOL. I.   C

classes was most notoriously neglected; except, perhaps, by romantic foreigners, who were the heroes of many a fashionable adventure that fed the clubs with ever-acceptable scandal. How could it be otherwise, when husbands spent their days in the hunting-field, or were entirely occupied with politics, and always away from home during the day; whilst the dinner-party, commencing at seven or eight, frequently did not break up before one in the morning. There were then four, and even five bottle-men; and the only thing that saved them was drinking very slowly, and out of very small glasses. The learned head of the law, Lord Eldon, and his brother, Lord Stowell, used to say that they had drunk more bad port than any two men in England; indeed, the former was rather apt to be overtaken, and to speak occasionally somewhat thicker than natural, after long and heavy potations. The late Lords Panmure, Dufferin, and Blayney, wonderful to relate, were six-bottle men at this time; and I really think that if the good society of 1815 could appear before their more moderate descendants in the state they were generally reduced to after dinner, the moderns would pronounce their ancestors fit for nothing but bed.

THE ITALIAN OPERA: CATALANI.—The greatest vocalist of whom I have a recollection is Madame Catalani. In her youth, she was the finest singer in Europe, and she was much sought after by all the great people during her *séjour* in London. She was extremely handsome, and was considered a model as wife and mother. Catalani was very fond of money, and would never sing unless paid beforehand. She

was invited, with her husband, to pass some time at
Stowe, where a numerous but select party had been
invited; and Madame Catalani, being asked to sing
soon after dinner, willingly complied. When the
day of her departure came, her husband placed in
the hands of the Marquis of Buckingham the following little billet :—" For seventeen songs, seventeen hundred pounds." This large sum was paid at
once, without hesitation; proving that Lord Buckingham was a refined gentleman, in every sense of
the word.

Catalani's husband, M. de Valabrèque, once fought
a duel with a German baron who had insulted the
prima donna; the weapons used were sabres, and
Valabrèque cut half of the baron's nose clean off.
Madame Catalani lived for many years, highly respected, at a handsome villa near Florence. Her
two sons are now distinguished members of the
Imperial court in Paris; the eldest being Préfet du
Palais, and the youngest colonel of a regiment of
hussars.

When George the Fourth was Regent, Her
Majesty's Theatre, as the Italian Opera in the
Haymarket is still called, was conducted on a very
different system from that which now prevails. Some
years previous to the period to which I refer, no
one could obtain a box or a ticket for the pit without a voucher from one of the lady patronesses,
who, in 1805, were the Duchesses of Marlborough,
Devonshire, and Bedford, Lady Carlisle, and some
others. In their day, after the singing and the
ballet were over, the company used to retire into the
concert-room, where a ball took place, accompanied
by refreshments and a supper. There all the rank

and fashion of England were assembled on a sort of neutral ground.

At a later period, the management of the Opera House fell into the hands of Mr. Waters, when it became less difficult to obtain admittance; but the strictest etiquette was still kept up as regarded the dress of the gentlemen, who were only admitted with knee-buckles, ruffles, and *chapeau bras*. If there happened to be a drawing-room, the ladies would appear in their court-dresses, as well as the gentlemen; and on all occasions the audience of Her Majesty's Theatre was stamped with aristocratic elegance. In the boxes of the first tier might have been seen the daughters of the Duchess of Argyle, four of England's beauties; in the next box were the equally lovely Marchioness of Stafford and her daughter, Lady Elizabeth Gore, now the Duchess of Norfolk: not less remarkable were Lady Harrowby and her daughters, Lady Susan and Lady Mary Ryder. The peculiar type of female beauty which these ladies so attractively exemplified, is such as can be met with only in the British Isles: the full, round, soul-inspired eye of Italy, and the dark hair of the sunny south, often combined with that exquisitely pearly complexion which seems to be concomitant with humidity and fog. You could scarcely gaze upon the peculiar beauty to which I refer without being as much charmed with its kindly expression as with its physical loveliness.

DINING AND COOKERY IN ENGLAND FIFTY YEARS AGO.—England can boast of a Spenser, Shakspeare, Milton, and many other illustrious poets, clearly indicating that the national character of Britons is

not deficient in imagination; but we have not had
one single masculine inventive genius of the kitchen.
It is the probable result of our national antipathy
to mysterious culinary compounds, that none of the
bright minds of England have ventured into the
region of scientific cookery. Even in the best
houses, when I was a young man, the dinners were
wonderfully solid, hot, and stimulating. The *menu*
of a grand dinner was thus composed:—Mulliga-
tawny and turtle soups were the first dishes placed
before you; a little lower, the eye met with the
familiar salmon at one end of the table, and the
turbot, surrounded by smelts, at the other. The
first course was sure to be followed by a saddle of
mutton or a piece of roast beef; and then you could
take your oath that fowls, tongue, and ham would
as assuredly succeed as darkness after day.

Whilst these never-ending *pièces de résistance*
were occupying the table, what were called French
dishes were, for custom's sake, added to the solid
abundance. The French, or side dishes, consisted
of very mild but very abortive attempts at Continental cooking; and I have always observed that
they met with the neglect and contempt that they
merited. The universally-adored and ever-popular
boiled potato, produced at the very earliest period
of the dinner, was eaten with everything, up to the
moment when sweets appeared. Our vegetables,
the best in the world, were never honoured by an
accompanying sauce, and generally came to the
table cold. A prime difficulty to overcome was the
placing on your fork, and finally in your mouth,
some half-dozen different eatables which occupied
your plate at the same time. For example, your

plate would contain, say, a slice of turkey, a piece
of stuffing, a sausage, pickles, a slice of tongue,
cauliflower, and potatoes. According to habit and
custom, a judicious and careful selection from this
little bazaar of good things was to be made, with
an endeavour to place a portion of each in your
mouth at the same moment. In fact, it appeared
to me that we used to do all our compound cookery
between our jaws.

The dessert,—generally ordered at Messrs. Grange's,
or at Owen's, in Bond Street,—if for a dozen people,
would cost at least as many pounds. The wines
were chiefly port, sherry, and hock; claret, and
even Burgundy, being then designated "poor, thin,
washy stuff." A perpetual thirst seemed to come
over people, both men and women, as soon as they
had tasted their soup; as from that moment everybody was taking wine with everybody else till the
close of the dinner; and such wine as produced
that class of cordiality which frequently wanders
into stupefaction. How all this sort of eating and
drinking ended was obvious, from the prevalence of
gout, and the necessity of every one making the pill-
box their constant bedroom companion.

THE PRINCE REGENT.—When the eldest son of
George the Third assumed the Regency, England
was in a state of political transition. The convul-
sions of the Continent were felt amongst us; the
very foundations of European society were shaking,
and the social relations of men were rapidly chang-
ing. The Regent's natural leanings were towards
the Tories; therefore, as soon as he undertook the
responsibility of power, he abruptly abandoned the

Whigs, and retained in office the admirers and partisans of his father's policy. This resolution caused
him to have innumerable and inveterate enemies,
who never lost an opportunity of attacking his
public acts and interfering with his domestic relations.

The Regent was singularly imbued with petty
royal pride. He would rather be amiable and
familiar with his tailor than agreeable and friendly
with the most illustrious of the aristocracy of Great
Britain; he would rather joke with a Brummell
than admit to his confidence a Norfolk or a Somerset. The Regent was always particularly well-bred
in public, and showed, if he chose, decidedly good
manners; but he very often preferred to address
those whom he felt he could patronise. His Royal
Highness was as much the victim of circumstances
and the child of thoughtless imprudence as the
most humble subject of the Crown. His unfortunate marriage with a Princess of Brunswick originated in his debts; as he married that unhappy
lady for one million sterling, William Pitt being
the contractor! The Princess of Wales married
nothing but an association with the Crown of England. If the Prince ever seriously loved any woman,
it was Mrs. Fitzherbert, with whom he had appeared
at the altar.

Public opinion in England, under the inspiration
of the Whigs, raised a cry of indignation against
the Prince. It was imagined, I presume, that a
royal personage should be born without heart or
feeling; that he should have been able to live only
for the good of the state and for the convenience
of his creditors. The Princess of Wales was one of

the most unattractive and almost repulsive women
for an elegant-minded man that could well have
been found amongst German royalty.   It is not my
intention to recall the events of the Regency.   It is
well known that the Prince became eventually so
unpopular as to exclude himself as much as possible
from public gaze.   His intimate companions, after
the trial of Queen Caroline, were Lords Conyngham
and Fife, Sir Benjamin Bloomfield, Sir William Mac-
mahon, Admiral Nagle, Sir Andrew Barnard, Lords
Glenlyon, Hertford, and Lowther.   These gentlemen
generally dined with him ; the dinner being the
artistic product of that famous gastronomic savant,
Wattier.   The Prince was very fond of listening
after dinner to the gossip of society.   When he
became George the Fourth, no change took place in
these *personnels* at the banquet, excepting that with
the fruits and flowers of the table was introduced
the beautiful Marchioness of Conyngham, whose
brilliant wit, according to the estimation of his
Majesty, surpassed that of any other of his friends,
male or female.

THE PRINCESS CHARLOTTE OF WALES AT A FÊTE
IN THE YEAR 1813 AT CARLTON HOUSE.—Carlton
House, at the period to which I refer, was a centre
for all the great politicians and wits who were the
favourites of the Regent.   The principal entrance
of this palace in Pall Mall, with its screen of
columns, will be remembered by many.   In the
rear of the mansion was an extensive garden that
reached from Warwick Street to Marlborough
House ; greensward, stately trees (probably two
hundred years old), and beds of the choicest flowers,

gave to the grounds a picturesque attraction perhaps unequalled. It was here that the heir to the
throne of England gave, in 1813, an open-air *fête*,
in honour of the battle of Vittoria. About three
o'clock P.M. the *élite* of London society, who had
been honoured with an invitation, began to arrive,
all in full dress; the ladies particularly displaying
their diamonds and pearls, as if they were going to
a drawing-room, the men, of course, in full dress,
wearing knee-breeches and buckles. The regal
circle was composed of the Queen, the Regent, the
Princesses Sophia and Mary, the Princess Charlotte, the Dukes of York, Clarence, Cumberland,
and Cambridge.

This was the first day that her Royal Highness
the Princess Charlotte appeared in public. She
was a young lady of more than ordinary personal
attractions; her features were regular, and her
complexion fair, with the rich bloom of youthful
beauty; her eyes were blue and very expressive,
and her hair was abundant, and of that peculiar
light brown which merges into the golden: in fact,
such hair as the Middle-Age Italian painters associate with their conceptions of the Madonna. In
figure her Royal Highness was somewhat over the
ordinary height of women, but finely proportioned
and well developed. Her manners were remarkable
for a simplicity and good-nature which would have
won admiration and invited affection in the most
humble walks of life. She created universal admiration, and I may say a feeling of national pride,
amongst all who attended the ball.

The Prince Regent entered the gardens giving
his arm to the Queen, the rest of the royal family

following. Tents had been erected in various parts of the grounds, where the bands of the Guards were stationed. The weather was magnificent, a circumstance which contributed to show off the admirable arrangements of Sir Benjamin Bloomfield, to whom had been deputed the organisation of the *fête*, which commenced by dancing on the lawn.

The Princess Charlotte honoured with her presence two dances. In the first she accepted the hand of the late Duke of Devonshire, and in the second that of the Earl of Aboyne, who had danced with Marie Antoinette, and who, as Lord Huntly, lived long enough to dance with Queen Victoria. The Princess entered so much into the spirit of the *fête* as to ask for the then fashionable Scotch dances. The Prince was dressed in the Windsor uniform, and wore the garter and star. He made himself very amiable, and conversed much with the Ladies Hertford, Cholmondeley, and Montford. Altogether, the *fête* was a memorable event.

A year afterwards, the Duke of York said to his royal niece, "Tell me, my dear, have you seen any one among the foreign princes whom you would like to have for a husband?" The Princess naïvely replied, "No one so much prepossesses me as Prince Leopold of Coburg. I have heard much of his bravery in the field, and I must say he is personally agreeable to me. I have particularly heard of his famous cavalry charge at the battle of Leipsic, where he took several thousand prisoners, for which he was rewarded with the Order of Maria Theresa." In a few months afterwards she became the wife of the man whom she so much admired, and from whom she was torn away not long after by the cruel hand of death. It will be remembered that she died in childbirth, and her offspring expired at the same time. The accoucheur who attended her was so much affected by the calamity that he committed suicide some short time afterwards.

BEAU BRUMMELL.—Amongst the curious freaks of fortune there is none more remarkable in my memory than the sudden appearance, in the highest and best society in London, of a young man whose antecedents warranted a much less conspicuous career: I refer to the famous Beau Brummell. We have innumerable instances of soldiers, lawyers, and men of letters elevating themselves from the most humble stations, and becoming the companions of princes and lawgivers; but there are comparatively few examples of men obtaining a similarly elevated position simply from their attractive personal appearance and fascinating manners. Brummell's father, who was a steward to one or two large estates, sent his son George to Eton. He was endowed with a handsome person, and distinguished himself at Eton as the best scholar, the best boatman, and the best cricketer; and, more than all, he was supposed to possess the comprehensive excellences that are represented by the familiar term of "good fellow." He made many friends amongst the scions of good families, by whom he was considered a sort of Crichton; and his reputation reached a circle over which reigned the celebrated Duchess of Devonshire. At a grand ball given by her Grace, George Brummell, then quite a youth,

appeared for the first time in such elevated society.
He immediately became a great favourite with the
ladies, and was asked by all the dowagers to as many
balls and *soirées* as he could attend.

At last the Prince of Wales sent for Brummell,
and was so much pleased with his manner and
appearance, that he gave him a commission in
his own regiment, the 10th Hussars. Unluckily,
Brummell, soon after joining his regiment, was
thrown from his horse at a grand review at Brighton,
when he broke his classical Roman nose. This
misfortune, however, did not affect the fame of the
beau; and although his nasal organ had undergone
a slight transformation, it was forgiven by his admirers, since the rest of his person remained intact.
When we are prepossessed by the attractions of a
favourite, it is not a trifle that will dispel the
illusion; and Brummell continued to govern society,
in conjunction with the Prince of Wales. He was
remarkable for his dress, which was generally con-
ceived by himself; the execution of his sublime
imagination being carried out by that superior
genius, Mr Weston, tailor, of Old Bond Street.
The Regent sympathised deeply with Brummell's
labours to arrive at the most attractive and gentlemanly mode of dressing the male form, at a period
when fashion had placed at the disposal of the
tailor the most hideous material that could possibly
tax his art. The coat may have a long tail or a
short tail, a high collar or a low collar, but it will
always be an ugly garment. The modern hat may
be spread out at the top, or narrowed, whilst the
brim may be turned up or turned down, made a
little wider or a little more narrow; still it is incon-

ceivably hideous. Pantaloons and Hessian boots
were the least objectionable features of the costume which the imagination of a Brummell and
the genius of a Royal Prince were called upon to
modify or change. The hours of meditative agony
which each dedicated to the odious fashions of
the day have left no monument save the coloured
caricatures in which these illustrious persons have
appeared.

Brummell, at this time, besides being the companion and friend of the Prince, was very intimate
with the Dukes of Rutland, Dorset, and Argyle,
Lords Sefton, Alvanley, and Plymouth. In the
zenith of his popularity he might be seen at the bay
window of White's Club, surrounded by the lions
of the day, laying down the law, and occasionally
indulging in those witty remarks for which he was
famous. His house in Chapel Street corresponded
with his personal "get up;" the furniture was in
excellent taste, and the library contained the best
works of the best authors of every period and of
every country. His canes, his snuff-boxes, his
Sèvres china, were exquisite; his horses and carriage were conspicuous for their excellence; and,
in fact, the superior taste of a Brummell was discoverable in everything that belonged to him.

But the reign of the king of fashion, like all
other reigns, was not destined to continue for ever.
Brummell warmly espoused the cause of Mrs.
Fitzherbert, and this of course offended the Prince
of Wales. I refer to the period when his Royal
Highness had abandoned that beautiful woman for
another favourite. A coldness then ensued between the Prince and his *protégé;* and finally,

the mirror of fashion was excluded from the royal presence.

A curious accident brought Brummell again to the dinner-table of his royal patron; he was asked one night at White's to take a hand at whist, when he won from George Harley Drummond £20,000. This circumstance having been related by the Duke of York to the Prince of Wales, the beau was again invited to Carlton House. At the commencement of the dinner, matters went off smoothly; but Brummell, in his joy at finding himself with his old friend, became excited, and drank too much wine. His Royal Highness—who wanted to pay off Brummell for an insult he had received at Lady Cholmondeley's ball, when the beau, turning towards the Prince, said to Lady Worcester, "Who is your fat friend?"—had invited him to dinner merely out of a desire for revenge. The Prince therefore pretended to be affronted with Brummell's hilarity, and said to his brother, the Duke of York, who was present, "I think we had better order Mr Brummell's carriage before he gets drunk." Whereupon he rang the bell, and Brummell left the royal presence. This circumstance originated the story about the beau having told the Prince to ring the bell. I received these details from the late General Sir Arthur Upton, who was present at the dinner.

The latter days of Brummell were clouded with mortifications and penury. He retired to Calais, where he kept up a ludicrous imitation of his past habits. At last he got himself named consul at Caen; but he afterwards lost the appointment, and eventually died insane, and in abject poverty, at Calais.

ROMEO COATES.—This singular man, more than forty years ago, occupied a large portion of public attention; his eccentricities were the theme of general wonder, and great was the curiosity to catch a glance at as strange a being as any that ever appeared in English society. This extraordinary individual was a native of one of the West India Islands, and was represented as a man of extraordinary wealth; to which, however, he had no claim.

About the year 1808, there arrived at the York Hotel, at Bath, a person about the age of fifty, somewhat gentlemanlike, but so different from the usual men of the day that considerable attention was directed to him. He was of a good figure; but his face was sallow, seamed with wrinkles, and more expressive of cunning than of any other quality. His dress was remarkable: in the daytime he was covered at all seasons with enormous quantities of fur; but the evening costume in which he went to the balls made a great impression, from its gaudy appearance; for his buttons, as well as his knee-buckles, were of diamonds. There was of course great curiosity to know who this stranger was; and this curiosity was heightened by an announcement that he proposed to appear at the theatre in the character of Romeo. There was something so unlike the impassioned lover in his appearance—so much that indicated a man with few intellectual gifts— that everybody was prepared for a failure. No one, however, anticipated the reality.

On the night fixed for his appearance, the house was crowded to suffocation. The playbills had given out that "an amateur of fashion" would for that night only perform in the character of Romeo;

besides, it was generally whispered that the rehearsals gave indication of comedy rather than tragedy, and that his readings were of a perfectly novel character.

The very first appearance of Romeo convulsed the house with laughter. Benvolio prepares the audience for the stealthy visit of the lover to the object of his admiration; and fully did the amateur give expression to one sense of the words uttered, for he was indeed the true representative of a thief stealing onwards in the night, " with Tarquin's ravishing strides," and disguising his face as if he were thoroughly ashamed of it. The darkness of the scene did not, however, show his real character so much as the masquerade, when he came forward with a hideous grin, and made what he considered his bow—which consisted in thrusting his head forward, and bobbing it up and down several times, his body remaining perfectly upright and stiff, like a toy mandarin with movable head.

His dress was *outré* in the extreme : whether Spanish, Italian, or English, no one could say; it was like nothing ever worn. In a cloak of sky-blue silk, profusely spangled, red pantaloons, a vest of white muslin, surmounted by an enormously thick cravat, and a wig *à la* Charles the Second, capped by an opera hat, he presented one of the most grotesque spectacles ever witnessed upon the stage. The whole of his garments were evidently too tight for him; and his movements appeared so incongruous, that every time he raised his arm, or moved a limb, it was impossible to refrain from laughter : but what chiefly convulsed the audience was the bursting of a seam in an inexpressible part of his dress, and the sudden extrusion through the red rent of a quantity of white linen sufficient to make a Bourbon flag, which was visible whenever he turned round. This was at first supposed to be a wilful offence against common decency, and some disapprobation was evinced; but the utter unconsciousness of the odd creature was soon apparent, and then unrestrained mirth reigned throughout the boxes, pit, and gallery. The total want of flexibility of limb, the awkwardness of his gait, and the idiotic manner in which he stood still, all produced a most ludicrous effect; but when his guttural voice was heard, and his total misapprehension of every passage in the play, especially the vulgarity of his address to Juliet, were perceived, every one was satisfied that Shakspeare's Romeo was burlesqued on that occasion.

The balcony scene was interrupted by shrieks of laughter, for in the midst of one of Juliet's impassioned exclamations, Romeo quietly took out his snuff-box and applied a pinch to his nose; on this a wag in the gallery bawled out, "I say, Romeo, give us a pinch," when the impassioned lover, in the most affected manner, walked to the side boxes and offered the contents of his box first to the gentlemen, and then, with great gallantry, to the ladies. This new interpretation of Shakspeare was hailed with loud bravos, which the actor acknowledged with his usual grin and nod. Romeo then returned to the balcony, and was seen to extend his arms; but all passed in dumb show, so incessant were the shouts of laughter. All that went on upon the stage was for a time quite inaudible, but previous to the soliloquy " I do remember an apothecary," there was for a moment a dead silence; for in rushed the hero with a precipitate step until he reached the stage lamps, when he commenced his speech in the lowest possible whisper, as if he had something to communicate to the pit that ought not to be generally known; and this tone was kept up throughout the whole of the soliloquy, so that not a sound could be heard.

The amateur actor showed many indications of aberration of mind, and seemed rather the object of pity than of amusement; he, however, appeared delighted with himself, and also with his audience, for at the conclusion he walked first to the left of the stage and bobbed his head in his usual grotesque manner at the side boxes; then to the right, performing the same feat; after which, going to the centre of the stage with the usual bob, and placing his hand upon his left breast, he exclaimed, "Haven't I done it well?" To this inquiry the house, convulsed as it was with shouts of laughter, responded in such a way as delighted the heart of Kean on one great occasion, when he said, "The pit rose at me." The whole audience started up as if with one accord, giving a yell of derision, whilst pocket-handkerchiefs waved from all parts of the theatre.

The dying scene was irresistibly comic, and I question if Liston, Munden, or Joey Knight, was ever greeted with such merriment; for Romeo dragged the unfortunate Juliet from the tomb, much in the same manner as a washerwoman thrusts into her cart the bag of foul linen. But how shall I describe his death? Out came a dirty silk handkerchief from his pocket, with which he carefully swept the ground; then his opera hat was carefully placed for a pillow, and down he laid

himself. After various tossings about, he seemed
reconciled to the position ; but the house vocifer-
ously bawled out, " Die again, Romeo ! " and, obe-
dient to the command, he rose up, and went
through the ceremony again. Scarcely had he
lain quietly down, when the call was again heard,
and the well-pleased amateur was evidently prepared to enact a third death ; but Juliet now rose
up from her tomb, and gracefully put an end to
this ludicrous scene by advancing to the front of
the stage and aptly applying a quotation from
Shakspeare—

> " Dying is such sweet sorrow,
> That he will die again until to-morrow."

Thus ended an extravaganza such as has seldom
been witnessed ; for although Coates repeated the
play at the Haymarket, amidst shouts of laughter
from the playgoers, there never was so ludicrous a
performance as that which took place at Bath on
the first night of his appearance. Eventually he
was driven from the stage with much contumely,
in consequence of its having been discovered that,
under pretence of acting for a charitable purpose,
he had obtained a sum of money for his performances. His love of notoriety led him to have a
most singular shell-shaped carriage built, in which,
drawn by two fine white horses, he was wont to
parade in the park ; the harness, and every available part of the vehicle (which was really handsome),
were blazoned over with his heraldic device—a cock
crowing ; and his appearance was heralded by the
gamins of London shrieking out, " Cock-a-doodle-
doo ! " Coates eventually quitted London and settled

at Boulogne, where a fair lady was induced to become the partner of his existence notwithstanding the ridicule of the whole world.

HYDE PARK AFTER THE PENINSULAR WAR.—That extensive district of park land, the entrances of which are in Piccadilly and Oxford Street, was far more rural in appearance in 1815 than at the present day. Under the trees cows and deer were grazing; the paths were fewer, and none told of that perpetual tread of human feet which now destroys all idea of country charms and illusions. As you gazed from an eminence, no rows of monotonous houses reminded you of the vicinity of a large city, and the atmosphere of Hyde Park was then much more like what God had made it than the hazy, grey, coal-darkened, half-twilight of the London of to-day. The company which then congregated daily about five was composed of dandies and women in the best society; the men mounted on such horses as England alone could then produce. The dandy's dress consisted of a blue coat with brass buttons, leather breeches, and top boots; and it was the fashion to wear a deep, stiff white cravat, which prevented you from seeing your boots while standing. All the world watched Brummell to imitate him, and order their clothes of the tradesman who dressed that sublime dandy. One day a youthful beau approached Brummell and said, " Permit me to ask you where you get your blacking ? " " Ah ! " replied Brummell, gazing complacently at his boots, " my blacking positively ruins me. I will tell you in confidence ; it is made with the finest champagne ! "

Many of the ladies used to drive into the park in a carriage called a *vis-à-vis*, which held only two persons. The hammer-cloth, rich in heraldic designs, the powdered footmen in smart liveries, and a coachman who assumed all the gaiety and appearance of a wigged archbishop, were indispensable. The equipages were generally much more gorgeous than at a later period, when democracy invaded the parks, and introduced what may be termed a "Brummagem society," with shabby-genteel carriages and servants. The carriage company consisted of the most celebrated beauties, amongst whom were remarked the Duchesses of Rutland, Argyle, Gordon, and Bedford, Ladies Cowper, Foley, Heathcote, Louisa Lambton, Hertford, and Mountjoy. The most conspicuous horsemen were the Prince Regent (accompanied by Sir Benjamin Bloomfield); the Duke of York and his old friend, Warwick Lake; the Duke of Dorset, on his white horse; the Marquis of Anglesea, with his lovely daughters; Lord Harrowby and the Ladies Ryder; the Earl of Sefton and the Ladies Molyneux; and the eccentric Earl of Morton, on his long-tailed grey. In those days, "pretty horse-breakers" would not have dared to show themselves in Hyde Park; nor did you see any of the lower or middle classes of London intruding themselves in regions which, with a sort of tacit understanding, were then given up exclusively to persons of rank and fashion.

LONDON HOTELS IN 1814.—There was a class of men, of very high rank,—such as Lords Wellington, Nelson, and Collingwood, Sir John Moore, and some few others,—who never frequented the clubs. The persons to whom I refer, and amongst whom were many members of the sporting world, used to congregate at a few hotels. The Clarendon, Limmer's, Ibbetson's, Fladong's, Stephens's, and Grillon's, were the fashionable hotels. The Clarendon was then kept by a French cook, Jacquiers, who contrived to amass a large sum of money in the service of Louis the Eighteenth in England, and subsequently with Lord Darnley. This was the only public hotel where you could get a genuine French dinner, and for which you seldom paid less than three or four pounds; your bottle of champagne or of claret, in the year 1814, costing you a guinea.

Limmer's was an evening resort for the sporting world; in fact, it was a midnight Tattersall's, where you heard nothing but the language of the turf, and where men with not very clean hands used to make up their books. Limmer's was the most dirty hotel in London; but in the gloomy, comfortless coffee-room might be seen many members of the rich squirearchy who visited London during the sporting season. This hotel was frequently so crowded, that a bed could not be obtained for any amount of money; but you could always get a very good plain English dinner, an excellent bottle of port, and some famous gin-punch.

Ibbetson's hotel was chiefly patronised by the clergy and young men from the universities. The charges there were more economical than at similar establishments. Fladong's, in Oxford Street, was chiefly frequented by naval men; for in those days there was no club for sailors. Stephens's, in Bond Street, was a fashionable hotel, supported by officers of the army and men about town. If a stranger asked to dine there, he was stared at by the servants, and very solemnly assured that there was no table vacant.   It was not an uncommon thing to see thirty or forty saddle-horses and tilburies waiting outside this hotel.   I recollect two of my old Welsh friends, who used each of them to dispose of five bottles of wine daily, residing here in 1815, when the familiar joints, boiled fish, and fried soles, were the only eatables you could order.

THE CLUBS OF LONDON IN 1814.—The members of the clubs in London, many years since, were persons, almost without exception, belonging exclusively to the aristocratic world.   "My tradesmen," as King Allen used to call the bankers and the merchants, had not then invaded White's, Boodle's, Brookes's, or Wattiers's, in Bolton Street, Piccadilly; which, with the Guards', Arthur's, and Graham's, were the only clubs at the West End of the town. White's was decidedly the most difficult of entry: its list of members comprised nearly all the noble names of Great Britain.

The politics of White's Club were then decidedly Tory.   It was here that play was carried on to an extent which made many ravages in large fortunes, the traces of which have not disappeared at the present day.   General Scott, the father-in-law of George Canning and the Duke of Portland, was known to have won at White's £200,000; thanks to his notorious sobriety and knowledge of the game of whist.   The general possessed a great advantage over his companions by avoiding those indulgences at the table which used to muddle other men's brains.   He confined himself to dining off something like a boiled chicken, with toast-and-water; by such a regimen he came to the whist-table with a clear head, and possessing as he did a remarkable memory, with great coolness and judgment, he was able honestly to win the enormous sum of £200,000.

At Brookes's, for nearly half a century, the play was of a more gambling character than at White's. Faro and macao were indulged in to an extent which enabled a man to win or to lose a considerable fortune in one night. It was here that Charles James Fox, Selwyn, Lord Carlisle, Lord Robert Spencer, General Fitzpatrick, and other great Whigs, won and lost hundreds of thousands; frequently remaining at the table for many hours without rising.

On one occasion, Lord Robert Spencer contrived to lose the last shilling of his considerable fortune, given him by his brother, the Duke of Marlborough; General Fitzpatrick being much in the same condition, they agreed to raise a sum of money in order that they might keep a faro bank. The members of the club made no objection, and ere long they carried out their design. As is generally the case, the bank was a winner, and Lord Robert bagged, as his share of the proceeds, £100,000. He retired, strange to say, from the fœtid atmosphere of play, with the money in his pocket, and never again gambled. George Harley Drummond, of the famous banking-house, Charing Cross, only played once in his whole life at White's Club at whist, on which occasion he lost £20,000 to Brummell. This event caused him to retire from the banking-house of which he was a partner.

Lord Carlisle was one of the most remarkable victims amongst the players at Brookes's, and Charles Fox, his friend, was not more fortunate, being subsequently always in pecuniary difficulties. Many a time, after a long night of hard play, the loser found himself at the Israelitish establishment of Howard and Gibbs, then the fashionable and patronised money-lenders. These gentlemen never failed to make hard terms with the borrower, although ample security was invariably demanded.

The Guards' Club was established for the three regiments of Foot Guards, and was conducted upon a military system. Billiards and low whist were the only games indulged in. The dinner was, perhaps, better than at most clubs, and considerably cheaper. I had the honour of being a member for several years, during which time I have nothing to remember but the most agreeable incidents. Arthur's and Graham's were less aristocratic than those I have mentioned; it was at the latter, thirty years ago, that a most painful circumstance took place. A nobleman of the highest position and influence in society was detected in cheating at cards, and after a trial, which did not terminate in his favour, he died of a broken heart.

Upon one occasion, some gentlemen of both White's and Brookes's had the honour to dine with the Prince Regent, and during the conversation, the prince inquired what sort of dinners they got at their clubs; upon which Sir Thomas Stepney, one of the guests, observed that their dinners were always the same, " the eternal joints, or beef-steaks, the boiled fowl with oyster sauce, and an apple-tart—this is what we have, sir, at our clubs, and very monotonous fare it is." The prince, without further remark, rang the bell for his cook, Wattier, and, in the presence of those who dined at the royal table, asked him whether he would take a house and organise a dinner club. Wattier assented, and named Madison, the prince's page, manager, and Labourie, the cook, from the royal kitchen. The club flourished only a few years, owing to the high play that was carried on there. The Duke of York patronised it, and was a member. I was a member in 1816, and frequently saw his Royal Highness there. The dinners were exquisite; the best Parisian cooks could not beat Labourie. The favourite game played there was macao. Upon one occasion, Jack Bouverie, brother of Lady Heytesbury, was losing large sums, and became very irritable: Raikes, with bad taste, laughed at Bouverie, and attempted to amuse us with some of his stale jokes; upon which Bouverie threw his play-bowl, with the few counters it contained, at Raikes's head; unfortunately it struck him, and made the city dandy angry, but no serious results followed this open insult.

REMARKABLE CHARACTERS OF LONDON ABOUT THE YEARS 1814, 1815, 1816.—It appears to be a law of natural history that every generation produces and throws out from the mob of society a few conspicuous men, that pass under the general appellation of "men about town." Michael Angelo Taylor was one of those remarkable individuals whom every one was glad to know; and those who had not that privilege were ever talking about him, although he was considered by many a bit of a bore. Michael

MARQUIS OF LONDONDERRY.　COL. "KANGAROO" COOKE.　CAPTAIN GRONOW.　LORD ALLEN.　COUNT D'ORSAY.

HABITUÉS OF WHITE'S.

Angelo was a member of Parliament for many years, and generally sat in one of the most important committees of the House of Commons; for he was a man of authority and an attractive speaker. In appearance he was one of that sort of persons whom you could not pass in the streets without exclaiming, "Who can that be?" His face blushed with port wine, the purple tints of which, by contrast, caused his white hair to glitter with silvery brightness; he wore leather breeches, top boots, blue coat, white waistcoat, and an unstarched and exquisitely white neckcloth, the whole surmounted by a very broad-brimmed beaver;—such was the dress of the universally-known Michael Angelo Taylor. If you met him in society, or at the clubs, he was never known to salute you but with the invariable phrase, "What news have you?" Upon one occasion, riding through St. James's Park, he met the great Minister, Mr. Pitt, coming from Wimbledon, where he resided. He asked Mr. Pitt the usual question, upon which the Premier replied, " I have not yet seen the morning papers."

" Oh, that won't do, Mr. Pitt. I am sure that you know something, and will not tell me."

Mr. Pitt good-humouredly replied : " Well, then, I am going to a Cabinet Council, and I will consult my colleagues whether I can divulge state secrets to you or not."

Upon another occasion, on entering Boodle's, of which he was a member, he observed the celebrated Lord Westmoreland at table, where the noble lord was doing justice to a roast fowl. Taylor, of course, asked him the news of the day, and Lord Westmoreland coolly told the little newsmonger to go into the other room and leave him to finish his dinner, promising to join him after he had done. The noble lord kept his word, and the first thing he heard from Mr. Taylor was, " Well, my lord, what news ? what had you for dinner ? "

His lordship replied, " A Welsh leg of mutton."

" What then—what then ? "

" Don't you think a leg of mutton enough for any man ? "

" Yes, my lord, but you did not eat it all ? "

" Yes, Taylor, I did."

" Well, I think you have placed the leg of mutton in some mysterious place, for I see no trace of it in your lean person."

Lord Westmoreland was remarkable for an appetite which made nothing of a respectable joint, or a couple of fowls.

I know not whether Mr. Poole, the author of *Paul Pry*, had Michael Angelo in his head when he wrote that well-known comedy ; but certainly he might have sat for a character whose intrusive and inquisitive habits were so notorious, that people on seeing him approach always prepared for a string of almost impertinent interrogations.

Another remarkable man about town was Colonel Cooke, commonly called Kangaroo Cooke, who was for many years the private aide-de-camp and secretary of H.R.H. the Duke of York. He was the brother of General Sir George Cooke and of the beautiful Countess of Cardigan, mother of the gallant Lord Cardigan, and the Ladies Howe, Baring, and Lucan. During his career he had been employed in diplomatic negotiations with the French, previous to the peace of Paris. He was in the best society, and always attracted attention by his dandified mode of dress.

Colonel Armstrong, another pet of the Duke of York's, was known, when in the Coldstream Guards, to be a thorough hard-working soldier, and his non-commissioned officers were so perfect, that nearly all the adjutants of the different regiments of the line were educated by him. He was a strict disciplinarian, but strongly opposed to corporal punishment, and used to boast that during the whole time that he commanded the regiment only two men had been flogged.

Colonel Mackinnon, commonly called "Dan," was an exceedingly well-made man, and remarkable for his physical powers in running, jumping, climbing, and such bodily exercises as demanded agility and muscular strength. He used to amuse his friends by creeping over the furniture of a room like a monkey. It was very common for his companions to make bets with him : for example, that he would not be able to climb up the ceiling of a room, or scramble over a certain house-top. Grimaldi, the famous clown, used to say, "Colonel Mackinnon has only to put on the motley costume, and he would totally eclipse me."

Mackinnon was famous for practical jokes ; which were, however, always played in a gentlemanly way. Before landing at St. Andero's, with some other officers who had been on leave in England, he agreed to personate the Duke of York, and make the Spaniards believe that his Royal Highness was amongst them. On nearing the shore, a royal standard was hoisted at the mast-head, and Mackinnon disembarked, wearing the star of his shako on his left breast, and accompanied by his friends, who agreed to play the part of aide-de-camp to royalty. The Spanish authorities were soon informed of the arrival of the Royal Commander-in-Chief of the British army; so they received Mackinnon with the usual pomp and circumstance attending such occasions. The mayor of the place, in honour of the illustrious arrival, gave a grand banquet, which terminated with the appearance of a huge bowl of punch. Whereupon Dan, thinking that the joke had gone far enough, suddenly dived his head into the porcelain vase, and threw his heels into the air. The surprise and indignation of the solemn Spaniards were such, that they made a most intemperate report of the hoax that had been played on them to Lord Wellington; Dan, however, was ultimately forgiven, after a severe reprimand.

Another of his freaks very nearly brought him to a court-martial. Lord Wellington was curious about visiting a convent near Lisbon, and the lady abbess made no difficulty; Mackinnon, hearing this, contrived to get clandestinely within the sacred walls, and it was generally supposed that it was neither his first nor his second visit. At all events, when Lord Wellington arrived, Dan Mackinnon was to be seen among the nuns, dressed out in their sacred costume, with his head and whiskers shaved; and as he possessed good features, he was declared to be one of the best-looking amongst those chaste dames. It was supposed that this adventure, which was known to Lord Byron, suggested a similar episode in *Don Juan*, the scene being laid in the East. I might say more about Dan's adventures in the convent, but have no wish to be scandalous.

Another dandy of the day was Sir Lumley Skeffington, who used to paint his face, so that he
looked like a French toy ; he dressed *à la* Robespierre, and practised other follies, although the consummate old fop was a man of literary attainments,
and a great admirer and patron of the drama.
Skeffington was remarkable for his politeness and
courtly manners ; in fact, he was invited everywhere, and was very popular with the ladies. You
always knew of his approach by an *avant-courier* of
sweet smells ; and when he advanced a little nearer,
you might suppose yourself in the atmosphere of a
perfumer's shop.   He is thus immortalised by Byron,
in *English Bards and Scotch Reviewers*, alluding
to the play written by Skeffington, *The Sleeping
Beauty* :—

> " In grim array though Lewis' spectres rise,
>   Still Skeffington and Goose divide the prize :
>   And sure great Skeffington must claim our praise,
>   For skirtless coats and skeletons of plays
>   Renown'd alike ; whose genius ne'er confines
>   Her flight to garnish Greenwood's gay designs,
>   Nor sleeps with ' sleeping beauties,' but anon
>   In five facetious acts comes thundering on,
>   While poor John Bull, bewilder'd with the scene,
>   Stares, wond'ring what the devil it can mean ;
>   But as some hands applaud—a venal few—
>   Rather than sleep, John Bull applauds it too."

Long Wellesley Pole was a fashionable who distinguished himself by giving sumptuous dinners at
Wanstead, where he owned one of the finest mansions in England. He used to ask his friends to
dine with him after the opera at midnight ; the
drive from London being considered *appétisant*.
Every luxury that money could command was placed

before his guests at this unusual hour of the night. He married Miss Tylney Pole, an heiress of fifty thousand a year, yet died quite a beggar : in fact, he would have starved, had it not been for the charity of his cousin, the present Duke of Wellington, who allowed him three hundred a year.

THE GUARDS MARCHING FROM ENGHIEN ON THE 15TH OF JUNE.—Two battalions of my regiment had started from Brussels ; the other (the 2nd), to which I belonged, remained in London, and I saw no prospect of taking part in the great events which were about to take place on the Continent. Early in June I had the honour of dining with Colonel Darling, the deputy adjutant-general, and I was there introduced to Sir Thomas Picton, as a countryman and neighbour of his brother, Mr. Turberville, of Evenney Abbey, in Glamorganshire. He was very gracious, and, on his two aides-de-camp—Major Tyler and my friend Chambers, of the Guards— lamenting that I was obliged to remain at home, Sir Thomas said, " Is the lad really anxious to go out ? " Chambers answered that it was the height of my ambition. Sir Thomas inquired if all the appointments to his staff were filled up ; and then added, with a grim smile, " If Tyler is killed, which is not at all unlikely, I do not know why I should not take my young countryman : he may go over with me if he can get leave." I was overjoyed at this, and, after thanking the general a thousand times, made my bow and retired.

I was much elated at the thoughts of being Picton's aide-de-camp, though that somewhat remote contingency depended upon my friends Tyler, or Chambers, or others, meeting with an untimely end; but at eighteen *on ne doute de rien.*   So I set about thinking how I should manage to get my outfit, in order to appear at Brussels in a manner worthy of the aide-de-camp of the great general. As my funds were at a low ebb, I went to Cox and Greenwood's, those stanch friends of the hard-up soldier.   Sailors may talk of the "little cherub that sits up aloft," but commend me for liberality, kindness, and generosity, to my old friends in Craig's Court.   I there obtained £200, which I took with me to a gambling-house in St. James's Square, where I managed, by some wonderful accident, to win £600; and, having thus obtained the sinews of war, I made numerous purchases, amongst others two first-rate horses at Tattersall's for a high figure, which were embarked for Ostend, along with my groom.   I had not got leave; but I thought I should get back, after the great battle that appeared imminent, in time to mount guard at St. James's.

On a Saturday I accompanied Chambers in his carriage to Ramsgate, where Sir Thomas Picton and Tyler had already arrived; we remained there for the Sunday, and embarked on Monday in a vessel which had been hired for the general and suite. On the same day we arrived at Ostend, and put up at a hotel in the square; where I was surprised to hear the general, in excellent French, get up a flirtation with our very pretty waiting-maid.

Sir Thomas Picton was a stern-looking, strong-built man, about the middle height, and considered very like the Hetman Platoff.   He generally wore a blue frock-coat, very tightly buttoned up to the throat; a very large black silk neckcloth, showing

little or no shirt-collar; dark trousers, boots, and a
round hat: it was in this very dress that he was
attired at Quatre Bras, as he had hurried off to the
scene of action before his uniform arrived. After
sleeping at Ostend, the general and Tyler went the
next morning to Ghent, and on Thursday to Brussels. I proceeded by boat to Ghent, and, without
stopping, hired a carriage, and arrived in time to
order rooms for Sir Thomas at the Hôtel d'Angleterre, Rue de la Madeleine, at Brussels: our horses
followed us.

While we were at breakfast, Colonel Canning
came to inform the general that the Duke of Wellington wished to see him immediately. Sir Thomas
lost not a moment in obeying the order of his chief,
leaving the breakfast-table and proceeding to the
park, where Wellington was walking with Fitzroy
Somerset and the Duke of Richmond. Picton's
manner was always more familiar than the duke
liked in his lieutenants, and on this occasion he
approached him in a careless sort of way, just as he
might have met an equal. The duke bowed coldly
to him, and said, "I am glad you are come, Sir
Thomas; the sooner you get on horseback the better:
no time is to be lost. You will take the command
of the troops in advance. The Prince of Orange
knows by this time that you will go to his assistance."
Picton appeared not to like the duke's manner; for
when he bowed and left, he muttered a few words,
which convinced those who were with him that he
was not much pleased with his interview.

QUATRE BRAS.—I got upon the best of my two
horses, and followed Sir Thomas Picton and his staff

to Quatre Bras at full speed. His division was already engaged in supporting the Prince of Orange, and had deployed itself in two lines in front of the road to Sombref when he arrived. Sir Thomas immediately took the command. Shortly afterwards, Kempt's and Pack's brigades arrived by the Brussels road, and part of Alten's division by the Nivelles road.

Ney was very strong in cavalry, and our men were constantly formed into squares to receive them. The famous Kellerman, the hero of Marengo, tried a last charge, and was very nearly being taken or killed, as his horse was shot under him when very near us. Wellington at last took the offensive;—a charge was made against the French, which succeeded, and we remained masters of the field. I acted as a mere spectator, and got, on one occasion, just within twenty or thirty yards of some of the cuirassiers; but my horse was too quick for them.

On the 17th, Wellington retreated upon Waterloo, about eleven o'clock. The infantry were masked by the cavalry in two lines, parallel to the Namur road. Our cavalry retired on the approach of the French cavalry, in three columns, on the Brussels road. A torrent of rain fell, upon the emperor's ordering the heavy cavalry to charge us; while the fire of sixty or eighty pieces of cannon showed that we had chosen our position at Waterloo. Chambers said to me, "Now, Gronow, the loss has been very severe in the Guards, and I think you ought to go and see whether you are wanted; for, as you have really nothing to do with Picton, you had better join your regiment, or you may get into a scrape."

Taking his advice, I rode off to where the Guards were stationed. The officers—amongst whom I remember Colonel Thomas and Brigade - Major Miller—expressed their astonishment and amazement on seeing me, and exclaimed, "What the deuce brought you here? Why are you not with your battalion in London? Get off your horse, and explain how you came here!"

Things were beginning to look a little awkward, when Gunthorpe, the adjutant, a great friend of mine, took my part and said, "As he is here, let us make the most of him : there's plenty of work for every one. Come, Gronow, you shall go with Captain Clements and a detachment to the village of Waterloo, to take charge of the French prisoners." "What the deuce shall I do with my horse?" I asked. Upon which Captain Stopford, aide-de-camp to Sir John Byng, volunteered to buy him. Having thus once more become a foot soldier, I started according to orders, and arrived at Waterloo.

GENERAL APPEARANCE OF THE FIELD OF WATERLOO.—The day on which the battle of Waterloo was fought seemed to have been chosen by some providential accident for which human wisdom is unable to account. On the morning of the 18th the sun shone most gloriously, and so clear was the atmosphere that we could see the long, imposing lines of the enemy most distinctly. Immediately in front of the division to which I belonged, and, I should imagine, about half a mile from us, were posted cavalry and artillery; and to the right and left the French had already engaged us, attacking Huguemont and La Haye Sainte. We heard incessantly the measured boom of artillery, accompanied by the incessant rattling echoes of musketry.

The whole of the British infantry not actually engaged were at that time formed into squares; and as you looked along our lines, it seemed as if we formed a continuous wall of human beings. I recollect distinctly being able to see Bonaparte and his staff; and some of my brother officers using the glass, exclaimed, "There he is on his white horse." I should not forget to state that when the enemy's artillery began to play on us, we had orders to lie down: we could hear the shot and shell whistling around us, killing and wounding great numbers; then again we were ordered on our knees to receive cavalry. The French artillery, which consisted of three hundred guns,—we did not muster more than half that number,—committed terrible havoc during the early part of the battle, whilst we were acting on the defensive.

THE DUKE OF WELLINGTON IN OUR SQUARE.— About four P.M. the enemy's artillery in front of us ceased firing all of a sudden, and we saw large masses of cavalry advance: not a man present who survived could have forgotten in after life the awful grandeur of that charge. You perceived at a distance what appeared to be an overwhelming, long moving line, which, ever advancing, glittered like a stormy wave of the sea when it catches the sunlight. On came the mounted host until they got near enough, whilst the very earth seemed to vibrate beneath their thundering tramp. One might suppose that nothing could have resisted the shock of this terrible moving mass. They were the famous cuirassiers, almost all old soldiers, who had distinguished themselves on most of the battle-fields of Europe. In an almost incredibly short period they were within twenty yards of us, shouting " *Vive l'Empereur!* " The word of command, " Prepare to receive cavalry," had been given, every man in the front ranks knelt, and a wall bristling with steel, held together by steady hands, presented itself to the infuriated cuirassiers.

I should observe that just before this charge the duke entered by one of the angles of the square, accompanied only by one aide-de-camp; all the rest of his staff being either killed or wounded. Our Commander-in-Chief, as far as I could judge, appeared perfectly composed; but looked very thoughtful and pale. He was dressed in a grey great-coat with a cape, white cravat, leather pantaloons, Hessian boots, and a large cocked hat *à la Russe.*

The charge of the French cavalry was gallantly executed; but our well-directed fire brought men and horses down, and ere long the utmost confusion arose in their ranks. The officers were exceedingly brave, and by their gestures and fearless bearing did all in their power to encourage their men to form again and renew the attack. The duke sat unmoved, mounted on his favourite charger. I recollect his asking Colonel Stanhope what o'clock it was, upon which Stanhope took out his watch, and said it was twenty minutes past four. The Duke replied, " The battle is mine; and if the Prussians arrive soon, there will be an end of the war."

THE FRENCH CAVALRY CHARGING THE BRUNS-WICKERS.—Soon after the cuirassiers had retired,

we observed to our right the red hussars of the
Garde Impériale charging a square of Brunswick
riflemen, who were about fifty yards from us. This
charge was brilliantly executed, but the well-sus-
tained fire from the square baffled the enemy, who
were obliged to retire after suffering a severe loss in
killed and wounded. The ground was completely
covered with those brave men, who lay in various
positions, mutilated in every conceivable way.
Among the fallen we perceived the gallant colonel
of the hussars lying under his horse, which had been
killed. All of a sudden two riflemen of the Bruns-
wickers left their battalion, and after taking from
their helpless victim his purse, watch, and other
articles of value, they deliberately put the colonel's
pistols to the poor fellow's head, and blew out his
brains. "Shame! shame!" was heard from our
ranks, and a feeling of indignation ran through
the whole line; but the deed was done: this brave
soldier lay a lifeless corpse in sight of his cruel foes,
whose only excuse perhaps was that their sovereign,
the Duke of Brunswick, had been killed two days
before by the French.

Again and again various cavalry regiments, heavy
dragoons, lancers, hussars, carabineers of the Guard,
endeavoured to break our walls of steel. The enemy's
cavalry had to advance over ground which was so
heavy that they could not reach us except at a trot;
they therefore came upon us in a much more com-
pact mass than they probably would have done if
the ground had been more favourable. When they
got within ten or fifteen yards they discharged their
carbines, to the cry of "*Vive l'Empereur!*" but
their fire produced little effect, as is generally the

case with the fire of cavalry. Our men had orders
not to fire unless they could do so on a near mass ;
the object being to economise our ammunition, and
not to waste it on scattered soldiers. The result
was, that when the cavalry had discharged their
carbines, and were still far off, we occasionally stood
face to face, looking at each other inactively, not
knowing what the next move might be.

The lancers were particularly troublesome, and
approached us with the utmost daring. On one
occasion I remember, the enemy's artillery having
made a gap in the square, the lancers were evidently
waiting to avail themselves of it, to rush among us,
when Colonel Staples, at once observing their intention, with the utmost promptness filled up the gap,
and thus again completed our impregnable steel
wall ; but in this act he fell mortally wounded. The
cavalry seeing this, made no attempt to carry out
their original intentions, and observing that we had
entirely regained our square, confined themselves to
hovering round us. I must not forget to mention
that the lancers in particular never failed to despatch
our wounded, whenever they had an opportunity of
doing so.

When we received cavalry, the order was to fire
low ; so that on the first discharge of musketry, the
ground was strewed with the fallen horses and their
riders, which impeded the advance of those behind
them, and broke the shock of the charge. It was
pitiable to witness the agony of the poor horses, which
really seemed conscious of the dangers that surrounded them : we often saw a poor wounded animal
raise its head, as if looking for its rider to afford him
aid. There is nothing perhaps amongst the episodes

of a great battle more striking than the *débris* of
a cavalry charge, where men and horses are seen
scattered and wounded on the ground in every
variety of painful attitude.   Many a time the heart
sickened at the moaning tones of agony which came
from man, and scarcely less intelligent horse, as they
lay in fearful agony upon the field of battle.

THE LAST CHARGE AT WATERLOO.—It was about
five o'clock on that memorable day, that we suddenly
received orders to retire behind an elevation in our
rear.   The enemy's artillery had come up *en masse*
within a hundred yards of us.   By the time they
began to discharge their guns, however, we were
lying down behind the rising ground, and protected
by the ridge before referred to.   The enemy's cavalry
was in the rear of their artillery, in order to be ready
to protect it if attacked ; but no attempt was made
on our part to do so.   After they had pounded away
at us for about half-an-hour, they deployed, and up
came the whole mass of the Imperial infantry of the
Guard, led on by the emperor in person.   We had
now before us probably about 20,000 of the best
soldiers in France, the heroes of many memorable
victories ; we saw the bear-skin caps rising higher
and higher, as they ascended the ridge of ground
which separated us and advanced nearer and nearer
to our lines.

It was at this moment that the Duke of Wellington gave his famous order for our bayonet charge,
as he rode along the line : these are the precise words
he made use of—"Guards, get up and charge!"   We
were instantly on our legs, and after so many hours
of inaction and irritation at maintaining a purely

defensive attitude,—all the time suffering the loss of comrades and friends,—the spirit which animated officers and men may easily be imagined. After firing a volley as soon as the enemy were within shot, we rushed on with fixed bayonets, and that hearty hurrah peculiar to British soldiers.

It appeared that our men, deliberately and with calculation, singled out their victims; for as they came upon the Imperial Guard our line broke, and the fighting became irregular. The impetuosity of our men seemed almost to paralyse their enemies: I witnessed several of the Imperial Guard who were run through the body apparently without any resistance on their parts. I observed a big Welshman of the name of Hughes, who was six feet seven inches in height, run through with his bayonet, and knock down with the butt-end of his firelock, I should think a dozen at least of his opponents. This terrible contest did not last more than ten minutes, for the Imperial Guard was soon in full retreat, leaving all their guns and many prisoners in our hands.

The famous General Cambronne was taken prisoner fighting hand to hand with the gallant Sir Colin Halkett, who was shortly after shot through the cheeks by a grape-shot. Cambronne's supposed answer of *"La Garde ne se rend pas"* was an invention of after times, and he himself always denied having used such an expression.

HUGUEMONT.—Early on the morning after the battle of Waterloo, I visited Huguemont, in order to witness with my own eyes the traces of one of the most hotly-contested spots of the field of battle. I came first upon the orchard, and there discovered heaps of dead men, in various uniforms: those of the Guards in their usual red jackets, the German Legion in green, and the French dressed in blue, mingled together. The dead and the wounded positively covered the whole area of the orchard; not less than two thousand men had there fallen. The apple-trees presented a singular appearance; shattered branches were seen hanging about their mother-trunks in such profusion, that one might almost suppose the stiff-growing and stunted tree had been converted into the willow: every tree was riddled and smashed in a manner which told that the showers of shot had been incessant. On this spot I lost some of my dearest and bravest friends, and the country had to mourn many of its most heroic sons slain here.

I must observe that, according to the custom of commanding-officers, whose business it is after a great battle to report to the Commander-in-Chief, the muster-roll of fame always closes before the rank of captain. It has always appeared to me a great injustice that there should ever be any limit to the roll of gallantry of either officers or men. If a captain, lieutenant, an ensign, a sergeant, or a private, has distinguished himself for his bravery, his intelligence, or both, their deeds ought to be reported, in order that the sovereign and nation should know who really fight the great battles of England. Of the class of officers and men to which I have referred, there were many even of superior rank who were omitted to be mentioned in the public despatches.

Thus, for example, to the individual courage of Lord Saltoun and Charley Ellis, who commanded the light companies, was mainly owing our success at Huguemont. The same may be said of Needham, Percival, Erskine, Grant, Vyner, Buckley, Master, and young Algernon Greville, who at that time could not have been more than seventeen years old. Excepting Percival, whose jaws were torn away by a grape-shot, every one of these heroes miraculously escaped.

I do not wish, in making these observations, to detract from the bravery and skill of officers whose names have already been mentioned in official despatches, but I think it only just that the services of those I have particularised should not be forgotten by one of their companions in arms.

BYNG WITH HIS BRIGADE AT WATERLOO. — No individual officer more distinguished himself than did General Byng at the battle of Waterloo. In the early part of the day he was seen at Huguemont leading his men in the thick of the fight; later he was with the battalion in square, where his presence animated to the utmost enthusiasm both officers and men. It is difficult to imagine how this courageous man passed through such innumerable dangers from shot and shell without receiving a single wound. I must also mention some other instances of courage and devotion in officers belonging to this brigade; for instance, it was Colonel Macdonell, a man of colossal stature, with Hesketh, Bowes, Tom Sowerby, and Hugh Seymour, who commanded from the inside the château of Huguemont. When the French had taken possession of the orchard, they made a rush at the principal door of the château, which had been turned into a fortress. Macdonell and the above officers placed themselves, accompanied by some of their men, behind the portal, and prevented the French from entering. Amongst other officers of that brigade who were most conspicuous for bravery, I would record the names of Montague, the "vigorous Gooch," as he was called, and the well-known Jack Standen.

THE LATE DUKE OF RICHMOND.—One of the most intimate friends of the Duke of Wellington was the Earl of March, afterwards Duke of Richmond. He was a genuine hard-working soldier, a man of extraordinary courage, and one who was ever found ready to gain laurels amidst the greatest dangers. When the 7th Fusiliers crossed the Bidassoa, the late duke left the staff and joined the regiment in which he had a company. At Orthes, in the thick of the fight, he received a shot which passed through his lungs; from this severe wound he recovered sufficiently to be able to join the Duke of Wellington, to whom he was exceedingly useful at the battle of Waterloo. On his return to England, he united himself to the most remarkably beautiful girl of the day, the eldest daughter of Lord Anglesea, and whose mother was the lovely Duchess of Argyle.

THE UNFORTUNATE CHARGE OF THE HOUSEHOLD BRIGADE.—When Lord Uxbridge gave orders to Sir W. Ponsonby and Lord Edward Somerset to charge the enemy, our cavalry advanced with the greatest bravery, cut through everything in their way, and gallantly attacked whole regiments of infantry; but eventually they came upon a masked battery of twenty guns, which carried death and destruction through our ranks, and our poor fellows were obliged to give way. The French cavalry followed on their retreat, when, perhaps, the severest hand-to-hand cavalry fighting took place within the memory of man. The Duke of Wellington was perfectly furious that this arm had been engaged without his orders, and lost not a moment in sending them to the rear, where they remained during the rest of the day. This disaster gave the French cavalry an opportunity of annoying and insulting us, and compelled the artillerymen to seek shelter in our squares; and if the French had been provided with tackle, or harness of any description, our guns would have been taken. It is, therefore, not to be wondered at that the duke should have expressed himself in no measured terms about the cavalry movements referred to. I recollect that, when his grace was in our square, our soldiers were so mortified at seeing the French deliberately walking their horses between our regiment and those regiments to our right and left, that they shouted, " Where are our cavalry ? why don't they come and pitch into those French fellows ? "

THE DUKE OF WELLINGTON'S OPINION OF THE ENGLISH CAVALRY.—A day or two after our arrival in Paris from Waterloo, Colonel Felton Hervey having entered the dining-room with the despatches which had come from London, the duke asked, " What news have you, Hervey ? " upon which Colonel Hervey answered, " I observe by the *Gazette* that the Prince Regent has made himself Captain-General of the Life Guards and Blues, for their brilliant conduct at Waterloo."

"Ah!" replied the duke, "his Royal Highness is our sovereign, and can do what he pleases; but this I will say, the cavalry of other European armies have won victories for their generals, but mine have invariably got me into scrapes. It is true that they have always fought gallantly and bravely, and have generally got themselves out of their difficulties by sheer pluck."

The justice of this observation has since been confirmed by the charge at Balaklava, where our cavalry undauntedly rushed into the face of death under the command of that intrepid officer Lord Cardigan.

MARSHAL EXCELMANN'S OPINION OF THE BRITISH CAVALRY.—Experience has taught me that there is nothing more valuable than the opinions of intelligent foreigners on the military and naval excellences, and the failures, of our united service. Marshal Excelmann's opinion about the British cavalry struck me as remarkably instructive: he used to say, "Your horses are the finest in the world, and your men ride better than any continental soldiers; with such materials, the English cavalry ought to have done more than has ever been accomplished by them on the field of battle. The great deficiency is in your officers, who have nothing to recommend them but their dash and sitting well in their saddles; indeed, as far as my experience goes, your English generals have never understood the use of cavalry: they have undoubtedly frequently misapplied that important arm of a grand army, and have never, up to the battle of Waterloo, employed the mounted soldier at the proper time and in the

proper place. The British cavalry officer seems to
be impressed with the conviction that he can dash
and ride over everything; as if the art of war were
precisely the same as that of fox-hunting. I need
not remind you of the charge of your two heavy
brigades at Waterloo: this charge was utterly useless, and all the world knows they came upon a
masked battery, which obliged a retreat, and entirely disconcerted Wellington's plans during the
rest of the day."

"Permit me," he added, "to point out a gross
error as regards the dress of your cavalry. I have
seen prisoners so tightly habited that it was impossible for them to use their sabres with facility."

The French marshal concluded by observing—
"I should wish nothing better than such material
as your men and horses are made of; since with
generals who wield cavalry, and officers who are
thoroughly acquainted with that duty in the field, I
do not hesitate to say I might gain a battle."

Such was the opinion of a man of cool judgment,
and one of the most experienced cavalry officers of
the day.

APPEARANCE OF PARIS WHEN THE ALLIES ENTERED.
—I propose giving my own impression of the aspect
of Paris and its vicinity when our regiment entered
that city on the 25th of June 1815. I recollect
we marched from the plain of St. Denis, my battalion being about five hundred strong, the sur-
vivors of the heroic fight of the 18th of June. We
approached near enough to be within fire of the
batteries of Montmartre, and bivouacked for three
weeks in the Bois de Boulogne. That now beautiful

CAMP DES ANGLAIS, IRLANDAIS, ECOSSAIS, AUX CHAMPS ELISEES A PARIS EN 1815.

a Paris, chez Mme Ve Chereau, rue St Jacques, N.^o

Déposé aux espérances

garden was at the period to which I refer a wild
pathless wood, swampy, and entirely neglected.
The Prussians, who were in bivouac near us, amused
themselves by doing as much damage as they could,
without any useful aim or object : they cut down
the finest trees, and set the wood on fire at several
points.   There were about three thousand of the
Guards then encamped in the wood, and I should
think about ten thousand Prussians.   Our camp was
not remarkable for its courtesy towards them ; in
fact, our intercourse was confined to the most ordinary demands of duty, as allies in an enemy's
country.

I believe I was one of the first of the British
army who penetrated into the heart of Paris after
Waterloo.   I entered by the Porte Maillot, and
passed the Arc de Triomphe, which was then building.   In those days the Champs Elysées only contained a few scattered houses, and the roads and
pathways were ankle-deep in mud.   The only attempt at lighting was the suspension of a few lamps
on cords, which crossed the roads.   Here I found
the Scotch regiments bivouacking ; their peculiar
uniform created a considerable sensation amongst
the Parisian women, who did not hesitate to declare
that the want of *culottes* was most indecent.   I
passed through the camp, and proceeded on towards
the gardens of the Tuileries.   This ancient palace
of the kings of France presented, so far as the old
front is concerned, the same aspect that it does at
the present day ; but there were then no flower-
gardens, although the same stately rows of trees
which now ornament the grounds were then in
their midsummer verdure.

Being in uniform, I created an immense amount of curiosity amongst the Parisians; who, by the way, I fancied regarded me with no loving looks. The first house I entered was a café in the garden of the Tuileries, called Legac's. I there met a man who told me he was by descent an Englishman, though he had been born in Paris, and had really never quitted France. He approached me, saying, "Sir, I am delighted to see an English officer in Paris, and you are the first I have yet met with." He talked about the battle of Waterloo, and gave me some useful directions concerning restaurants and cafés. Along the Boulevards were handsome houses, isolated, with gardens interspersed, and the roads were bordered on both sides with stately, spreading trees, some of them probably a hundred years old. There was but an imperfect pavement, the stepping-stones of which were adapted to display the Parisian female ankle and boot in all their calculated coquetry; and the road showed nothing but mother earth, in the middle of which a dirty gutter served to convey the impurities of the city to the river. The people in the streets appeared sulky and stupified : here and there I noticed groups of the higher classes evidently discussing the events of the moment.

How strange humanity would look in our day in the costume of the first empire. The ladies wore very scanty and short skirts, which left little or no waist; their bonnets were of exaggerated proportions, and protruded at least a foot from their faces; and they generally carried a fan. The men wore blue or black coats, which were baggily made, and reached down to their ankles; their hats were enormously large, and spread out at the top.

I dined the first day of my entrance into Paris at the Café Anglais, on the Boulevard des Italiens; where I found, to my surprise, several of my brother officers. I recollect the charge for the dinner was about one-third what it would be at the present day. I had a potage, fish—anything but fresh, and, according to English predilections and taste, of course I ordered a beef-steak and *pommes de terre*. The wine, I thought, was sour. The dinner cost about two francs.

The theatres at this time, as may easily be imagined, were not very well attended. I recollect going to the Français, where I saw for the first time the famous Talma. There was but a scanty audience; in fact, all the best places in the house were empty.

It may easily be imagined that, at a moment like this, most of those who had a stake in the country were pondering over the great and real drama that was then taking place. Napoleon had fled to Rochfort; the wreck of his army had retreated beyond the Loire; no list of killed and wounded had appeared; and, strange to say, the official journal of Paris had made out that the great imperial army at Waterloo had gained a victory. There were, nevertheless, hundreds of people in Paris who knew to the contrary, and many were already aware that they had lost relations and friends in the great battle.

Louis XVIII. arrived, as well as I can remember, at the Tuileries on the 26th of July 1815, and his reception by the Parisians was a singular illustration of the versatile character of the French nation, and the sudden and often inexplicable changes which take place in the feeling of the populace. When the Bourbon, in his old lumbering state-carriage, drove down the Boulevards, accompanied by the Gardes du Corps, the people in the streets and at the windows displayed the wildest joy, enthusiastically shouting " *Vive le Roi !*" amidst the waving of hats and handkerchiefs, while white sheets or white rags were made to do the duty of a Bourbon banner. The king was dressed in a blue coat with a red collar, and wore also a white waistcoat, and a cocked hat with a white cockade in it. His portly and good-natured appearance seemed to be appreciated by the crowd, whom he saluted with a benevolent smile. I should here mention that two great devotees of the Church sat opposite to the King on this memorable occasion. The *cortège* proceeded slowly down the Rue de la Paix until the Tuileries was reached, where a company of the Guards, together with a certain number of the Garde Nationale of Paris, were stationed.

It fell to my lot to be on duty the day after, when the Duke of Wellington and Lord Castlereagh arrived to pay their respects to the restored monarch. I happened to be in the Salle des Maréchaux when these illustrious personages passed through that magnificent apartment. The respect paid to the Duke of Wellington on this occasion may be easily imagined, from the fact that a number of ladies of the highest rank, and of course partisans of the legitimate dynasty, formed an avenue through which the hero of Waterloo passed, exchanging with them courteous recognitions. The king was waiting in the grand reception apartment to receive the great British captain. The interview, I have every reason to believe, was not confined to the courtesies of the palace.

The position of the duke was a difficult one. In the first place, he had to curb the vindictive vandalism of Blucher and his army, who would have levelled the city of Paris to the ground, if they could have done so ; on the other hand, he had to practise a considerable amount of diplomacy towards the newly-restored king. At the same time, the duke's powers from his own Government were necessarily limited. A spirit of vindictiveness pervaded the restored Court against Napoleon and his adherents, which the duke constantly endeavoured to modify. I must not forget to give an illustration of this state of feeling. It was actually proposed by Talleyrand, Fouché, and some important ecclesiastics of the ultra-royalist party, to arrest and shoot the Emperor Napoleon, who was then at Rochfort. So anxious were they to commit this criminal, inhuman, and cowardly act, on an illustrious fallen enemy, who had made the arms of France glorious throughout Europe, that they suggested to the duke, who had the command of the old woodenarmed semaphores, to employ the telegraph to order what I should have designated by no other name than the assassination of the Cæsar of modern history.

MARSHAL NEY AND WELLINGTON.—As an illustration of the false impressions which are always disseminated concerning public men, I must record the following fact :—The Duke of Wellington was accused of being implicated in the military murder of Ney. Now, so far from this being the truth, I know positively that the Duke of Wellington used every endeavour to prevent this national disgrace; but the Church party, ever crafty and ever ready to profit by the weakness and passions of humanity, supported the king in his moments of excited revenge. It is a lamentable fact, but no less historical truth, that the Roman Catholic Church has ever sought to make the graves of its enemies the foundations of its power. The Duke of Wellington was never able to approach the king or use his influence to save Marshal Ney's life; but everything he could do was done, in order to accomplish his benevolent views. I repeat, the influence of the ultramontane party triumphed over the Christian humanity of the illustrious duke.

THE PALAIS ROYAL AFTER THE RESTORATION.—France has often been called the centre of European fashion and gaiety; and the Palais Royal, at the period to which I refer, might be called the very heart of French dissipation. It was a theatre in which all the great actors of fashion of all nations met to play their parts: on this spot were congregated daily an immense multitude, for no other purpose than to watch the busy comedy of real life that animated the corridors, gardens, and saloons of that vast building, which was founded by Richelieu and Mazarin, and modified by Philippe Egalité. Mingled together, and moving about the area of this oblong-square block of buildings, might be seen, about seven o'clock P.M., a crowd of English, Russian, Prussian, Austrian, and other officers of the Allied armies, together with countless foreigners from all parts of the world. Here, too, might have been seen

the present King of Prussia, with his father and
brother, the late king, the Dukes of Nassau, Baden,
and a host of continental princes, who entered
familiarly into the amusements of ordinary mortals,
dining *incog.* at the most renowned restaurants, and
flirting with painted female frailty.

A description of one of the houses of the Palais
Royal will serve to portray the whole of this French
pandemonium.   On the ground-floor is a jeweller's
shop, where may be purchased diamonds, pearls,
emeralds, and every description of female ornament,
such as only can be possessed by those who have
very large sums of money at their command.   It was
here that the successful gambler often deposited
a portion of his winnings, and took away some
costly article of jewellery, which he presented to
some female friend who had never appeared with
him at the altar of marriage.   Beside this shop was
a staircase, generally very dirty, which communicated with the floors above.   Immediately over the
shop was a café, at the counter of which presided a
lady, generally of more than ordinary female attractions, who was very much *décolletée,* and wore an
amount of jewellery which would have made the
eye of an Israelite twinkle with delight.   And there
la crème de la crème of male society used to meet,
sip their ice and drink their cup of mocha, whilst
holding long conversations, almost exclusively about
gambling and women.

Men's thoughts, in this region, seemed to centre
night and day upon the *tapis vert,* and at the entrance of this *salon* was that fatal chamber, over
which might have been written the famous line of
Dante, " *Voi che entrate lasciate ogni speranza.*"

The reader will at once understand that I am referring to the gambling-house, the so-called "hell" of modern society. In one room was the *rouge-et-noir* table, which, from the hour of twelve in the morning, was surrounded by men in every stage of the gambling malady. There was the young pigeon, who, on losing his first feather, had experienced an exciting sensation which, if followed by a bit of good luck, gave him a confidence that the parasites around him, in order to flatter his vanity, would call pluck. There were others in a more advanced stage of the fever, who had long since lost the greater part of their incomes, having mortgaged their property, and been in too frequent correspondence with the Jews. These men had not got to the last stage of gambling despair, but they were so far advanced on the road to perdition that their days were clouded by perpetual anxiety, which reproduced itself in their very dreams. The gambler who has thus far advanced in his career, lives in an *inferno* of his own creation : the charms of society, the beauty of woman, the attractions of the fine arts, and even the enjoyment of a good dinner, are to him rather a source of irritation than delight. The confirmed gamester is doing nothing less than perpetually digging a grave for his own happiness.

The third and most numerous group of men round the *tapis vert* consisted of a class most of whom had already spent their fortunes, exhausted their health, and lost their position in society, by the fatal and demoralising thirst for gold which still fascinated them. These became the hawks of the gambling table ; their quick and wild-glancing eyes were constantly looking out for suitable game during the day, and leaving it where it might be bagged at night. Both at the *rouge-et-noir* table and *roulette* the same sort of company might be met with.   These gambling-houses were the very fountains of immorality : they gathered together, under the most seductive circumstances, the swindler and the swindled.   There were tables for all classes—the workman might play with 20 sous, or the gentleman with 10,000 francs.   The law did not prevent any class from indulging in a vice that assisted to fill the coffers of the municipality of Paris.

The floor over the gambling-house was occupied by unmarried women.   I will not attempt to picture some of the saddest evils of the society of large cities ; but I may add that these Phrynes lived in a style of splendour which can only be accounted for by the fact of their participating in the easily-earned gains of the gambling-house régime.

At that time the Palais Royal was externally the only well-lighted place in Paris.   It was the rendez-vous of all idlers, and especially of that particular class of ladies who lay out their attractions for the public at large.   These were to be seen at all hours in full dress, their bare necks ornamented with mock diamonds and pearls ; and thus decked out in all their finery, they paraded up and down, casting their eyes significantly on every side.

Some strange stories are told in connection with the gambling-houses of the Palais Royal.   An officer of the Grenadier Guards came to Paris on leave of absence, took apartments here, and never left it until his time of absence had expired.   On his arrival in London, one of his friends inquired whether this was true, to which he replied, " Of course it is ; for I found everything I wanted there, both for body and mind."

Such was the state of the Palais Royal under Louis XVIII. and Charles X. ; the Palais Royal of the present day is simply a tame and legitimately commercial mart, compared with that of olden times. Society has changed ; Government no longer patronises such nests of immorality ; and though vice may exist to the same extent, it assumes another garb, and does not appear in the open streets, as at the period to which I have referred.

THE ENGLISH IN PARIS AFTER THE RESTORATION OF THE BOURBONS.—There is no more ordinary illusion belonging to humanity than that which enables us to discover, in the fashions of the day, an elegance and comeliness of dress which a few years after we ourselves regard as odious caricatures of costumes. Thousands of oddly-dressed English flocked to Paris immediately after the war : I remember that the burden of one of the popular songs of the day was, " All the world's in Paris ; " and our countrymen and women having so long been excluded from French modes, had adopted fashions of their own quite as remarkable and eccentric as those of the Parisians, and much less graceful. British beauties were dressed in long, straight pelisses of various colours ; the body of the dress was never of the same colour as the skirt ; and the bonnet was of the bee-hive shape, and very small. The characteristic of the dress of the gentleman was a coat of light blue, or snuff-colour, with brass buttons, the tail reaching nearly to the heels ; a gigantic bunch of seals dangled from his fob, whilst his pantaloons

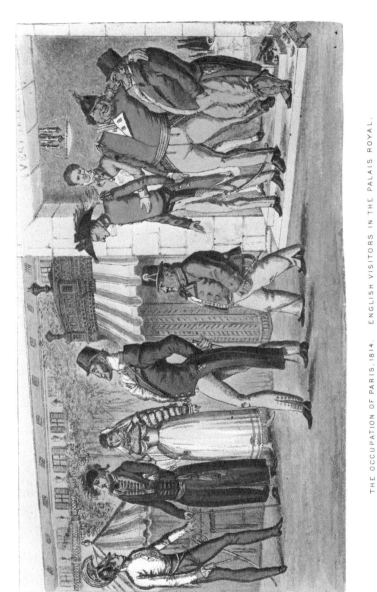

THE OCCUPATION OF PARIS, 1814.   ENGLISH VISITORS IN THE PALAIS ROYAL.

were short and tight at the knees ; and a spacious
waistcoat, with a voluminous muslin cravat and a
frilled shirt, completed the toilette. The dress of
the British military, in its stiff and formal ugliness,
was equally cumbrous and ludicrous.

Lady Oxford—that beautiful and accomplished
woman, who lived in her hotel in the Rue de Clichy
—gave charming soirées, at which were gathered
the *élite* of Paris society. Among these were Edward Montague, Charles Standish, Hervey Aston,
Arthur Upton, "Kangaroo" Cook, Benjamin Constant, Dupin, Casimir Perier, as well as the chief
Orleanists.   On one occasion, I recollect seeing
there George Canning and the celebrated Madame
de Staël.   Cornwall, the eldest son of the Bishop of
Worcester, had, from some unaccountable cause, a
misunderstanding with Madame de Staël, who appeared very excited, and said to Lady Oxford, in a
loud voice, "*Notre ami, M. Cornewal, est grosso,
rosso, e furioso.*"   It should be observed that the
gentleman thus characterised was red-haired, and
hasty in temper. All who heard this denunciation
were astounded at the lady's manner, for she looked
daggers at the object of her sarcasm.

Fox, the secretary of the embassy, was an excellent man, but odd, indolent, and careless in the extreme ; he was seldom seen in the daytime, unless
it was either at the embassy in a state of *négligé*,
or in bed.   At night he used to go to the Salon des
Étrangers ; and, if he possessed a napoleon, it was
sure to be thrown away at hazard, or *rouge et noir*.
On one occasion, however, fortune favoured him in
a most extraordinary manner.   The late Henry
Baring having recommended him to take the dice-

box, Fox replied, "I will do so for the last time, for all my money is thrown away upon this infernal table." Fox staked all he had in his pockets; he threw in *eleven* times, breaking the bank, and taking home for his share 60,000 francs. After this, several days passed without any tidings being heard of him; but upon my calling at the embassy to get my passport *visé*, I went into his room, and saw it filled with Cashmere shawls, silk, Chantilly veils, bonnets, gloves, shoes, and other articles of ladies' dress. On my asking the purpose of all this millinery, Fox replied, in a good-natured way, "Why, my dear Gronow, it was the only means to prevent those rascals at the *salon* winning back my money."

LES ANGLAISES POUR RIRE.—An order had been given to the managers of all the theatres in Paris to admit a certain number of soldiers of the army of occupation, free of expense. It happened that a party of the Guards, composed of a sergeant and a few men, went to the Théâtre des Variétés on the Boulevards, where one of the pieces, entitled *Les Anglaises pour Rire*, was admirably acted by Potier and Brunet. In this piece Englishwomen were represented in a very ridiculous light by those accomplished performers. This gave great offence to our soldiers, and the sergeant and his men determined to put a stop to the acting; accordingly they stormed the stage, and laid violent hands upon the actors, eventually driving them off. The police were called in, and foolishly wanted to take our men to prison; but they soon found to their cost that they had to deal with unmanageable opponents, for the whole posse of gendarmes were charged and

LES MODES ANGLAISES A PARIS.

Le Suprême Bon Ton. N.° 22.

A Paris chez Marchent, Libraire, Rue du Coq.

D.p. a la Direc de la Lib.

driven out of the theatre. A crowd assembled on the Boulevards; which, however, soon dispersed when it became known that English soldiers were determined, *coûte que coûte*, to prevent their countrywomen from being ridiculed. It must be remembered that the only revenge which the Parisians were able to take upon the conquerors was to ridicule them; and the English generally took it in good humour, and laughed at the extravagant drollery of the burlesque.

The English soldiers generally walked about Paris in parties of a dozen, and were quiet and well-behaved. They usually gathered every day on the Boulevard du Temple, where they were amused with the mountebanks and jugglers there assembled.

This part of Paris is now completely changed: but at the time I speak of, it was an extensive open place, where every species of fun was carried on, as at fairs: there were gambling, rope-dancing, wild beasts, and shows; booths for the sale of cakes, ginger-bread, fruit, and lemonade, and every species of attraction that pleases the multitude; but that space has now been built upon, and these sports have all migrated to the barriers.

During the time our troops remained, we had only one man found dead in the streets: it was said that he had been murdered; but of that there was considerable doubt, for no signs of violence were found. This was strongly in contrast to what occurred to the Prussian soldiers. It was asserted, and indeed proved beyond a doubt, that numbers of them were assassinated; and in some parts of France it was not unusual to find in the morning, in deep wells or cellars, several bodies of soldiers of that nation

who had been killed during the night; so strong
was the hatred borne against them by the French.

COACHING AND RACING IN 1815.—Stage-coaches,
or four-in-hand teams, were introduced in Paris in
1815 by Captain Bacon of the 10th Hussars (afterwards a general in the Portuguese service), Sir
Charles Smith, Mr. Roles the brewer, and Arnold,
of the 10th. They used to meet opposite Demidoff's
house, afterwards the Café de Paris, and drive to
the Boulevard Beaumarchais, and then back again,
proceeding to the then unfinished Arc de Triomphe.
Crowds assembled to witness the departure of the
teams; and it created no little amusement to the
Parisian to see perched upon Sir C. Smith's coach
one or two smartly-dressed ladies, who appeared
quite at home. Sir Charles was likewise a great
supporter of the turf, and was the first man who
brought over from England thoroughbred horses.
By his indefatigable energy he contrived to get up
very fair racing in the neighbourhood of Valenciennes; his trainer at this time being Tom Hurst,
who is now, I believe, at Chantilly. All the officers
of our several cavalry and infantry regiments contributed their efforts to make these races respectable
in the eyes of foreigners : certainly they were superior
to those in the Champ de Mars, though under the
patronage of the king.

I shall not forget the first time I witnessed racing
in Paris, for it was more like a review of Gendarmes
and National Guards; the course was kept by a
forest of bayonets, while mounted police galloped
after the running horses, and, in some instances,
reached the goal before them. The Duc d'An-

goulême, with the Duc de Guiche and the Préfet, were present ; but there was only one small stand, opposite to a sentry-box, where the judge was placed. The running, to say the least of it, was ridiculous : horses and riders fell ; and the *fête*, as it was called, ended with a flourish of trumpets. Wonderful changes have taken place since that time, and at the Bois de Boulogne and at Chantilly may be seen running equal to that of our best races in England ; and our neighbours produce horses, bred in France, that can carry off some of the great prizes in our own " Isthmian games."

PARISIAN CAFÉS IN 1815.—At the present day, Paris may be said to be a city of cafés and restaurants. The railroads and steamboats enable the rich of every quarter of the globe to reach the most attractive of all European cities with comparative economy and facility. All foreigners arriving in Paris seem by instinct to rush to the restaurateurs', where strangers may be counted by tens of thousands. It is not surprising that we find in every important street these gaudy modern *triclinia*, which, I should observe, are as much frequented by a certain class of French people as by foreigners, for Paris is proverbially fond of dining out ; in fact, the social intercourse may be said to take place more frequently in the public café than under the domestic roof.

In 1815, I need scarcely remark that the condition of the roads in Europe, and the enormous expense of travelling, made a visit to Paris a journey which could only be indulged in by a very limited and wealthy class of strangers. Hotels and cafés

were then neither so numerous nor so splendid as at
the present day : Meurice's Hotel was a very insignificant establishment in the Rue de l'Echiquier ;
and in the Rue de la Paix, at that time unfinished,
there were but two or three hotels, which would not
be considered even second-rate at the present time.
The site of the Maison Dorée, at the corner of the
Rue Lafitte, was then occupied by a shabby building which went by the name of the Hôtel d'Angleterre, and was kept by the popular and once beautiful Madame Dunan.   The most celebrated restaur-
ant was that of Beauvilliers, in the Rue de Richelieu ;
mirrors and a little gilding were the decorative characteristics of this house, the *cuisine* was far superior
to that of any restaurateur of our day, and the wines
were first-rate.   Beauvilliers was also celebrated
for his *suprême de volaille*, and for his *côtelettes à
la Soubise*. The company consisted of the most
distinguished men of Paris ; here were to be seen
Chateaubriand, Bailly de Ferrette, the Dukes of
Fitzjames, Rochefoucauld, and Grammont, and many
other remarkable personages. It was the custom
to go to the theatres after dinner, and then to
the Salon des Étrangers, which was the Parisian
Crockford's.

Another famous dining-house was the Rocher de
Cancale, in the Rue Mandar, kept by Borel, formerly one of the cooks of Napoleon. Here the
cuisine was so refined that people were reported to
have come over from England expressly for the purpose of enjoying it : indeed, Borel once showed me
a list of his customers, amongst whom I found the
names of Robespierre, Charles James Fox, and the
Duke of Bedford. In the Palais Royal the still

well-known Trois Frères Provençaux was in vogue, and frequented much by the French officers; being celebrated chiefly for its wines and its Provence dishes. It was in the Palais Royal that General Lannes, Junot, Murat, and other distinguished officers, used to meet Bonaparte just before and during the Consulate; but the cafés, with the exception of the Mille Colonnes, were not nearly so smartly fitted up as they now are. The Café Turc, on the Boulevard du Temple, latterly visited chiefly by shopkeepers, was much frequented: smoking was not allowed, and then, as now, ladies were seen here; more especially when the theatres had closed.

REVIEW OF THE ALLIED ARMIES BY THE ALLIED SOVEREIGNS IN PARIS.—In July 1815, it was agreed by the sovereigns of Russia, Austria, Prussia, Bavaria, Wurtemberg, and a host of petty German powers,—who had become wonderfully courageous and enthusiastically devoted to England, a few hours after the battle of Waterloo,—that a grand review should be held on the plains of St Denis, where the whole of the allied forces were to meet. Accordingly, at an early hour on a fine summer morning, there were seen issuing from the various roads which centre on the plains of St Denis, numerous English, Russian, Prussian, and Austrian regiments of horse and foot, in heavy marching order, with their bands playing; and finally, a mass of men, numbering not less than two hundred thousand, took up their positions on the wide-spreading field.

About twelve o'clock, the Duke of Wellington, commander-in-chief of the allied army, approached,

mounted on a favourite charger; and, strange as it
may appear, on his right was observed a lady in a
plain riding-habit, who was no other than Lady
Shelley, the wife of the late Sir John Shelley. Immediately behind the duke followed the emperors
of Austria and Russia; the kings of Prussia, Holland, Bavaria, and Wurtemberg; several German
princes, and general officers—the whole forming one
of the most illustrious and numerous staffs ever
brought together. The Duke of Wellington, thus
accompanied, took up his position, and began manœuvring, with a facility and confidence which
elicited the admiration of all the experienced soldiers around him. Being on duty near his grace, I
had an opportunity of hearing Prince Schwartzen-
berg say to the duke, "You are the only man who
can so well play at this game." The review lasted
two hours; then the men marched home to their
quarters, through a crowd of spectators which included the whole population of Paris. The most
mournful silence was observed throughout on the
part of the French.

CONDUCT OF THE RUSSIAN AND PRUSSIAN SOLDIERS
DURING THE OCCUPATION OF PARIS BY THE ALLIES.
—It is only just to say that the moderation shown
by the British army, from the Duke of Wellington
down to the private soldier, during our occupation
of Paris, contrasted most favourably with that of
the Russian and Prussian military. Whilst we
simply did our duty, and were civil to all those
with whom we came in contact, the Russians and
Prussians were frequently most insubordinate, and
never lost an opportunity of insulting a people whose

armies had almost always defeated them on the day of battle. I remember one particular occasion, when the Emperor of Russia reviewed his Garde Impériale, that the Cossacks actually charged the crowd, and inflicted wounds on the unarmed and inoffensive spectators. I recollect, too, a Prussian regiment displaying its bravery in the Rue St. Honoré on a number of hackney coachmen; indeed, scarcely a day passed without outrages being committed by the Russian and Prussian soldiers on the helpless population of the lower orders.

THE BRITISH EMBASSY IN PARIS.—England was represented at this period by Sir Charles Stuart, who was one of the most popular ambassadors Great Britain ever sent to Paris. He made himself acceptable to his countrymen, and paid as much attention to individual interests as to the more weighty duties of State. His *attachés*, as is always the case, took their tone and manner from their chief, and were not only civil and agreeable to all those who went to the Embassy, but knew everything and everybody, and were of great use to the ambassador, keeping him well supplied with information on whatever event might be taking place. The British Embassy, in those days, was a centre where you were sure to find all the English gentlemen in Paris collected, from time to time. Dinners, balls, and receptions were given with profusion throughout the season: in fact, Sir Charles spent the whole of his private income in these noble hospitalities. England was then represented, as it always should be in France, by an ambassador who worthily expressed the intelligence, the amiability, and the wealth of the great country to which he belonged. At the present day, the British Embassy emulates the solitude of a monastic establishment; with the exception, however, of that hospitality and courtesy which the traveller and stranger were wont to experience even in monasteries.

ESCAPE OF LAVALETTE FROM PRISON.—Few circumstances created a greater sensation than the escape of Lavalette from the Conciergerie, after he had been destined by the French Government to give employment to the guillotine. The means by which the prisoner avoided his fate and disappointed his enemies produced a deep respect for the English character, and led the French to believe that, however much the Governments of France and England might be disposed to foster feelings either of friendship or of enmity, individuals could entertain the deepest sense of regard for each other, and that a chivalrous feeling of honour would urge them on to the exercise of the noblest feelings of our nature. This incident likewise had a salutary influence in preventing acts of cruelty and of bloodshed, which were doubtless contemplated by those in power.

Lavalette had been, under the Imperial Government, head of the Post-Office, which place he filled on the return of the Bourbons; and when the Emperor Napoleon arrived from Elba, he continued still to be thus employed. Doubtless, on every occasion when opportunity presented itself, he did all in his power to serve his great master; to whom, indeed, he was allied by domestic ties, having married into the Beauharnais family. When Louis the Eighteenth returned to Paris after the battle of Waterloo,

Lavalette and the unfortunate Marshal Ney were singled out as traitors to the Bourbon cause, and tried, convicted, and sentenced to death.

The 26th of December was the day fixed for the execution of Lavalette, a man of high respectability and of great connections, whose only fault was fidelity to his chief. On the evening of the 21st, Madame Lavalette, accompanied by her daughter and her governess, Madame Dutoit, a lady of seventy years of age, presented herself at the Conciergerie, to take a last farewell of her husband. She arrived at the prison in a sedan chair. On this very day the Procureur-Général had given an order that no one should be admitted without an order signed by himself; the *greffier* having, however, on previous occasions been accustomed to receive Madame Lavalette with the two ladies who now sought also to enter the cell, did not object to it ; so these three ladies proposed to take coffee with Lavalette. The under-gaoler was sent to a neighbouring café to obtain it, and during his absence Lavalette exchanged dresses with his wife. He managed to pass undetected out of the prison, accompanied by his daughter, and entered the chair in which Madame Lavalette had arrived ; which, owing to the management of a faithful valet, had been placed so that no observation could be made of the person entering it. The bearers found the chair somewhat heavier than usual, but were ignorant of the change that had taken place, and were glad to find, after proceeding a short distance, that the individual within preferred walking home, and giving up the sedan to the young lady. On the *greffier* entering the cell, he quickly discovered the *ruse*, and gave the alarm; the under-gaoler was despatched to stop the chair, but he was too late.

Lavalette had formed a friendship with a young Englishman of the name of Bruce, to whom he immediately had recourse, throwing himself upon his generosity and kind feeling for protection, which was unhesitatingly afforded. But as Bruce could do nothing alone, he consulted two English friends who had shown considerable sympathy for the fate of Marshal Ney—men of liberal principles and undoubted honour, and both of them officers in the British service: these were Captain Hutchinson and General Sir Robert Wilson. To the latter was committed the most difficult task, that of conveying out of France the condemned prisoner; and for this achievement few men were better fitted than Sir Robert Wilson, a man of fertile imagination, ready courage, great assurance, and singular power of command over others; who spoke French well, and was intimately acquainted with the military habits of different nations.

Sir Robert Wilson's career was a singular one: he had commenced life an ardent enemy of Bonaparte, and it was upon his evidence, collected in Egypt and published to the world, that the great general was for a long time believed to have poisoned his wounded soldiers at Jaffa. Afterwards he was attached to the allied sovereigns in their great campaign; but upon his arrival in Paris, his views of public affairs became suddenly changed; he threw off the yoke of preconceived opinions, became an ardent liberal, and so continued to the last hours of his life. The cause of this sudden change of opinion has never been thoroughly

known, but certain it is that on every occasion he
supported liberal opinions with a firmness and
courage that astonished those who had known him
in his earlier days.

Sir Robert undertook, in the midst of great
dangers and difficulties, to convey Lavalette out of
France. Having dressed him in the uniform of an
English officer, and obtained a passport under a
feigned name, he took him in a cabriolet past the
barriers as far as Compiègne, where a carriage was
waiting for them. They passed through sundry
examinations at the fortified towns, but fortunately
escaped; the great difficulty being that, owing to
Lavalette's having been the director of the posts,
his countenance was familiar to almost all the post-
masters who supplied relays of horses. At Cambray
three hours were lost, from the gates being shut, and
at Valenciennes they underwent three examinations;
but eventually they got out of France.

The police, however, became acquainted with the
fact that Lavalette had been concealed in the Rue
du Helder for three days, at the apartments of Mr.
Bruce; and this enabled them to trace all the circumstances, showing that it was at the apartments
of Hutchinson that Lavalette had changed his
dress, and that he had remained there the night
before he quitted Paris. The consequence was that
Sir Robert Wilson, Bruce, and Hutchinson were
tried for aiding the escape of a prisoner; and each
of them was condemned to three months' imprison-
ment: the under-gaoler, who had evidently been
well paid for services rendered, had two years' con-
finement allotted to him.

I went to see Sir Robert Wilson during his stay

in the Conciergerie—a punishment not very difficult to bear, but which marked him as a popular
hero for his life.   A circumstance, I remember,
made a strong impression on me, proving that, however great may be the courage of a man in trying
circumstances, a trifling incident might severely
shake his nerves.   I was accompanied by a favourite
dog of the Countess of Oxford's, which, being un-
aware of the high character of Sir Robert, or dissatisfied with his physiognomy, or for some good
canine reason, took a sudden antipathy to him, and
inserted his teeth into a somewhat fleshy part, but
without doing much injury.   The effect, however,
on the general was extraordinary : he was most
earnest to have the dog killed.   I, being certain
that the animal was in no way diseased, avoided
obeying his wishes, and fear that I thus lost the
good graces of the worthy man.

DUELLING IN FRANCE IN 1815.—When the restoration of the Bourbons took place, a variety of
circumstances combined to render duelling so common, that scarcely a day passed without one at
least of these hostile meetings.   Amongst the
French themselves there were two parties always
ready to distribute to each other "*des coups
d'épée*"—the officers of Napoleon's army and the
Bourbonist officers of the *Garde du Corps*.   Then,
again, there was the irritating presence of the
English, Russian, Prussian, and Austrian officers
in the French capital.   In the duels between these
soldiers and the French, the latter were always the
aggressors.

At Tortoni's, on the Boulevards, there was a

room set apart for such quarrelsome gentlemen, where, after these meetings, they indulged in riotous champagne breakfasts. At this café might be seen all the most notorious duellists, amongst whom I can call to mind an Irishman in the *Garde du Corps*, W * * *, who was a most formidable fire-eater. The number of duels in which he had been engaged would seem incredible in the present day : he is said to have killed nine of his opponents in one year !

The Marquis de H * * *, descended of an ancient family in Brittany, also in the *Garde du Corps*, likewise fought innumerable duels, killing many of his antagonists. I have heard that on entering the army he was not of a quarrelsome disposition, but being laughed at and bullied into fighting by his brother officers, he, from the day of his first duel, like a wild beast that had once smelt blood, took a delight in such fatal scenes, and was ever ready to rush at and quarrel with any one. The marquis has now, I am glad to say, subsided into a very quiet, placable, and peace-making old gentleman ; but at the time I speak of he was much blamed for his duel with F * * *, a young man of nineteen. While dining at a café he exclaimed, "*J'ai envie de tuer quelqu'un,*" and rushed out into the street and to the theatres, trying to pick a quarrel ; but he was so well known that no one was found willing to encounter him. At last, at the Théâtre de la Porte St. Martin, he grossly insulted this young man, who was, I think, an *élève* of the École Polytechnique, and a duel took place, under the lamp-post near the theatre, with swords. He ran F * * * through the body, and left him dead upon the ground.

The late Marshal St. A * * * and General J * * *
were great duellists at this time, with a whole host
of others whose names I forget. The meetings
generally took place in the Bois de Boulogne, and
the favourite weapon of the French was the small
sword or the sabre; but foreigners, in fighting with
the French, who were generally capital swordsmen,
availed themselves of the use of pistols. The ground
for a duel with pistols was marked out by indicating
two spots, which were twenty-five paces apart; the
seconds then generally proceeded to toss up who
should have the first shot; the principals were then
placed, and the word was given to fire.

The Café Foy, in the Palais Royal, was the principal place of rendezvous for the Prussian officers,
and to this café the French officers on half-pay
frequently proceeded in order to pick quarrels with
their foreign invaders; swords were quickly drawn,
and frequently the most bloody frays took place:
these originated not in any personal hatred, but from
national jealousy on the part of the French, who could
not bear the sight of foreign soldiers in their capital;
which, when ruled by the great captain of the age,
had, like Rome, influenced the rest of the world.
On one occasion, our Guards, who were on duty at
the Palais Royal, were called out to put an end to
one of these encounters, in which fourteen Prussians
and ten Frenchmen were either killed or wounded.

The French took every opportunity of insulting
the English; and very frequently, I am sorry to say,
those insults were not met in a manner to do honour
to our character. Our countrymen in general were
very pacific; but the most awkward customer the
French ever came across was my fellow-countryman

the late gallant Colonel Sir Charles S***, of the
Engineers, who was ready for them with anything:
sword, pistol, sabre, or fists—he was good at all; and
though never seeking a quarrel, he would not put up
with the slightest insult. He killed three Frenchmen
in Paris, in quarrels forced upon him. I remember,
in October 1815, being asked by a friend to dine at
Beauvillier's, in the Rue Richelieu, when Sir Charles
S***, who was well known to us, occupied a table
at the farther end of the room. About the middle
of the dinner we heard a most extraordinary noise,
and, on looking up, perceived that it arose from
S***'s table; he was engaged in beating the head
of a smartly-dressed gentleman with one of the long
French loaves so well known to all who have visited
France. On being asked the reason of such rough
treatment, he said he would serve all Frenchmen in
the same manner if they insulted him. The offence,
it seems, proceeded from the person who had just
been chastised in so summary a manner, and who
had stared and laughed at S*** in a rude way, for
having ordered three bottles of wine to be placed
upon his table. The upshot of this was a duel, which
took place next day at a place near Vincennes, and
in which S*** shot the unfortunate jester.

When Sir Charles returned to Valenciennes, where
he commanded the Engineers, he found on his arrival
a French officer waiting to avenge the death of his
relation, who had only been shot ten days before at
Vincennes. They accordingly fought before S***
had time even to shave himself or eat his breakfast;
he having only just arrived in his *coupé* from Paris.
The meeting took place in the fosse of the fortress,
and the first shot from S***'s pistol killed the

French officer, who had actually travelled in the
diligence from Paris for the purpose, as he boasted
to his fellow-travellers, of killing an Englishman.

I recollect dining, in 1816, at Hervey Aston's, at
the Hôtel Breteuil in the Rue de Rivoli, opposite the
Tuileries, where I met Seymour Bathurst and Captain
E * * *, of the Artillery, a very good-looking man.
After dinner, Mrs. Aston took us as far as Tortoni's,
on her way to the Opera. On entering the café,
Captain E * * * did not touch his hat according to
the custom of the country, but behaved himself *à la*
John Bull, in a noisy and swaggering manner; upon
which General, then Colonel J * * *, went up to E * * *
and knocked off his hat, telling him that he hoped
he would in future behave himself better. Aston,
Bathurst, and I, waited for some time, expecting to
see E * * * knock J * * * down, or, at all events, give
him his card as a preliminary to a hostile meeting,
on receiving such an insult; but he did nothing.
We were very much disgusted and annoyed at a
countryman's behaving in such a manner, and, after
a meeting at my lodgings, we recommended Captain
E * * *, in the strongest terms, to call out Colonel
J * * *; but he positively refused to do so, as he said
it was against his principles. This specimen of the
white feather astonished us beyond measure. Captain E * * * shortly after received orders to start for
India, where I believe he died of cholera—in all
probability of FUNK.

I do not think that Colonel J * * * would altogether
have escaped with impunity, after such a gratuitous
insult to an English officer; but he retired into the
country almost immediately after the incident at
Tortoni's, and could not be found.

There were many men in our army who did not thus disgrace the British uniform when insulted by the French. I cannot omit the names of my old friends, Captain Burges, Mike Fitzgerald, Charles Hesse, and Thoroton; each of whom, by their willingness to resent gratuitous offences, showed that insults to Englishmen were not to be committed with impunity. The last-named officer having been grossly insulted by Marshal V*** without giving him the slightest provocation, knocked him down: this circumstance caused a great sensation in Paris, and brought about a court of inquiry, which ended in the acquittal of Captain Thoroton. My friend, B***, though he had only one leg, was a good swordsman, and contrived to kill a man at Lyons who had jeered him about the loss of his limb at Waterloo. My old and esteemed friend, Mike Fitzgerald, son of Lord Edward and the celebrated Pamela, was always ready to measure swords with the Frenchmen; and, after a brawl at Silves's, the then fashionable Bonapartist café at the corner of the Rue Lafitte and the Boulevard, in which two of our Scotch countrymen showed the white feather, he and another officer placed their own cards over the chimney-piece in the principal room of the café, offering to fight any man, or number of men, for the frequent public insults offered to Britons. This challenge, however, was never answered.

A curious duel took place at Beauvais during the occupation of France by our army. A Captain B***, of one of our cavalry regiments quartered in that town, was insulted by a French officer. B*** demanded satisfaction, which was accepted; but the Frenchman would not fight with pistols. B*** would not fight with swords; so at last it was agreed that they should fight on horseback, with lances. The duel took place in the neighbourhood of Beauvais, and a crowd assembled to witness it. B *** received three wounds; but, by a lucky prod, eventually killed his man. B *** was a fine-looking man and a good horseman. My late friend the Baron de P ***, so well known in Parisian circles, was second to the Frenchman on this occasion.

A friend of mine—certainly not of a quarrelsome turn, but considered by his friends, on the contrary, as rather a good-natured man—had three duels forced upon him in the course of a few weeks. He had formed a *liaison* with a person whose extraordinary beauty got him into several scrapes and disputes. In January 1817, a few days after this acquaintance had been formed, Jack B ***, well known at that time in the best society in London, became madly in love with the fair lady, and attempted one night to enter her private box at Drury Lane. This my friend endeavoured to prevent: violent language was used, and a duel was the consequence. The parties met a few miles from London, in a field close to the Uxbridge Road, where B ***, who was a hot-tempered man, did his best to kill my friend; but, after the exchange of two shots, without injury to either party, they were separated by their seconds. B *** was the son of Lady Bridget B ***, and the seconds were Payne, uncle to George Payne, and Colonel Joddrell of the Guards.

Soon after this incident, my friend accompanied the lady to Paris, where they took up their residence at Meurice's, in the Rue de l'Echiquier. The day after their arrival, they went out to take a walk in the Palais Royal, and were followed by a half-pay

officer of Napoleon's army, Colonel D * * *, a notorious
duellist, who observed to the people about him that
he was going to bully " *un Anglais*." This man was
exceedingly rude in his remarks, uttered in a loud
voice; and after every sort of insult expressed in
words, he had the impudence to put his arm round
the lady's waist. My friend indignantly asked the
colonel what he meant; upon which the ruffian spat
in my friend's face : but he did not get off with impunity, for my friend, who had a crab-stick in his
hand, caught him a blow on the side of the head,
which dropped him. The Frenchman jumped up,
and rushed at the Englishman; but they were
separated by the bystanders. Cards were exchanged,
and a meeting was arranged to take place the next
morning in the neighbourhood of Passy. When my
friend, accompanied by his second, Captain H * * *,
of the 18th, came upon the ground, he found the
colonel boasting of the number of officers of all
nations whom he had killed, and saying, " I'll now
complete my list by killing an Englishman : *Mon
petit, tu auras bientôt ton compte, car je tire fort
bien*." My friend quietly said, " *Je ne tire pas mal
non plus*," and took his place. The colonel, who
seems to have been a horrible ruffian, after a good
deal more swaggering and bravado, placed himself
opposite, and, on the signal being given, the colonel's
ball went through my friend's whiskers, whilst his
ball pierced his adversary's heart, who fell dead
without a groan.

This duel made much noise in Paris, and the survivor
left immediately for Chantilly, where he passed some
time. On his return to Paris, the second of the man
who had been killed, Commander P * * *, insulted and

challenged my friend. A meeting was accordingly
agreed upon, and pistols were again the weapons
used. Again my friend won the toss, and told his
second, Captain H***, that he would not kill his
antagonist, though he richly deserved death for
wishing to take the life of a person who had never
offended him; but that he would give him a lesson
which he should remember. My friend accordingly
shot his antagonist in the knee; and I remember to
have seen him limping about the streets of Paris
twenty years after this event.

When the result of this second duel was known,
not less than eleven challenges from Bonapartists
were received by the gentleman in question; but
any further encounters were put a stop to by the
Minister of War, or the Duc d'Angoulême (I forget
which), who threatened to place the officers under
arrest if they followed up this quarrel any further.
When the news reached England, the Duke of
York said that my friend could not have acted
otherwise than he had done in the first duel, con-
sidering the gross provocation that he had received; but he thought it would have been better
if the second duel had been avoided.

In the deeds I have narrated, the English seem
to have had the advantage; but many others took
place, in which Englishmen were killed or wounded.
These I have not mentioned, as their details do not
recur to my memory; but I do not remember an occasion on which Frenchmen were not the aggressors.

At a somewhat later period than this, the present
Marquis of H***, then Lord B***, had a duel
with the son of the Bonapartist General L***.
General S*** was Lord B***'s second, and the

principals exchanged several shots without injury to either party.   This duel, like the preceding, originated with the Frenchman, who insulted the Englishman at the Théâtre Français in the most unprovoked manner.   At the present day our fiery neighbours are much more amenable to reason, and if you are but civil, they will be civil to you; duels consequently are of rare occurrence.   Let us hope that the frequency of these hostile meetings and the *animus* displayed in them originated in national wounded vanity rather than in personal animosity.

In the autumn of 1821 I was living in Paris, when my old friend H***, adjutant of the 1st Foot Guards, called upon me, and requested that I would be his second in a duel with Mr. N***, an officer in the same regiment.   After hearing what he had to say, and thinking I could serve him, I consented.   It was agreed by Captain F***, R.N., of Pitfour, Mr. N***'s second, that the duel should take place in the Bois de Boulogne.   After an exchange of shots, Captain F*** and myself put an end to the duel.   The cause of the quarrel was, that Mr. N***, now Lord G***, proclaimed in the presence of Captain H*** and other officers, that a lady, the wife of a brother officer, was "what she ought not to be."   When the report reached the ear of the colonel, H.R.H. the Duke of York requested Mr. N*** to leave the regiment, or be brought to a court-martial; and then the duel took place, happily without bloodshed.   Both of the officers, it need scarcely be stated, behaved with courage and coolness.

PISTOL - SHOOTING.—From 1820 to 1830 pistol-shooting was not much practised. One evening, in the Salon des Étrangers, I was introduced to General F * * *, a very great duellist, and the terror of every regiment he commanded ; he was considered by Napoleon to be one of his best cavalry officers, but was never in favour in consequence of his duelling propensities. It was currently reported that F * * *, in a duel with a very young officer, lost his toss, and his antagonist fired first at him ; when, finding he had not been touched, he deliberately walked close up to the young man, saying, "*Je plains ta mère*," and shot him dead. But there were some doubts of the truth of this story ; and I trust, for the honour of humanity, that it was either an invention or a gross exaggeration.

The night I was introduced to F * * *, I was told to be on my guard, as he was a dangerous character. He was very fond of practising with pistols, and I frequently met him at Lepage's, the only place at that time where gentlemen used to shoot. F * * *, in the year 1822, was very corpulent, and wore an enormous cravat, in order, it was said, to hide two scars received in battle. He was a very slow shot.

The famous Junot, Governor-General of Paris, whom I never saw, was considered to be the best shot in France. My quick shooting surprised the *habitués* at Lepage's, where we fired at a spot chalked on the figure of a Cossack painted on a board, and by word of command, "One—two—three." F * * *, upon my firing and hitting the mark forty times in succession, at the distance of twenty paces, shrieked out, "*Tonnerre de Dieu,* *c'est magnifique!*" We were ever afterwards on good terms, and supped frequently together at the Salon. At Manton's, on one occasion, I hit the wafer nineteen times out of twenty. When my battalion was on duty at the Tower in 1819, it happened to be very cold, and much snow covered the parade and trees. For our amusement it was proposed to shoot at the sparrows in the trees from Lady Jane Grey's room; and it fell to my lot to bag eleven, without missing one. This, I may say, without flattering myself, was considered the best pistol-shooting ever heard of.

Manton assigned as the reason why pistols had become the usual arms for duels, the story (now universally laughed at) of Sheridan and Captain Matthews fighting with swords on the ground, and mangling each other in a frightful way. These combatants narrated their own story; but its enormous exaggeration has been proved even on Sheridan's own evidence, and the blood that poured from him seems merely to have been the excellent claret of the previous night's debauch. The number of wounds said to have been inflicted on each other was something so incredible that nothing but the solemn asseverations of the parties could have gained belief; and in those days Sheridan had not obtained that reputation for rodomontade which he afterwards enjoyed by universal consent.

THE FAUBOURG ST. GERMAIN.—The distinguishing characteristics of the residents of the "noble faubourg," as it was called at the time I am speaking of, were indomitable pride and exclusiveness, with a narrow-minded ignorance of all beyond the circle in which its members moved. In our day of comparative equality and general civility, no one who has not arrived at my age, and lived in Paris, can form any idea of the insolence and hauteur of the higher classes of society in 1815. The glance of unutterable disdain which the painted old duchesse of the Restoration cast upon the youthful belles of the Chaussée d'Antin, or the handsome widows of Napoleon's army of heroes, defies description. Although often responded to by a sarcastic sneer at the antediluvian charms of the *émigrée*, yet the look of contempt and disgust often sank deep into the victim's heart, leaving there germs which showed themselves fifteen years later in the revolution of 1830. In those days, this privileged class was surrounded by a charmed circle, which no one could by any means break through. Neither personal attractions nor mental qualifications formed a passport into that exclusive society; to enter which the small nobility of the provinces, or the *nouveau riche*, sighed in vain. It would have been easier for a young Guardsman to make his way into the Convent des Oiseaux—the fashionable convent in Paris—than for any of these *parvenus* to force an entrance into the Faubourg St. Germain.

One of the first acts which followed the Restoration of the Bourbons was the grant of a pecuniary indemnity, amounting to a milliard, or forty millions sterling, to be distributed amongst the *émigrés* who had lost fortunes or estates by their devotion to the royal family. They had now, therefore, the means of receiving their friends, political partisans, and foreigners, with more than usual splendour; and it must be admitted that those who were thought worthy to be received were treated like spoiled children, and petted and flattered to their hearts' content. In their own houses they were really *des grands seigneurs*, and quite incapable of treating their invited guests with the insolence that became the fashion among the Jewish *parvenus* during the reign of the "citizen king." It is one thing to disdain those whom one does not think worthy of our acquaintance, and another to insult those whom one has thought proper to invite.

In their own houses, the inhabitants of the Faubourg St. Germain were scrupulously polite : even if some enterprising foreigner should have got in surreptitiously, as long as he was under his host's roof he was treated with perfect courtesy ; though ignominiously " cut " for the remainder of his days. All this was not very amiable ; but the inhabitants of the " noble faubourg " were never distinguished for their amiability. Their best characteristics were the undaunted courage with which they met death upon the scaffold, and the cheerfulness and resignation with which they ate the bitter bread of exile.

In general, *les grandes dames* were not remarkable for their personal attractions, nor for the elegance of their appearance or dress. The galaxy of handsome women that formed the court of the emperor had perhaps sent beauty somewhat out of fashion ; for the high-born ladies who took their place were what we should call dowdy, and had nothing distinguished in their appearance. Many of those who belonged to the most ancient families were almost vulgar in outward form and feature :

their manner had a peculiar off-hand, easy style;
and they particularly excelled in setting down any
unlucky person who had happened to offend them.
Their main object, at this time, was to stand well
at court; therefore they adapted themselves to circumstances, and could be devout with the Dauphine
and sceptical with Louis the Eighteenth.

The men of the aristocracy of the Revolution
were less clever and satirical than the women;
but on the other hand, they had far more of the
distinguished bearing and graceful urbanity of the
grands seigneurs of the olden time. The *émigré*
nobles would have gazed with unutterable horror
at their degenerate descendants of the present day;
but these young, booted, bearded, cigar-smoking
scions of *la jeune France* would have run round
their courteous, though perhaps rather slow ancestors, in all the details of daily life.

The principal houses of reception in those days
were those of the Montmorencys, the Richelieus,
Birons, Rohans, Gontaut - Talleyrands, Beauffre-
monts, Luxembourgs, Crillons, Choiseuls, Chabots,
Fitzjameses, Grammonts, Latour du Pins, Coislins,
and Maillys. Most of these mansions are now
occupied as public offices, or Jesuitical schools, or
by foreign Ministers. Those who are now supposed to be the great people of the Faubourg St.
Germain are nothing more than actors, who put on
a motley dress, and appear before the public with a
view of attracting that attention to which they are
not entitled; it is, therefore, an error to suppose
that the modern faubourg is anything like what it
was during the days of the Bourbons. At the
present moment the only practical aid the in-

habitants of this locality can accord to the legiti-
mist cause in Europe, is by getting up subscrip-
tions for the Papacy, and such exiled sovereigns as
Francis II. ; and, in order to do so, they generally
address themselves to married women and widows :
in fact, it is from the purses of susceptible females,
many of whom are English, that donations are obtained for legitimacy and Popery in distress.

It is to be regretted that the most renowned
and ancient families of France have, in society and
politics, yielded their places to another class. That
refinement of perception, sensitiveness, and gentle
bearing, which take three or four generations to
produce, are no longer the characteristics of Parisian
society. The gilded saloons of the Tuileries, and
those magnificent hotels whose architects have not
been geniuses of art, but the children of mammon,
are occupied by the Jew speculator, the political
parasite, the clever schemer, and those who—whilst
following the fortune of the great man who rules
France—are nothing better than harpies. Most
of these pretended devotees of imperialism have,
speaking figuratively, their portmanteaus perpetually
packed, ready for flight. The emperor's good-nature,
as regards his *entourage*, has never allowed him
to get rid of men who, perhaps, ought not to be
seen so near the imperial throne of France. The
weakest feature of Napoleon III.'s Government is
the conspicuous presence of a few persons in high
places, whose cupidity is so extravagant that, in
order to gratify their lust of wealth, they would not
hesitate, indirectly at least, to risk a slur on the
reputation of their master and benefactor, in order
to gain their own ends.

THE SALON DES ÉTRANGERS IN PARIS.—When the allies entered Paris, after the battle of Waterloo, the English gentlemen sought, instinctively, something like a club. Paris, however, possessed nothing of the sort; but there was a much more dangerous establishment than the London clubs—namely, a rendezvous for confirmed gamblers. The Salon des Étrangers was most gorgeously furnished, provided with an excellent kitchen and wines, and was conducted by the celebrated Marquis de Livry, who received the guests and did the honours with a courtesy which made him famous throughout Europe. The Marquis presented an extraordinary likeness to the Prince Regent of England, who actually sent Lord Fife over to Paris to ascertain this momentous fact. The play which took place in these saloons was frequently of the most reckless character; large fortunes were often lost, the losers disappearing, never more to be heard of. Amongst the English *habitués* were the Hon. George T***, the late Henry Baring, Lord Thanet, Tom Sowerby, Cuthbert, Mr. Steer, Henry Broadwood, and Bob Arnold.

The Hon. George T***, who used to arrive from London with a very considerable letter of credit expressly to try his luck at the Salon des Étrangers, at length contrived to lose his last shilling at *rouge et noir*. When he had lost everything he possessed in the world, he got up and exclaimed, in an excited manner, "If I had Canova's Venus and Adonis from Alton Towers, my uncle's country seat, it should be placed on the *rouge*, for black has won fourteen times running!"

The late Henry Baring was more fortunate at hazard than his countryman, but his love of gambling

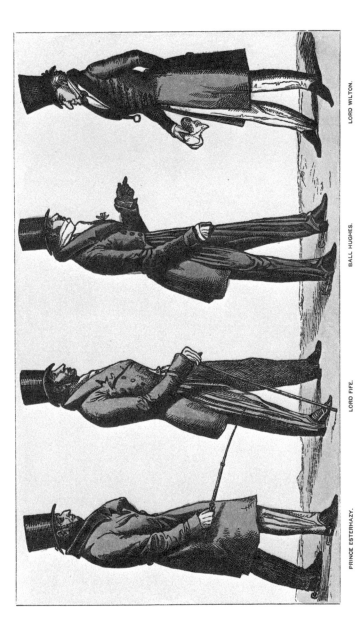

PRINCE ESTERHAZY.   LORD FIFE.   BALL HUGHES.   LORD WILTON.

PILLARS OF THE OPERA.

was the cause of his being excluded from the bank-
ing establishment.   Colonel Sowerby, of the Guards,
was one of the most inveterate players in Paris;
and, as is frequently the case with a fair player, a
considerable loser.   But perhaps the most incurable
gamester amongst the English was Lord Thanet,
whose income was not less than £50,000 a year,
every farthing of which he lost at play.   Cuthbert
dissipated the whole of his fortune in like manner.
In fact, I do not remember any instance where those
who spent their time in this den did not lose all they
possessed.

The Marquis de Livry had a charming villa at
Romainville, near Paris, to which, on Sundays, he
invited not only those gentlemen who were the most
prodigal patrons of his *salon,* but a number of ladies,
who were dancers and singers conspicuous at the
opera; forming a society of the strangest character,
the male portion of which were bent on losing their
money, whilst the ladies were determined to get rid
of whatever virtue they might still have left.   The
dinners on these occasions were supplied by the *chef*
of the Salon des Étrangers, and were such as few
renommés of the kitchens of France could place upon
the table.

Amongst the constant guests was Lord Fife, the
intimate friend of George IV., with Mdlle. Noblet, a
danseuse, who gave so much satisfaction to the
habitués of the pit at the opera, both in Paris and
London.   His lordship spent a fortune upon her;
his presents in jewels, furniture, articles of dress, and
money, exceeded £40,000.   In return for all this
generosity, Lord Fife asked nothing more than the
lady's flattery and professions of affection.

Hull Standish was always to be seen in this circle; and his own hotel in the Rue Lepelletier was often lighted up, and *fêtes* given to the theatrical and *demi-monde*. Standish died in Spain, leaving his gallery of pictures to Louis Philippe.

Amongst others who visited the Salon des Étrangers were Sir Francis Vincent, Gooch, Green, Ball Hughes, and many others whose names I no longer remember. Of foreigners, the most conspicuous were Blucher, General Ornano, step-father to Count Walewski, Pactot, and Clary, as well as most of the ambassadors at the court of the Tuileries. As at Crockford's, a magnificent supper was provided every night for all who thought proper to avail themselves of it. The games principally played were *rouge et noir* and hazard; the former producing an immense profit, for not only were the whole of the expenses of this costly establishment defrayed by the winnings of the bank, but a very large sum was paid annually to the municipality of Paris. I recollect a young Irishman, Mr. Gough, losing a large fortune at this *tapis vert*. After returning home about two A.M., he sat down and wrote a letter, giving reasons as to why he was about to commit suicide: these, it is needless to say, were simply his gambling reverses. A pistol shot through the brain terminated his existence. Sir Francis Vincent—a man of old family and considerable fortune—was another victim of this French hell, who contrived to get rid of his magnificent property, and then disappeared from society.

In calling up my recollections of the Salon des Étrangers, some forty years since, I see before me the noble form and face of the Hungarian Count

PREMIÈRES DANSEUSES AND THEIR ADMIRERS — THE GREEN ROOM OF THE OPERA HOUSE (KINGS THEATRE) 1822.

EARL OF FIFE   BALL HUGHES   MDLLE MERCANDOTTI   MDLLE NOBLET.   PRINCE V. ESTERHAZY.   MDLLE. HULLIN.   LORD PETERSHAM.

THE REMINISCENCES OF CAPTAIN GRONOW, II

In this final volume of Gronow's Reminiscences we meet again many old friends — Byron and Brummel, the Duke, the outrageous Dan Mackinnon, the habitues of Almacks and the army of the Peninsula. There are amusing descriptions of life in Paris, French manners and French cooking ("It suits the French; but it would never do in England.") and Gronow gives a first hand account of the coup d'etat of 1851. He returns often to his favourite themes of the Napoleonic wars and Regency London and there is a full supporting cast, drawn both from the beau monde and the demi-monde, of emperors, actresses, dandies, lunatics, etc, including some "shocking bad hats".

1

Repeat the prescription – a Gronow ancedote after lunch, two before dinner and not more than six or seven at bed-time.

The R.S. Surtees Society intends to publish in a single volume Gronow's "Celebrities of London and Paris" and "Last Recollections".

The second volume, like the first, will be based on the limited edition of 1889 and will include the 12 full-page coloured plates of that edition.

The Society's edition will be available **by the end of September, 1985**

Pre-publication prices

For those who subscribe **before 31st May, 1985,** the prices will be:

(a) **£11.50** per copy for books which are collected from J. A. Allen & Co., 1 Grosvenor Place, Buckingham Palace Road, London, S.W.1 (subscribers collecting their books will be notified when they are available), and

(b) **£13.50** per copy for books which are posted, the price including packing and postage.

The post-publication price will be substantially higher.

A list of those subscribing before 31st May, 1985, will be printed at the end of the book.

Minimum of pre-publication subscribers and ordering

A minimum of 1500 subscribers must be obtained by 31st May, 1985. All cheques will be acknowledged. All pre-publication money will be kept in a separate *Gronow* bank account and will be returned in the event of publication not going ahead. An Order Form is on page 6.

Illustrations

Complete sets of the full-page illustrations mentioned above will be available at the end of September, 1985. These are offered at £5 a set, packing and postage included.

W. W. JACOBS

W. W. Jacobs was immensely popular with high, middle and low brows from about 1895 to 1930. Like Conrad, Kipling and E. Nesbit he was a contributor to the *Strand Magazine* in its great days. P. G. Wodehouse was a fan and owned a complete collection of his works. Like Surtees, Jacobs was very well served by his illustrators.

The R.S. Surtees Society intends to publish a fascimile W. W. Jacobs' **Ship's Company,** a collection of 12 short stories with 23 black and white illustrations by **Will Owen,** one of the best *Punch* illustrators of the day, Auberon Waugh has agreed to write a Foreword.

The pre-publication price will be about £5 for books which are collected and a little over £6 for books which are posted. It is intended that the book shall be ready at the end of September, 1985.

2

HILLINGDON HALL

OR

THE COCKNEY SQUIRE

"IT'S SIR ROBERT PEEL'S GRAND BOOLE!"

Jorrocks becomes a squire, a scientific farmer and a Justice of the Peace. He tells his tenants and neighbours they are "a long way behind the intelligence o' the day".

Hillingdon Hall is the last of the Jorrocks books. It deserves to be much better known. Surtees mocks pseudo-scientific farming, his fellow J.P.s, complacent Whig noblemen (the then Duke of Northumberland, according to John Welcome, instantly struck the Surtees family off his visiting list), the wearing of the kilt ("jest one of Walter Scott's wagaries") and an unintended *double-entendre* in Sir Robert Peel's Agricultural Speech at Tamworth.

James Pigg rescues Jorrocks from his farming difficulties and William Bowker, now an unscrupulous agent of the Anti-Corn Law League, betrays a confidence from the Duke of Donkeyton so that a contested election at Sellborough is inevitable. Jorrocks, a Whig when he arrived at Hillingdon Hall, becomes the farmer's friend and the Anti-Repeal candidate.

3

SOME EXPERIENCES
and
FURTHER EXPERIENCES OF AN IRISH R.M.
by E. Œ. Somerville and Martin Ross

Some Experiences and *Further Experiences* each contain twelve episodes in which Major Sinclair Yeates recounts, with sober dignity, humour and tolerance, his social, sporting and professional discomfitures as a Resident Magistrate in South-West Ireland at the turn of the century. The rhetoric and deceit of the natives provide the wit and drama. Circumstances make Major Yeates a connoisseur of whole-hearted insincerity.

The R. S. Surtees Society's editions of *Some Experiences* and *Further Experiences* are as nearly as practicable facsimilies of the first editions, of 1899 and 1908 respectively. They include the black and white illustrations by **Miss Somerville** from the first editions (30 in *Some Experiences* and 35 in *Further Experiences*) and an Introduction by **Molly Keane** who wrote the best-seller *Good Behaviour* and has lived most of her life in Southern Ireland.

Price **£7.95,** in each case, packing and postage included.

R. S. SURTEES

Mr. Sponge's Sporting Tour. Facsimile of 1853 edition. 13 full-page coloured plates and 90 engravings by **John Leach.** Introduction by **Auberon Waugh.**

Mr. Facey Romford's Hounds. 24 plates by **Leach** and **'Phiz'.** 50 engravings. Introduction by **Enoch Powell.** *Special Offer:* Romford with uncut pages (which some members prefer) at **£12.20.**

''Ask Mamma''. Facsimile of 1858 edition, 13 plates and 70 engravings by **Leach.** Introduction by **Rebecca West.**

Handley Cross; or, Mr. Jorrocks' Hunt. Facsimile of 1854 edition. 17 plates and 100 engravings by **Leach.** Introduction by **Raymond Carr.**

Jorrocks' Jaunts and Jollities. Facsimile of 1874 edition. 31 plates by **Henry Alken, 'Phiz'** and **W. Heath.** Introduction by **Michael Wharton** ('Peter Simple').

Price £14.95 in each case, post free. Prices for separate sets of coloured plates are *Sponge* £5, *Romford* £8, *''Ask Mamma''* £5, *Handley Cross* £6 and *Jaunts and Jollities* £8.

The Horseman's Manual: being a treatise on Soundness, the Law of Warranty and generally on the Laws relating to Horses.
Surtees' first book, published in 1831. Hugh Davidson has published a numbered facsimile edition of 600 copies, of which 170 remain.
Price £10.50, packing and postage included.

Hunyady, the chief gambler of the day, who created considerable sensation in his time.   He became *très à la mode:* his horses, carriage, and house were considered perfect, while his good looks were the theme of universal admiration; there were ladies' cloaks *à la Huniade;* and the illustrious Borel, of the Rocher de Cancale, named new dishes after the famous Hungarian.   Hunyady's luck for a long time was prodigious: no bank could resist his attacks; and at one time he must have been a winner of nearly two millions of francs.   His manners were particularly calm and gentlemanlike; he sat apparently unmoved, with his right hand in the breast of his coat, whilst thousands depended upon the turning of a card or the hazard of a die.   His valet, however, confided to some indiscreet friend that his nerves were not of such iron temper as he would have made people believe, and that the count bore in the morning the bloody marks of his nails, which he had pressed into his chest in the agony of an unsuccessful turn of fortune.   The streets of Paris were at that time not very safe; consequently, the count was usually attended to his residence by two gendarmes, in order to prevent his being attacked by robbers. Hunyady was not wise enough (what gamblers are?) to leave Paris with his large winnings, but continued as usual to play day and night.   A run of bad luck set in against him, and he lost not only the whole of the money he had won, but a very large portion of his own fortune.   He actually borrowed £50 of the well-known Tommy Garth—who was himself generally more in the borrowing than the lending line—to take him back to Hungary.

THE DUCHESSE DE BERRI AT MASS AT THE CHA-
PELLE ROYALE.—I had the honour of being invited
to an evening party at the Tuileries in the winter of
1816, and was in conversation with the Countess de
l'Espinasse, when the duchesse did me the honour to
ask me if I intended going to St. Germain to hunt.
I replied in the negative, not having received an
invitation; upon which the duchesse graciously
observed that if I would attend mass the following
morning in the royal chapel, she would manage it.
Accordingly, I presented myself there dressed in a
black coat and trousers and white neckcloth; but at
the entrance, a huge Swiss told me I could not enter
the chapel without knee-buckles. At that moment
Alexandre de Girardin, the grand *veneur*, came to my
assistance; he spoke to the duchesse, who immediately
gave instructions that Mr. Gronow was to be admitted
" *sans culottes.*" The card for the hunt came; but
the time to get the uniform was so short, that I
was prevented going to St. Germain. At that time
the fascinating Duchesse de Berri was the theme
of admiration of every one. All who could obtain
admission to the chapelle were charmed with the
grace with which, on passing through the happy
group who had been fortunate enough to gain the
privilege, she cast her glance of recognition upon
those who were honoured with her notice. When
again I had the honour of being in the presence of
the duchesse, she inquired whether the hunt amused
me; and upon my telling her that I had been
unable to go, in consequence of the want of the
required uniform, the duchesse archly remarked—
"*Ah! M. le Capitaine, parceque vous n'avez jamais
des culottes.*"

LORD WESTMORELAND.—When I was presented at the Court of Louis XVIII., Lord Westmoreland, the grandfather of the present lord, accompanied Sir Charles Stewart to the Tuileries. On our arrival in the room where the king was, we formed ourselves into a circle, when the king good-naturedly inquired after Lady Westmoreland, from whom his lordship was divorced, and whether she was in Paris. Upon this, the noble lord looked sullen, and refused to reply to the question put by the king. His majesty, however, repeated it, when Lord Westmoreland hallooed out, in bad French, "*Je ne sais pas, je ne sais pas, je ne sais pas.*" Louis, rising, said, "*Assez, milord; assez, milord.*"

On one occasion, Lord Westmoreland, who was Lord Privy Seal, being asked what office he held, replied, "*Le Chancelier est le grand sceau (sot); moi je suis le petit sceau d'Angleterre.*" On another occasion, he wished to say "I would if I could, but I can't," and rendered it, "*Je voudrais si je coudrais, mais je ne cannais pas.*"

ALDERMAN WOOD.—Among the many English who then visited Paris was Alderman Wood, who had previously filled the office of Lord Mayor of London. He ordered a hundred visiting cards, inscribing upon them, "Alderman Wood, *feu Lord Maire de Londres,*" which he had largely distributed amongst people of rank—having translated the word "late" into "*feu,*" which I need hardly state means "dead."

THE OPERA.—A few years after the restoration of the Bourbons, the opera was the grand resort of all the fashionable world. Sosthène de la Rochefoucould was Minister of the Household, and his office placed him at the head of all the theatres.   M. de la Rochefoucauld was exceedingly polite to our country-men, and gave permission to most of our dandies to go behind the scenes, where Bigottini, Fanny Bias, Vestris, Anatole, Paul, Albert, and the other princi-pal dancers congregated.   One of our countrymen having been introduced by M. de la Rochefoucauld to Mademoiselle Bigottini, the beautiful and graceful dancer, in the course of conversation with this gentleman, asked him in what part of the theatre he was placed; upon which he replied, "Mademoiselle, *dans une loge rôtie*," instead of "*grillée*." The lady could not understand what he meant, until his introducer explained the mistake, observing, "*Ces diables d'Anglais pensent toujours à leur rosbif.*"

FANNY ELSSLER.—In 1822 I saw this beautiful person for the first time.   She was originally one of the *figurantes* at the opera at Vienna, and was at this time about fourteen years of age, and of delicate and graceful proportions.   Her hair was auburn, her eyes blue and large, and her face wore an expression of great tenderness.   Some years after the Duke of Reichstadt, the son of the great Napoleon, was captivated with her beauty; in a word, he became her acknowledged admirer, while her marvellous act-ing and dancing drew around her all the great men of the German court.   The year following she went to Naples, where a brother of the king's fell desper-ately in love with her.   Mademoiselle Elssler went soon afterwards to Paris, where her wit electrified all the fashionable world, and her dancing and acting in the "Diable Boiteux" made the fortune of the *entrepreneur.*   In London her success was not so striking; but her *cachucha* will long be remembered as one of the most exquisite exhibitions of female grace and power ever seen at her Majesty's Theatre, and in expressiveness, her pantomimic powers were unrivalled.

CHARLES X. AND LOUIS PHILIPPE.—When the father of the present ex-king of Naples came to Paris during the reign of Charles X., Louis Philippe, then Duke of Orleans, living at the Palais Royal, gave a very grand *fête* to his royal cousin. I had the honour to be one of the party invited, and witnessed an extraordinary scene, which I think worth relating.   About eleven o'clock, when the rooms were crowded, Charles X. arrived, with a numerous suite.   On entering, he let fall his pocket-handkerchief—it was then supposed by accident; upon this, Louis Philippe fell upon one knee and presented the handkerchief to his sovereign, who smiled and said, " *Merci, mon cher; merci.*"   This incident was commented upon for many days, and several persons said that the handkerchief was purposely thrown down to see whether Louis Philippe would pick it up.

At that period, the Orleans family were *en mauvaise odeur* at the Tuileries, and consequently this little incident created considerable gossip among the courtly quidnuncs.   I remember that when Lord William Bentinck was asked what he thought of the circumstance, he good-naturedly answered, "The king most probably wanted to know how the wind blew."

It was known that a large number of persons

hostile to the court were invited, and among these were Casimir Périer, the Dupins, Lafitte, Benjamin Constant, and a host of others who a few years afterwards drove out the eldest branch that occupied the throne to make way for Louis Philippe.

LORD THANET.—The late Lord Thanet, celebrated for having been imprisoned in the Tower for his supposed predilection for republicanism, passed much of his time in Paris, particularly at the Salon des Étrangers. His lordship's infatuation for play was such, that when the gambling-tables were closed, he invited those who remained to play at chicken-hazard and *écarté*; the consequence was, that one night he left off a loser of £120,000. When told of his folly and the probability of his having been cheated, he exclaimed, "Then I consider myself lucky in not having lost twice that sum!"

LORD GRANVILLE, THE BRITISH AMBASSADOR.— Soon after Lord Granville's appointment, a strange occurrence took place at one of the public gambling-houses. A colonel, on half-pay, in the British service, having lost every farthing that he possessed, determined to destroy himself, together with all those who were instrumental in his ruin. Accordingly, he placed a canister full of fulminating powder under the table, and set it on fire: it blew up, but fortunately no one was hurt. The police arrested the colonel, and placed him in prison; he was, however, through the humane interposition of our ambassador, sent out of France as a madman.

MARSHAL BLUCHER.—Marshal Blucher, though a
very fine fellow, was a very rough diamond, with
the manners of a common soldier. On his arrival
in Paris, he went every day to the *salon*, and played
the highest stakes at *rouge et noir*. The *salon*,
during the time that the marshal remained in
Paris, was crowded by persons who came to see him
play. His manner of playing was anything but
gentlemanlike, and when he lost, he used to swear
in German at everything that was French, looking
daggers at the croupiers. He generally managed to
lose all he had about him, also all the money his servant, who was waiting in the ante-chamber, carried.
I recollect looking attentively at the manner in
which he played; he would put his right hand
into his pocket, and bring out several rouleaus of
Napoleons, throwing them on the red or the black.
If he won the first coup, he would allow it to
remain; but when the croupier stated that the
table was not responsible for more than ten thousand francs, then Blucher would roar like a lion,
and rap out oaths in his native language which
would doubtless have met with great success at
Billingsgate, if duly translated : fortunately, they
were not heeded, as they were not understood by
the lookers-on.

At that period there were rumours—and reliable
ones, too—that Blucher and the Duke of Wellington were at loggerheads. The Prussians wanted to
blow up the Bridge of Jena; but the. duke sent a
battalion of our regiment to prevent it, and the
Prussian engineers who were mining the bridge
were civilly sent away : this circumstance created
some ill-will between the chiefs.

A sort of congress of the Emperors of Austria and Russia and the King of Prussia, with Blucher and Wellington, met at the Hotel of Foreign Affairs, on the Boulevard, when, after much ado, the Duke of Wellington emphatically declared that if any of the monuments were destroyed he would take the British army from Paris : this threat had the desired effect. Nevertheless, Blucher levied contributions on the poor Parisians, and his army was newly clothed. The Bank of France was called upon to furnish him with several thousand pounds, which, it was said, were to reimburse him for the money lost at play. This, with many other instances of extortion and tyranny, was the cause of Blucher's removal, and he took his departure by order of the king.

THE PRUSSIANS IN PARIS.—The French had behaved so ill at Berlin, after the battle of Jena, in 1806, that the Prussians had sworn to be revenged, if ever they had the opportunity to visit upon France the cruelties, the extortion, insults, and hard usage their own capital had suffered ; and they kept their word.

I once saw a regiment of Prussians march down the Rue St. Honoré when a line of half-a-dozen hackney-coachmen were quietly endeavouring to make their way in a contrary direction ; suddenly some of the Prussian soldiers left their ranks, and with the butt-end of their muskets knocked the poor coachmen off their seats. I naturally felt ashamed at what I had seen, and, being in uniform, some Frenchmen came up to me and requested me to report what I had witnessed to the Duke of Wellington. Upon my telling them it would be of no avail, they one and all said the English ought to blush at having allies and friends capable of such wanton brutality.

One afternoon, when upwards of a hundred Prussian officers entered the galleries of the Palais Royal, they visited all the shops in turn, insulting the women and striking the men, breaking the windows, and turning everything upside down : nothing, indeed, could have been more outrageous than their conduct. When information was brought to Lord James Hay of what was going on, he went out, and arrived just as a troop of French gendarmes were on the point of charging the Prussians, then in the garden. He lost no time in calling out his men, and, placing himself between the gendarmes and the officers, said he should fire upon the first who moved. The Prussians then came to him and said, "We had all vowed to return upon the heads of the French in Paris the insults that they had heaped upon our countrymen in Berlin ; we have kept our vow, and we will now retire." Nothing could equal the bitter hatred which existed, and still exists, between the French and the Prussians.

JEW MONEY-LENDERS.—One of the features of high society after the long war was a passion for gambling ; so universal was it, that there are few families of distinction who do not even to the present day retain unpleasant reminiscences of the period. When people become systematic players, they are often obliged to raise money at an exorbitant interest, and usually under such circumstances fly to the Israelites. I have often heard players wish these people in almost every uncomfortable quarter of the known and unknown worlds. The mildness and civility with which the Christian in difficulties always addresses the moneyed Israelite, contrast forcibly with the opprobrious epithets lavished on him when the day for settlement comes. When a man requires money to pay his debts of honour, and borrows from the Jews, he knows perfectly well what he is doing; though one of the last things which foolish people learn is how to trace their own errors to their proper source. Hebrew money-lenders could not thrive if there were no borrowers : the gambler brings about his own ruin.

The characteristics of the Jew are never more perceptible than when he comes in contact with gentlemen to ruin them. On such occasions, the Jew is humble, supercilious, blunderingly flattering : and if he can become the agent of any dirty work, is only too happy to be so, in preference to a straightforward and honest transaction. No man is more vulgarly insulting to those dependent upon him than the Jew, who invariably cringes to his superiors ; above all, he is not a brave man. It will be seen from these observations what is my opinion of a class of traders who in all parts of the world are sure to embrace what may be termed illicit and illegitimate commerce. At the same time, I suspect that the Jew simply avails himself of the weakness and vices of mankind, and will continue in this line of business so long as imprudent and extravagant humanity remains what it is.

Two usurers, who obtained much notoriety from the high game which was brought to them, were men known by the names of Jew King and Solomon. These were of very different characters. King was a man of some talent, and had good taste in the fine arts ; he had made the peerage a complete study, knew the exact position of every one who was connected with a coronet, the value of their property, how deeply the estates were mortgaged, and what incumbrances weighed upon them. Nor did his knowledge stop there : by dint of sundry kind attentions to the clerks of the leading banking-houses, he was aware of the balances they kept, and the credit attached to their names ; so that, to the surprise of the borrower, he let him into the secrets of his own actual position. He gave excellent dinners, at which many of the highest personages of the realm were present ; and when they fancied that they were about to meet individuals whom it would be upon their conscience to recognise elsewhere, were not a little amused to find clients quite as highly placed as themselves, and with purses quite as empty.

King had a well-appointed house in Clarges Street ; but it was in a villa upon the banks of the Thames, which had been beautifully fitted up by Walsh Porter in the Oriental style, and which I believe is now the seat of one of the most favoured votaries of the Muses, Sir Edward Bulwer Lytton, that his hospitalities were most lavishly and luxuriously exercised. Here it was that Sheridan told his host that he liked his table better than his multiplication table ; to which his host, who was not only witty, but often the cause of wit in others, replied, " I know, Mr. Sheridan, your taste is more for Joking than for Jew King : " alluding to King the actor's admirable performance in Sheridan's *School for Scandal.*

King kept a princely establishment, and a splendid equipage, which he made to serve as an advertisement of his calling. A yellow carriage, with panels emblazoned with a well-executed shield and armorial bearings, and drawn by two richly-caparisoned steeds, the Jehu on the box wearing, according to the fashion of those days, a coat of many capes, a powdered wig, and gloves *à la Henri Quatre*, and two spruce footmen in striking but not gaudy livery, with long canes in their hands, daily made its appearance in the Park from four to seven in the height of the season. Mrs. King was a fine-looking woman, and being dressed in the height of fashion, she attracted innumerable gazers, who pronounced the whole turn-out to be a work of refined taste, and worthy a man of " so much principal and interest."

It happened that, during one of these drives, Lord William L***, a man of fashion, but, like other of the great men of the day, an issuer of paper money discounted at high rates by the usurers, was thrown off his horse. Mr. and Mrs. King immediately quitted the carriage, and placed the noble lord within. On this circumstance being mentioned in the clubs, Brummell observed it was only " a Bill *Jewly* (duly) taken up and honoured."

Solomon indulged in many *aliases*, being known by the names of Goldsched, Slowman, as well as by other *noms de guerre;* and he was altogether of a different caste from King, being avaricious, distrustful, and difficult to deal with. He counted upon his gains with all the grasping feverishness of the miser; and owing to his great caution, he had an immense command of money, which the confidence of his brethren placed in his hands. To the jewellers, the coachmakers, and the tailors, who were obliged to give exorbitant accommodation to their aristocratic customers, and were eventually paid in bills of an incredibly long date, Solomon was of inestimable use. Hamlet, Houlditch, and other dependants upon the nobility were often compelled to seek his assistance.

Hamlet, the jeweller, was once looked up to as the richest tradesman at the West End. His shop at the corner of Cranbourne Alley exhibited a profuse display of gold and silver plate, whilst in the jewel room sparkled diamonds, amethysts, rubies, and other precious stones, in every variety of setting. He was constantly called on to advance money upon such objects, which were left in pawn, only to be taken out on the occasion of a great banquet, or when a court dress was to be worn. His gains were enormous, though it was necessary to give long credit; and his bills for twenty or thirty thousand pounds were eagerly discounted. In fact, he was looked upon as a second Crœsus, or a Crassus, who could have bought the Roman empire; and his daughter's hand was sought in marriage by peers. But all at once the mighty bubble collapsed. He had advanced money to the Duke of York, and had received as security property in Nova Scotia, consisting chiefly of mines, which, when he began to work them, turned out valueless, after entailing enormous expense. Loss upon loss succeeded, and in the end bankruptcy. I have even heard that this man, once so envied for his wealth, died the inmate of an almshouse.

Some persons of rank, tempted by the offers of these usurers, lent their money to them at a very high interest. A lady of some position lent a thousand pounds to King, on the promise of receiving annually 15 per cent.; which he continued to pay with the utmost regularity. Her son being in want of money, applied for a loan of a thousand pounds, which King granted at the rate of 80 per cent.; lending him, of course, his mother's money. In a moment of tenderness the young man told his tale to her, when she immediately went to King and upbraided him for not making her a party to his gains, and demanded her money back. King refused to return it, saying that he had never engaged to return the principal; and dared her to take any proceedings against him, as, being a married woman, she had no power over the money. She, however, acknowledged it to her husband, obtained his forgiveness; and, after threats of legal interference, King was compelled to refund the money, besides losing much of his credit and popularity by the transaction.

LORD ALVANLEY.—To Lord Alvanley was awarded the reputation, good or bad, of all the witticisms in the clubs after the abdication of the throne of dandyism by Brummell; who, before that time, was always quoted as the sayer of good things, as Sheridan had been some time before. Lord Alvanley had the talk of the day completely under his control, and was the arbiter of the school for scandal in St. James's. A *bon mot* attributed to him gave rise to the belief that Solomon caused the downfall and disappearance of Brummell; for on some friends of the prince of dandies observing that if he had remained in London something might have been done for him by his old associates, Alvanley replied, " He has done quite right to be off: it was Solomon's judgment."

When Sir Lumley Skeffington, who had been a lion in his day—and whose spectacle, the *Sleeping Beauty*, produced at a great expense on the stage, had made him looked up to as deserving all the blandishments of fashionable life—reappeared some years after his complete downfall and seclusion in the Bench, he fancied that by a very gay external appearance he would recover his lost position ; but he found his old friends very shy of him. Alvanley being asked, on one occasion, who that smart-looking individual was, answered, " It is a second edition of the *Sleeping Beauty*, bound in calf, richly gilt, and illustrated by many cuts."

One of the gay men of the day, named Judge, being incarcerated in the Bench, some one observed he believed it was the first instance of a Judge reaching the bench without being previously called to the bar ; to which Alvanley replied, " Many a bad judge has been taken from the bench and placed at the bar." He used to say that Brummell was the only *Dande*lion that flourished year after year in the hot-bed of the fashionable world : he had taken root. Lions were generally annual, but Brummell was perennial, and he quoted a letter from Walter Scott :—" If you are celebrated for writing verses, or for slicing cucumbers, for being two feet taller, or two feet less, than any other biped, for acting plays when you should be whipped at school, or for attending schools and institutions when you should be preparing for your grave, your notoriety becomes a talisman, an ' open sesame,'

which gives way to everything, till you are voted a
bore, and discarded for a new plaything." This
passage appeared in a letter from Walter Scott to
the Earl of Dalkeith, when he himself, Belzoni,
Master Betty the Roscius, and old Joseph Lancaster
the schoolmaster, were the lions of the season, and
were one night brought together by my indefatigable old friend, Lady Cork, who was " the Lady of
Lyons " of that day.

GENERAL PALMER.—This excellent man had the
last days of his life embittered by the money-lenders.
He had commenced his career surrounded by every
circumstance that could render existence agreeable ;
fortune, in his early days, having smiled most
benignantly on him.   His father was a man of
considerable ability, and was to the past generation
what Rowland Hill is in the present day—the great
benefactor of correspondents.   He first proposed
and carried out the mail-coach system ; and letters,
instead of being at the mercy of postboys, and a
private speculation in many instances, became the
care of Government, and were transmitted under its
immediate direction.
    During the lifetime of Mr. Palmer, the reward
due to him for his suggestions and his practical
knowledge was denied ; he accordingly went to
Bath, and became the manager and proprietor of
the theatre.   He occasionally trod the boards himself, for which his elegant deportment and good
taste eminently qualified him; and he has often
been mistaken for Gentleman Palmer, whose portrait
is well drawn in the Memoir of Sheridan by Dr.
Sigmond, prefixed to Bohn's edition of Sheridan's

plays. Mr. Palmer was successful in his undertaking, and at his death his son found himself the
inheritor of a handsome fortune, and became a
universal favourite in Bath.

The corporation of that city, consisting of thirty
apothecaries, were, in those borough-mongering days,
the sole electors to the House of Commons, and
finding young Palmer hospitable, and intimate with
the Marquis of Bath and Lord Camden, and likewise desiring for themselves and their families free
access to the most agreeable theatre in England,
they returned him to Parliament. He entered the
army, and became a conspicuous officer in the
10tn Hussars, which regiment being commanded
by the Prince Regent, Palmer was at once introduced at Carlton House, the Pavilion at Brighton,
and consequently into the highest society of the
country; for which his agreeable manners, his
amiable disposition, and his attainments, admirably
qualified him. His fortune was sufficiently large
for all his wants; but, unfortunately, as it turned
out, the House of Commons voted to him, as the
representative of his father, £100,000, which he
was desirous of laying out to advantage.

A fine opportunity, as he imagined, had presented
itself to him; for, in travelling in the diligence
from Lyons to Paris—a journey then requiring
three days—he met a charming widow, who told a
tale that had not only a wonderful effect upon his
susceptible heart, but upon his amply-filled purse.
She said her husband, who had been the proprietor
of one of the finest estates in the neighbourhood
of Bordeaux, was just dead, and that she was on
her way to Paris to sell the property, that it might

be divided, according to the laws of France,
amongst the family. Owing, however, to the absolute necessity of forcing a sale, that which was
worth an enormous sum would realise one quarter
only of its value. She described the property as
one admirably fitted for the production of wine ;
that it was, in fact, the next estate to the Château
Lafitte, and would prove a fortune to any capitalist.
The fascinations of this lady, and the temptation
of enormous gain to the speculator, impelled the
gallant colonel to offer his services to relieve her
from her embarrassment ; so by the time the diligence arrived in Paris he had become the proprietor
of a fine domain, which was soon irrevocably fixed
on him by the lady's notary, in return for a large
sum of money : and, had the colonel proved a man
of business, he would no doubt have been amply
repaid, and his investment might have become the
source of great wealth.

Palmer, however, conscious of his inaptitude for
business, looked around him for an active agent,
and believed he had found one in a Mr. Gray, a
man of captivating manners and good connections,
but almost as useless a person as the general himself. Fully confident in his own abilities, Gray had
already been concerned in many speculations ; but
not one of them had ever succeeded, and all had
led to the demolition of large fortunes. Plausible
in his address, and possessing many of those superficial qualities that please the multitude, he appeared to be able to secure for the claret—which
was the production of the estate—a large *clientèle*.
Palmer's claret, under his auspices, began to be
talked of in the clubs ; and the *bon vivant* was

anxious to secure a quantity of this highly-prized wine.

The patronage of the Prince Regent being considered essential, was solicited, and the prince, with his egotistical good-nature, and from a kindly feeling for Palmer, gave a dinner at Carlton House, when a fair trial was to be given to his claret. A select circle of *gastronomes* was to be present, amongst whom was Lord Yarmouth, well known in those days by the appellation of "Red-herrings," from his rubicund whiskers, hair, and face, and from the town of Yarmouth deriving its principal support from the importation from Holland of that fish; Sir Benjamin Bloomfield, Sir William Knighton, and Sir Thomas Tyrwhitt, were also of the party. The wine was produced, and was found excellent, and the spirits of the party ran high; the light wine animating them without intoxication. The Prince was delighted, and, as usual upon such occasions, told some of his best stories, quoted Shakspeare, and was particularly happy upon the bouquet of the wine as suited "to the holy Palmer's kiss."

Lord Yarmouth alone sat in moody silence, and, on being questioned as to the cause, replied that whenever he dined at his Royal Highness's table, he drank a claret which he much preferred—that which was furnished by Carbonell. The prince immediately ordered a bottle of this wine; and to give them an opportunity of testing the difference, he desired that some anchovy sandwiches should be served up. Carbonell's wine was placed upon the table: it was a claret made expressly for the London market, well dashed with Hermitage, and infi-

nitely more to the taste of the Englishmen than
the delicately-flavoured wine they had been drinking. The banquet terminated in the prince declar-
ing his own wine superior to that of Palmer's, and
suggesting that he should try some experiments
on his estate to obtain a better wine. Palmer
came from Carlton House much mortified. On Sir
Thomas Tyrwhitt attempting to console him, and
saying that it was the anchovies that had spoiled
the taste of the connoisseurs, the general said,
loudly enough to be heard by Lord Yarmouth,
"No; it was the confounded red herrings." A
duel was very nearly the consequence.

General Palmer, feeling it his duty to follow the
advice of the prince, rooted out his old vines,
planted new ones, and tried all sorts of experiments
at an immense cost, but with little or no result.
He and his agent, in consequence, got themselves
into all sorts of difficulties, mortgaged the property,
borrowed largely, and were at last obliged to have
recourse to usurers, to life assurances, and every
sort of expedient, to raise money. The theatre at
Bath was sold, the Reform in Parliament robbed
him of his seat, and at last he and his agent became ruined men. A subscription would have
been raised to relieve him, but he preferred ending
his days in poverty to living upon the bounty of
his friends. He sold his commission, and was
plunged in the deepest distress; while the accumu-
lation of debt to the usurers became so heavy,
that he was compelled to pass through the In-
solvent Court.

Thus ended the career of a man who had been
courted in society, idolised in the army, and figured

as a legislator for many years. His friends, of
course, fell off, and he was to be seen a mendicant in
the streets of London—shunned where he once was
courted. Gray, his agent, became equally involved;
but, marrying a widow with some money, he was
enabled to make a better fight. Eventually, however, he became a prey to the money-lenders, and
his life ended under circumstances distressing to
those who had known him in early days.

" MONK " LEWIS.—One of the most agreeable men
of the day was " Monk " Lewis. As the author of
The Monk and *Tales of Wonder*, he not only found
his way into the best circles, but gained a high reputation in the literary world. His poetic talent
was undoubted, and he was intimately connected
with Walter Scott in his ballad researches : his
Alonzo the Brave and the Fair Imogene was recited
at the theatres. Wherever he went he found a welcome reception ; his West Indian fortune and connections, and his seat in Parliament, giving him
access to all the aristocratic circles. From these,
however, he was banished upon the appearance of
the fourth and last dialogue of the *Pursuits of
Literature*. Had a thunderbolt fallen upon him, he
could not have been more astonished than he was
by the onslaught of Mr. Matthias, which led to his
ostracism from fashionable society.

It is not for me to appreciate the value of this
satirical poem, which created such an extraordinary
sensation, not only in the fashionable, but in the
political world ; I, however, remember that whilst
at Canning's, at the Bishop of London's, and at
Gifford's, it was pronounced the most classical and

spirited production that had ever issued from the
press, it was held up at Lord Holland's, at the
Marquis of Lansdowne's, and at Brookes's, as one of
the most spiteful and ill-natured satires that had
ever disgraced the literary world, and one which no
talent or classic lore could ever redeem.   Certain it
is that Matthias fell foul of poor "Monk" Lewis
for his romance : obscenity and blasphemy were
the charges laid at his door; he was acknowledged
to be a man of genius and fancy, but this added
only to his crime, to which was superadded that of
being a very young man. The charges brought
against him cooled his friends and heated his enemies; the young ladies were forbidden to speak to
him, matrons even feared him, and from being one
of the idols of the world, he became one of the objects of its disdain.   Even his father was led to
believe that his son had abandoned the paths of
virtue, and was on the high road to ruin.

"Monk" Lewis, unable to stand against the out-
cry thus raised against him, determined to try the
effects of absence, and took his departure for the
island in which his property was ; but unfortunately
for those who dissented from the ferocious judgment
that was passed upon him, and for those who had
discrimination enough to know that after all there
was nothing very objectionable in his romance, and
felt assured that posterity would do him justice, this
amiable and kind-hearted man died on his passage
out ; leaving a blank in one variety of literature
which has never been filled up.

The denunciation was not followed by any other
severe criticism ; but editors have, in compliance
with the insinuations of Matthias, omitted the pas-

SIR LUMLEY SKEFFINGTON.   LORD PETERSHAM.

DANDIES OF OTHER DAYS.

sages which he pointed out as objectionable, so that the original text is seldom met with.

"Monk" Lewis had a black servant, affectionately attached to his master; but so ridiculously did this servant repeat his master's expressions, that he became the laughing-stock of all his master's friends. Brummell used often to raise a hearty laugh at Carlton House by repeating witticisms which he pretended to have heard from Lewis's servant: some of these were very stale; yet they were considered so good as to be repeated at the clubs, and greatly added to the reputation of the Beau as a teller of good things. "On one occasion," said Brummell, "I called to inquire after a young lady who had sprained her ankle; Lewis, on being asked how she was, had said, in the black's presence, 'The doctor has seen her, put her legs straight, and the poor chicken is doing well.' The servant, therefore, told me, with a mysterious and knowing look, 'Oh, sir, the doctor has been here; she has laid eggs, and she and the chickens are doing well.'"

Such extravagances in those days were received as the essence of wit, and to such stories did the public give a willing ear, repeating them with unwearying zest. Even Sheridan's wit partook of this character, making him the delight of the prince, who ruled over the fashionable world, and whose approbation was sufficient to give currency to anything, however ludicrous and absurd.

Sir Thomas Turton.—There is a pleasure in recalling to memory even the schoolboy pranks of men who make a figure in the world. The career of Turton promised to be a brilliant one; and had

he not offended against the moral feeling of the
country, and lost his position, he would have
mounted to the highest step in the ladder of fortune.   At Eton he showed himself a dashing and a
daring boy, and was looked upon by Dr. Goodall,
the then head master, as one of his best classical
scholars ; by his schoolfellows he was even more
highly regarded, being the acknowledged " cock of
the school."   Amongst the qualities that endeared
him to them, was a fearlessness which led him into
dangers and difficulties, from which his pluck only
could extricate him.   He was a determined poacher:
not one of the skulking class, but of a daring that
led him to exert his abilities in Windsor Park itself;
where he contrived to bag game, in spite of the
watchfulness of the keepers and the surveillance of
the well-paid watchers of the night.   On one occasion, however, by some unlucky chance, tidings of his
successes reached the ears of the royal gamekeeper,
who formed a plan by which to entrap him ; and
so nearly were they pouncing upon Turton that he
was obliged to take to his heels and fly, carrying
with him a hare which he had caught.   The keepers
followed close upon his heels until they came to the
Thames, into which Turton plunged, and, still holding his prize by his teeth, swam to the other side,
to the astonishment and dismay of his pursuers, who
had no inclination for a cold bath, and whose mortification was great at seeing Turton safely landed on
the other side.   He reached the college in safety;
and the hare served for the enjoyment of merry
friends.

Turton's history in after life I will not pursue ; but
must express my regret that he threw away golden

opportunities of showing his love for classic lore, and
his ability to meet the difficulties of life, in the same
bold way in which he swam the Thames and baffled
the Windsor gamekeepers.

GEORGE SMYTHE, THE LATE LORD STRANGFORD.—
This is another friend to whom I am pleased to
pay the tribute of a reminiscence, and who, if he
was not as well known as most of those I have
spoken of, was yet highly prized by many of the
most distinguished persons, and formed one of a
circle that had great influence in England. Being
the son of the well-known Lord Strangford, the
translator of *Camoens*, he had a first place in
aristocratic society, and had he not given himself
up to indulgences and amusements, might have
reached the rank of statesman. The late Lord
Strangford was distinguished by those external
qualifications which are everywhere acceptable; his
manners were polished and easy, his conversation
elegant and witty, and these, added to great personal attractions, gave him a charm which was
generally felt. Disraeli, Sir Edward Bulwer Lytton,
and the leading men of the day, were his associates.
When Lord Aberdeen became Minister for Foreign
Affairs he selected George Smythe as under-secre-
tary; in which capacity he acquitted himself with
great ability. He could not, however, act under
Lord Palmerston, and rather than do so gave up
his position. He did not long survive, but died very
young; just as he was beginning to learn the value
of his rare abilities, and had ascertained how best
they might have been of use to his country.

THE HONOURABLE GEORGE TALBOT. — I have a very vivid recollection of George Talbot, a brother of the late Earl of Shrewsbury, and who was a fashionable man about town, of whom there are many anecdotes in circulation. The only one that took my fancy was related to me in Paris, where he was as usual in the midst of the gayest of the gay, recklessly spending his money, and oftentimes re-sorting for resources to the gambling-table, where at last he was thoroughly pigeoned.

Talbot had tried in vain all the usual means of recruiting his empty purse. Being a Roman Catho-lic, like most of the members of one of the oldest families in Great Britain, he was a regular attendant upon the ceremonies of his Church, and acquainted with all the clergy in Paris; so he took the resolu-tion of going to his confessor, unburdening his con-science, and at the same time seeking counsel from the holy father, as to the best way of raising the wind. After entering minutely into his condition, and asking the priest how he could find funds to pay his debts and take him home, the confessor seemed touched by his tale of woe, and after much apparent consideration recommended him to trust in Providence. Talbot seemed struck with such sensible advice, and promised to call again in a few days. This second visit was made in due course; he again mourned over his condition, and requested the priest's advice and assistance. His story was listened to as before, with much commiseration, but he was again recommended to trust in Providence. Talbot came away quite crestfallen, and evidently with little hope of any immediate relief. After the lapse of a few days, however, he appeared again before his confessor, apparently much elated, and invited the worthy abbé to dine with him at the Rocher de Cancale. This invitation was gladly accepted, the holy father not doubting but that he should have all the delicacies in the land; to which, in common with the rest of the clergy, he had no objection: nor was he disappointed. The dinner was *recherché*; the best the establishment could furnish was placed before them, and most heartily and lovingly did the worthy abbé devote himself to what was offered. At the end of the repast the *carte à payer* was duly furnished; but what was the astonishment of the reverend guest when Talbot declared that his purse was completely *à sec*, and that it had been a long time empty, but that upon this occasion, as upon all others, he trusted, as the abbé had advised him, in Providence.

The Abbé Pecheron, recovering from his surprise, and being of a kind and generous disposition, laughed heartily at Talbot's impudence, and feeling that he had deserved this rebuke, he pulled out his purse, paid for the dinner, and did what he should have done at first—wrote to the members of Talbot's family, and obtained for him such assistance as enabled him to quit Paris, and return home, where he afterwards led a more sober life.

A DINNER AT SIR JAMES BLAND BURGES'S, IN LOWER BROOK STREET, AUTUMN, 1815.—I was once invited to dinner by Sir James Burges, father of my friend, Captain Burges of the Guards: it was towards the end of the season 1815. I there met, to my great delight, Lord Byron and Sir Walter Scott; and amongst the rest of the company were

Lord Caledon, and Croker, the Secretary to the Admiralty. Sir James had been private secretary to Pitt at the time of the French Revolution, and had a fund of curious anecdotes about everything and everybody of note at the end of the last century. I remember his telling us the now generally-received story of Pitt dictating a king's speech off-hand— then a more difficult task than at the present day— without the slightest hesitation ; this speech being adopted by his colleagues nearly word for word as it was written down.

Walter Scott was quite delightful ; he appeared full of fire and animation, and told some interesting anecdotes connected with his early life in Scotland. I remember that he proved himself, what would have been called in the olden times he delighted to portray, "a stout trencher-man ; " nor were his attentions confined by any means to the eatables ; on the contrary, he showed himself worthy to have made a third in the famous carousal in *Ivanhoe*, between the Black Knight and the Holy Clerk of Copmanhurst.

Byron, whom I had before seen at the shooting-galleries and elsewhere, was then a very handsome man, with remarkably fine eyes and hair ; but was, as usual, all show-off and affectation. I recollect his saying that he disliked seeing women eat, or to have their company at dinner, from a wish to believe, if possible, in their more ethereal nature ; but he was rallied into avowing that his chief dislike to their presence at the festive board arose from the fact of their being helped first, and consequently getting all the wings of the chickens, whilst men had to be content with the legs or other parts.

Byron, on this occasion, was in great good-humour, and full of boyish and even boisterous mirth.

Croker was also agreeable, notwithstanding his bitter and sarcastic remarks upon everything and everybody. The sneering, ill-natured expression of his face, struck me as an impressive contrast to the frank and benevolent countenance of Walter Scott.

I never assisted at a more agreeable dinner. According to the custom of the day, we sat late; the poets, statesmen, and soldiers all drank an immense quantity of wine, and I for one felt the effects of it next day. Walter Scott gave one or two recitations, in a very animated manner, from the ballads that he had been collecting, which delighted his auditory; and both Lord Byron and Croker added to the hilarity of the evening by quotations from, and criticisms on, the more prominent writers of the period.

LORD BYRON.—I knew very little of Lord Byron personally, but lived much with two of his intimate friends, Scrope Davies and Wedderburn Webster, from whom I frequently heard many anecdotes of him. I regret that I remember so few; and wish that I had written down those told me by poor Scrope Davies, one of the most agreeable men I ever met.

When Byron was at Cambridge, he was introduced to Scrope Davies by their mutual friend, Matthews, who was afterwards drowned in the river Cam. After Matthews's death, Davies became Byron's particular friend, and was admitted to his rooms at all hours. Upon one occasion he found the poet in bed with his hair *en papillote*, upon which Scrope cried, "Ha, ha! Byron, I have at last caught you acting the part of the Sleeping Beauty."

Byron, in a rage, exclaimed, "No, Scrope; the part of a d——d fool, you should have said."

"Well, then, anything you please; but you have succeeded admirably in deceiving your friends, for it was my conviction that your hair curled naturally."

"Yes, naturally every night," returned the poet; "but do not, my dear Scrope, let the cat out of the bag, for I am as vain of my curls as a girl of sixteen."

When in London, Byron used to go to Manton's shooting-gallery, in Davies Street, to try his hand, as he said, at a wafer. Wedderburn Webster was present when the poet, intensely delighted with his own skill, boasted to Joe Manton that he considered himself the best shot in London. "No, my lord," replied Manton, "not the best; but your shooting to-day was respectable." Whereupon Byron waxed wroth, and left the shop in a violent passion.

Lords Byron, Yarmouth, Pollington, Mountjoy, Wallscourt, Blandford, Captain Burges, Jack Bouverie, and myself, were in 1814, and for several years afterwards, amongst the chief and most constant frequenters of this well-known shooting-gallery, and frequently shot at the wafer for considerable sums of money. Manton was allowed to enter the betting list, and he generally backed me. On one occasion I hit the wafer nineteen times out of twenty.

Byron lived a great deal at Brighton, his house being opposite the Pavilion. He was fond of boating, and was generally accompanied by a lad, who was said to be a girl in boy's clothes. This report was confirmed to me by Webster, who was then living at Brighton. The vivid description of the page in *Lara*, no doubt, gave some plausibility to this often-told tale. I myself witnessed the dexterous manner in which Byron used to get into his boat; for, while standing on the beach, I once saw him vault into it with the agility of a harlequin, in spite of his lame foot.

On one occasion, whilst his lordship was dining with a few of his friends in Charles Street, Pall Mall, a letter was delivered to Scrope Davies, which required an immediate answer. Scrope, after reading its contents, handed it to Lord Byron. It was thus worded :—

" MY DEAR SCROPE,—Lend me £500 for a few days ; the funds are shut for the dividends, or I would not have made this request.

"G. BRUMMELL."

The reply was :—

" MY DEAR BRUMMELL,—All my money is locked up in the funds.

" SCROPE DAVIES."

This was just before Brummell's escape to the Continent.

I have frequently asked Scrope Davies his private opinion of Lord Byron, and invariably received the same answer—that he considered Lord Byron very agreeable and clever, but vain, overbearing, conceited, suspicious, and jealous. Byron hated Palmerston, but liked Peel, and thought that the whole

world ought to be constantly employed in admiring
his poetry and himself; he never could write a
poem or a drama without making himself its hero,
and he was always the subject of his own conversation.

During one of Hobhouse's visits to Byron, at his
villa near Genoa, and whilst they were walking in
the garden, his lordship suddenly turned upon his
guest, and, *à propos* of nothing, exclaimed, " Now,
I know, Hobhouse, you are looking at my foot."
Upon which Hobhouse kindly replied, "My dear
Byron, nobody thinks of or looks at anything but
your head."

SHELLEY.—Shelley, the poet, cut off at so early
an age, just when his great poetical talents had been
matured by study and reflection, and when he probably would have produced some great work, was
my friend and associate at Eton. He was a boy of
studious and meditative habits, averse to all games
and sports, and a great reader of novels and roman-
ces. He was a thin, slight lad, with remarkably
lustrous eyes, fine hair, and a very peculiar shrill
voice and laugh. His most intimate friend at Eton
was a boy named Price, who was considered one of
the best classical scholars amongst us. At his tutor,
Bethell's, where he lodged, he attempted many me-
chanical and scientific experiments. By the aid of
a common tinker, he contrived to make something
like a steam-engine, which, unfortunately, one day
suddenly exploded, to the great consternation of the
neighbourhood and to the imminent danger of a
severe flogging from Dr. Goodall.

Soon after leaving school, and about the year

1810, he came, in a state of great distress and difficulty, to Swansea, when we had an opportunity of rendering him a service; but we could never ascertain what had brought him to Wales, though we had reason to suppose it was some mysterious *affaire du cœur*.

The last time I saw Shelley was at Genoa, in 1822, sitting on the sea-shore, and, when I came upon him, making a true poet's meal of bread and fruit. He at once recognised me, jumped up, and appearing greatly delighted, exclaimed, " Here you see me at my old Eton habits; but instead of the green fields for a couch, I have here the shores of the Mediterranean. It is very grand, and very romantic. I only wish I had some of the excellent brown bread and butter we used to get at Spiers's : but I was never very fastidious in my diet." Then he continued, in a wild and eccentric manner: " Gronow, do you remember the beautiful Martha, the Hebe of Spiers's ? She was the loveliest girl I ever saw, and I loved her to distraction."

Shelley was looking careworn and ill; and, as usual, was very carelessly dressed. He had on a large and wide straw hat, his long brown hair, already streaked with grey, flowing in large masses from under it, and presented a wild and strange appearance.

During the time I sat by his side he asked many questions about myself and many of our schoolfellows; but on my questioning him in turn about himself, his way of life, and his future plans, he avoided entering into any explanation : indeed, he gave such short and evasive answers, that, thinking my inquisitiveness displeased him, I rose to take my leave. I observed that I had not been lucky enough to see Lord Byron in any of my rambles, to which he replied, " Byron is living at his villa, surrounded by his court of sycophants; but I shall shortly see him at Leghorn." We then shook hands. I never saw him again ; for he was drowned shortly afterwards, with his friend, Captain Williams, and his body was washed ashore near Via Reggio. Every one is familiar with the romantic scene which took place on the sea-shore, when the remains of my poor friend and Captain Williams were burnt, in the presence of Byron and Trelawny, in the Roman fashion. His ashes were gathered into an urn, and buried in the Protestant cemetery at Rome. He was but twenty-nine years of age at his death.

ROBERT SOUTHEY, THE POET.—In the year 1803 my father received a letter of introduction from Mr. Rees, of the well-known firm of Longman, Paternoster Row, presenting Robert Southey, the poet, to him. He came into Wales with the hope of finding a cottage to reside in. Accordingly a cavalcade was formed, consisting of Mr. W. Gwynne, the two brothers Southey, my father, and myself, and we rode up the Valley of Neath to look at a cottage about eight miles from the town. The poet, delighted with the scenery and situation, decided upon taking it ; but the owner, unfortunately for the honour of Welshmen, actually declined to let it to Robert Southey, fearing that a poet could not find security for the small annual rent of twenty-five pounds. This circumstance led the man of letters, who eventually became one of the most distinguished men of his day, to seek a home elsewhere, and the Lakes were at length chosen as his residence. Probably the picturesque beauties of Cumberland compensated the Laureate for the indignity put upon him by the Welshman.

An act of Vandalism perpetrated in the same Vale of Neath, and reflecting no honour on my countrymen, deserves here to be noted with reprobation. A natural cascade, called Dyllais, which was so beautiful as to excite the admiration of travellers, was destroyed by an agent to Lord Jersey, the proprietor of the estate, in order to build a few cottages and the lock of a canal. The rock down which this beautiful cascade had flowed from the time of the Flood, and which had created a scene of beauty universally admired, was blown up with gunpowder by this man, who could probably appreciate no more beautiful sight than that which presents itself from a window in Gray's or Lincoln's Inn, of which he was a member.

CAPTAIN HESSE, FORMERLY OF THE 18TH HUSSARS. —One of my most intimate friends was the late Captain Hesse, generally believed to be a son of the Duke of York, by a German lady of rank. Though it is not my intention to disclose certain family secrets of which I am in possession, I may, nevertheless, record some circumstances connected with the life of my friend, which were familiar to a large circle with whom I mixed. Hesse, in early youth, lived with the Duke and Duchess of York; he was treated in such a manner by them as to indicate an interest in him by their Royal Highnesses which could scarcely be attributed to ordinary regard, and was gazetted a cornet in the 18th Hussars at seventeen years of age. Shortly afterwards he went to Spain, and was present in all the battles in which his regiment was engaged; receiving a severe wound in the wrist at the battle of Vittoria. When this became known in England, a royal lady wrote to Lord Wellington, requesting that he might be carefully attended to; and, at the same time, a watch, with her portrait, was forwarded, which was delivered to the wounded hussar by Lord Wellington himself. When he had sufficiently recovered, Hesse returned to England, and passed much of his time at Oatlands, the residence of the Duchess of York; he was also honoured with the confidence of the Princess Charlotte and her mother, Queen Caroline.

Many delicate and important transactions were conducted through the medium of Captain Hesse; in fact, it was perfectly well known that he played a striking part in many scenes of domestic life which I do not wish to reveal. I may, however, observe that the Prince Regent sent the late Admiral Lord Keith to Hesse's lodgings, who demanded, in his Royal Highness's name, the restitution of the watch and letters which had been sent him when in Spain. After a considerable amount of hesitation, the admiral obtained what he wanted the following day; whereupon Lord Keith assured him that the Prince Regent would never forget so great a mark of confidence, and that the heir to the throne would ever afterwards be his friend. I regret to say, from personal knowledge, that upon this occasion the prince behaved most ungratefully and unfeelingly; for, after having obtained all he

wanted, he positively refused to receive Hesse at
Carlton House.

Hesse's life was full of singular incidents. He
was a great friend of the Queen of Naples, grandmother of the ex-Sovereign of the Two Sicilies;
in fact, so notorious was that *liaison*, that Hesse
was eventually expelled from Naples under an
escort of gendarmes. He was engaged in several
affairs of honour, in which he always displayed the
utmost courage; and his romantic career terminated
by his being killed in a duel by Count Léon, natural
son of the first Napoleon. He died as he had lived,
beloved by his friends, and leaving behind him little
but his name and the kind thoughts of those who
survived him.

VISITING IN THE COUNTRY.—When I returned to
London from Paris, in 1815, upon promotion, I was
accompanied by Colonel Brooke, who was good
enough to invite me to pass some time at his brother's,
Sir R. Brooke, in Cheshire, upon the occasion of the
christening of his eldest son. The *fête* was truly
magnificent, and worthy of our excellent host; and
all the great people of the neighbouring counties
were present.

Soon afterwards I went to the Hale, a country
house near Liverpool, belonging to Mr. Blackburn,
one of the oldest members of the House of Commons, where many persons, who had been at Sir
Richard Brooke's, met again. Mr. Blackburn was
extremely absent and otherwise odd: upon one occasion I gave him a letter to frank, which he deliberately opened and read in my presence; and on
my asking him if it amused him, he replied that he

did not understand what it meant. Upon another occasion, the Duke of Gloucester, accompanied by Mr. Blackburn, went out to shoot pheasants in the preserves near the Hale ; when all of a sudden, Mr. B., observing that the duke's gun was cocked, asked his Royal Highness whether he always carried his gun cocked. "Yes, Blackburn, always," was the reply. "Well then, good morning, your Royal Highness ; I will no longer accompany you."

At dinner Mr. Blackburn was very eccentric : he would never surrender his place at table even to royalty ; so the Duke was obliged to sit near him. Whenever the royal servant filled the duke's glass with wine-and-water, Mr. B. invariably drank it off ; until at length the duke asked his servant for more wine-and-water, and anticipating a repetition of the farce that had so often been played, drank it off, and said, "Well, Blackburn, I have done you at last." After dinner the duke and the men went to join the ladies in the drawing-room, where the servant in royal livery was waiting, holding a tray, upon which was a cup of tea for the duke. Mr. Blackburn, observing the servant in waiting, and that nobody took the cup of tea, determined on drinking it ; but the domestic retired a little, to endeavour to prevent it. Mr. Blackburn, however, followed and persisted ; upon which the servant said, "Sir, it is for his Royal Highness." "D——his Royal Highness ; I will have this tea." The duke exclaimed, " That's right, Blackburn," and ordered the servant to hand it to him.

COLONEL KELLY AND HIS BLACKING. — Among the odd characters I have met with, I do not re-

collect any one more eccentric than the late Lieutenant-Colonel Kelly, of the First Foot Guards, who
was the vainest man I ever encountered.   He was
a thin, emaciated-looking dandy, but had all the
bearing of the gentleman.   He was haughty in the
extreme, and very fond of dress; his boots were so
well varnished that the polish now in use could not
surpass Kelly's blacking in brilliancy; his pantaloons were made of the finest leather, and his
coats were inimitable: in short, his dress was considered perfect.

His sister held the place of housekeeper to the
Custom-house, and when it was burnt down, Kelly
was burnt with it, in endeavouring to save his
favourite boots.   When the news of his horrible
death became known, all the dandies were anxious
to secure the services of his valet, who possessed
the mystery of the inimitable blacking.   Brummell
lost no time in discovering his place of residence,
and asked what wages he required; the servant
answered, his late master gave him £150 a year,
but it was not enough for his talents, and he should
require £200; upon which Brummell said, "Well, if
you will make it guineas, I shall be happy to attend
upon *you*."   The late Lord Plymouth eventually
secured this phœnix of valets at £200 a year, and
bore away the sovereignty of boots.

LORD ALLEN AND COUNT D'ORSAY.—Lord Allen
being rather the worse for drinking too much wine
at dinner, teased Count d'Orsay, and said some
very disagreeable things, which irritated him;
when suddenly John Bush entered the club and
shook hands with the count, who exclaimed, "*Voilà*

la différence entre une bonne bouche *et une mauvaise* haleine."

The following *bon mot* was also attributed to the count: General Ornano, observing a certain nobleman—who, by some misfortune in his youth, lost the use of his legs—in a Bath chair, which he wheeled about, inquired the name of the English peer; D'Orsay answered, "Père la Chaise."

The count had many disciples among our men of fashion, but none of them succeeded in copying the original. His death produced, both in London and in Paris, a deep and universal regret. The count's life has been so well delineated in the public prints, that nothing I could say would add to the praise that has been bestowed upon him. Perfectly natural in manners and language, highly accomplished, and never betraying the slightest affectation or pretension, he had formed friendships with some of the noblest and most accomplished men in England. He was also a great favourite in Paris, where he had begun to exercise his talent as an artist, when death prematurely removed him from society.

Mr. Phelps.—Mr. Phelps, a chorus singer, and an excellent musician, with good looks and address, contrived to ingratiate himself with the Marchioness of Antrim, and was fortunate enough to marry her ladyship, by whose influence he was created a baronet, and, through his marriage, he became allied to some of our most aristocratic families.

The late Lord Bloomfield.—The late Lord Bloomfield likewise owed his elevation to the Peerage to his musical talents. When the Prince of

Wales was living at the Pavilion at Brighton, he wanted some one who could accompany him on the violoncello, and having ascertained that Captain Bloomfield, of the Royal Artillery, who was then at Brighton with his troop, was an accomplished violoncello player, the captain was accordingly summoned to appear before the prince at the Pavilion.   From that night commenced an intimacy which for many years existed between the prince and Captain Bloomfield, who for a considerable length of time was well known in fashionable circles under the title of Sir Benjamin Bloomfield. A court intrigue, headed by a fascinating marchioness, caused him to be sent into splendid exile : this lady attributing to Sir Benjamin Bloomfield her being compelled to send back some jewels which had been presented to her by the Prince Regent, but which, it was discovered, belonged to the Crown, and could not be alienated.   Sir Benjamin was created a peer, and sent to Stockholm as ambassador, where his affable manners and his unostentatious hospitality rendered him exceedingly popular ; and he became as great a favourite with Bernadotte as he had been with the Prince Regent. The name of Bloomfield is to this day respected in Sweden.

THE RIGHT HON. GEORGE CANNING.—When Mr. Canning retired from Portugal, he was received at Paris with a distinction and a deference perhaps never before bestowed on a foreign diplomatist ; he dined with Charles X. almost *tête-à-tête*, and was scrambled for by the leading aristocracy of France.   It happened that he also dined, on one occasion, with the Bailli de Ferrete, who was the oldest foreign ambassador in Paris; and it was generally understood that Canning, who had the reputation of being a *gourmand*, and was not in robust health at the time, never thoroughly recovered from these Parisian hospitalities. A short time after, this great orator, and the most brilliant statesman of the day, breathed his last at Chiswick, in the same room in which Charles James Fox died.

MRS. BOEHM, OF ST. JAMES'S SQUARE.—This lady used to give fashionable balls and masquerades, to which I look back with much pleasure. The Prince Regent frequently honoured her *fêtes* with his presence. Mrs. Boehm, on one occasion, sent invitations to one of her particular friends, begging him to fill them up, and tickets were given by him to Dick Butler (afterwards Lord Glengal) and to Mr. Raikes. Whilst they were deliberating in what character they should go, Dick Butler—for by that name he was only then known—proposed that Raikes should take the part of Apollo;* which the latter agreed to, provided Dick would be his *lyre*. The noble lord's reputation for stretching the long bow rendered this repartee so applicable, that it was universally repeated at the clubs.

DR. GOODALL, OF ETON.—This gentleman was proverbially fond of punning. About the same time that he was made Provost of Eton, he received, also, a stall at Windsor. A young lady of his acquaintance, while congratulating him on his elevation, and

---

* Raikes, being a city merchant as well as a dandy, was called "Apollo," because he rose in the East and set in the West.

requesting him to give the young ladies of Eton and Windsor a ball during the vacation, happened to touch his wig with her fan, and caused the powder to fly about. Upon which the doctor exclaimed, "My dear, you see you can get the powder out of the *canon*, but not the ball."

LORD MELBOURNE, THE DUKE OF LEINSTER, AND LORD NORMANBY.—When Lord Melbourne offered the garter to the Duke of Leinster, his grace is reported to have answered that he did not want it; adding, "It will, no doubt, be eagerly accepted by one of your lordship's supporters in the Upper House." On another occasion, when Lord Normanby was soliciting Lord Melbourne to be made a marquis, the noble Premier observed, in his jocular way, "Why, Normanby, you are not such a d——d fool as to want that!" The favour, however, was eventually granted.

THE DUKE OF GLOUCESTER.—His Royal Highness, who was in the habit of saying very ludicrous things, asked one of his friends in the House of Lords, on the occasion when William IV. assented to Lord Grey's proposition to pass the Reform Bill *coûte que coûte*, "Who is Silly Billy now?" This was in allusion to the general opinion that was prevalent of the royal duke's weakness, and which had obtained for him the sobriquet of "Silly Billy."

The duke frequently visited Cheltenham during the season. Upon one occasion he called upon Colonel Higgins, brother to the equerry of his Royal Highness the Prince Regent, and, on inquiring of the servant if his master was at home, received

for answer, " My master is dyeing."   " Dying !" repeated the duke ; "have you sent for a doctor ?"

" No, sir."   His Royal Highness immediately ran
back into the street, and, having the good fortune
to find a medical man, he requested him to come at
once to Colonel Higgins, as he was on the point of
death.   The duke and the doctor soon reached the
colonel's house, and, after again asking the servant
how his master was, that functionary replied, " I
told you, sir, that he is dyeing."   They mounted
the staircase, and were rather amused to find the
reported invalid busily occupied in dyeing his hair.

LADY CORK.—In 1819 this venerable lady lived
in Old Burlington Street, where she gave many
parties, to persons of all nations, and contrived to
bring together foreigners from the wilds of America,
the Cape of Good Hope, and even savages from the
isles of the Pacific ; in fact, she was the notorious
lion-hunter of her age.   It was supposed that she
had a peculiar ignorance of the laws of *meum* and
tuum, and that her monomania was such that she
would try to get possession of whatever she could
place her hands upon ; so that it was dangerous to
leave in the ante-room anything of value.   On
application being made, however, the articles were
usually returned the following day, the fear of the
law acting strongly upon her ladyship's bewildered
brain.

THE DUCHESS OF GORDON.—This leader of fashion,
who was wont to be the admiration of all circles,
was looked upon as the most ambitious of women,
and her vanity was fully gratified by the marriage

of her daughters to the first people in the realm—
the Dukes of Richmond, Manchester, and Bedford,
and the Marquis of Cornwallis.

THE LATE MRS. BRADSHAW (MARIA TREE).—The
two Miss Trees, Maria and Ellen (the latter now
Mrs. Kean), were the great favourites of the Bath
stage for many seasons before they became leading
stars in London; Miss Ellen Tree made her first
appearance in a grand entertainment, called the
Cataract of the Ganges, in a magnificent car, drawn
by six horses. Her beauty made a deep impression
on the audience, which was naturally increased by
her subsequent exhibition of great talents.

Miss Maria Tree was much admired as a vocalist,
and her Viola, in *Twelfth Night*, was one of the
most popular performances of the day. Mr. Bradshaw
became desperately enamoured of her during her
engagement in London, and having learnt that she
was about to go by the mail coach to Birmingham,
where she was to perform her principal characters,
thought it a favourable opportunity of enjoying her
society; so he sent his servant to secure him a place
by the mail, under the name of Tomkins. At the
appointed time for departure, Mr. Bradshaw was at
the office, and jumping into the coach was soon
whirled away; but great was his disappointment at
finding that the fair object of his admiration was
not a fellow-passenger: he was not consoled by discovering that there were two mails, the one the
Birmingham mail, the other, the Birmingham and
Manchester, and that whilst he was journeying by
the latter, Miss Tree was travelling in the other.

On arriving at Birmingham, early in the morning,

he left the coach and stepped into the hotel, determined to remain there and go to the theatre on the
following evening. He went to bed, and slept late
the following day; but on waking he remembered
that his trunk with all his money had gone on to
Manchester, and that he was without the means of
paying his way. Seeing the Bank of Birmingham
opposite the hotel, he went over and explained his
position to one of the partners, giving his own
banker's address in London, and showing letters
addressed to him as Mr. Bradshaw. Upon this he
was told that with such credentials he might have
a loan; and the banker said he would write the
necessary letter and cheque, and send the money
over to him at the hotel. Mr. Bradshaw, pleased
with this kind attention, sat himself down comfortably to breakfast in the coffee-room. According to
promise, the cashier made his appearance at the hotel,
and asked the waiter for Mr. Bradshaw. "No such
gentleman here," was the reply. "Oh, yes, he came
by the London mail." "No, sir; no one came but
Mr. Tomkins, who was booked as inside passenger to
Manchester." The cashier was dissatisfied; but the
waiter added, " Sir, you can look through the window
of the coffee-room door, and see the gentleman
yourself." On doing so, he beheld the supposed Mr.
Tomkins, *alias* Mr. Bradshaw, and immediately returned to the bank, telling what he himself had
heard and seen. The banker went over to the hotel,
had a consultation with the landlord, and it was determined that a watch should be placed upon the
suspicious person who had two names and no lug-
gage, and who was booked to Manchester but had
stopped at Birmingham.

The landlord then summoned "boots,"—a little lame fellow, of most ludicrous appearance,—and pointing to the gentleman in the coffee-room, told him his duty for the day was to follow him wherever he went, and never to lose sight of him; but above all to take care that he did not get away. Boots nodded assent, and immediately mounted guard. Mr. Bradshaw having taken his breakfast and read the papers, looked at his watch, and sallied forth to see something of the goodly town of Birmingham. He was much surprised at observing a little odd-looking man surveying him most attentively, and watching his every movement; stopping whenever he stopped, and evidently taking a deep interest in all he did. At last, observing that he was the object of this incessant *espionnage*, and finding that he had a shilling left in his pocket, he hailed one of the coaches that ran short distances in those days when omnibuses were not. This, however, did not suit little boots, who went up to him and insisted that he must not leave the town.

Mr. Bradshaw's indignation was naturally excessive, and he immediately returned to the hotel, where he found a constable ready to take him before the mayor as an impostor and swindler. He was compelled to appear before his worship, and had the mortification of being told that unless he could give some explanation, he must be content with a night's lodging in a house of detention. Mr. Bradshaw had no alternative but to send to the fair charmer of his heart to identify him; which she most readily did, as soon as rehearsal was over. Explanations were then entered into; but he was forced to give the reason of his being in Birmingham, which of course made a due impression on the lady's heart, and led to that happy result of their interviews—a marriage which resulted in the enjoyment of mutual happiness for many years.

LADIES' JEWELLERY AND LOVERS.—Some of the most magnificent fortunes in England have, in the first instance, been undermined by an extravagant expenditure on jewellery, which has been given to ladies, married and unmarried, who have fascinated their wealthy admirers and made them their slaves. Hamlet, and Rundell, and Bridge were in my day patronised by the great, and obtained large sums of money from their enamoured clients, to whom they often became bankers.

On the day after the coronation of George IV., Hamlet made his appearance at the house of Mr. Coutts, in Piccadilly, the corner of Stratton Street. It was during dinner; but, owing no doubt to a previous arrangement, he was at once admitted, when he placed before the rich banker a magnificent diamond cross, which had been worn the previous day by the Duke of York. It at once attracted the admiration of Mrs. Coutts, who loudly exclaimed, "How happy I should be with such a splendid specimen of jewellery." "What is it worth?" immediately exclaimed Mr. Coutts. "I could not allow it to pass out of my possession for less than £15,000," said the wary tradesman. "Bring me a pen and ink," was the only answer made by the doting husband; and he at once drew a cheque for that amount upon the bank in the Strand, and with much delight the worthy old gentleman placed the jewel upon the fair bosom of the lady :—

"Upon her breast a sparkling cross she wore,
Which Jews might kiss, and infidels adore."

The Earl of C***, whose reputation in the sporting world was of the highest order, and who had
obtained some notoriety by his amours, fell into the
hands of Hamlet, who was known to the aristocracy
by his mock title of "Prince of Denmark." Hamlet
placed before him on one occasion jewels to the
amount of thirty thousand pounds, and volunteered,
as his client was not of age, to give him credit for
several months. The offer was accepted, and the
brilliant present became the possession of a young
lady, one of the Terpsichorean tribe (Mademoiselle
le G.), whose charms had captivated the youthful
nobleman: she had irrevocably fascinated him by
the expression of her love, awakened by the prospect
of a rich remuneration, and she accepted him as the
sole possessor of a heart which had been before at
the disposal of any rich admirer whose purse was
worthy her consideration.

This lady, who is now somewhat advanced in
years, but has still the remains of beauty, is living
in France upon her estate; the produce of the many
charms which she once possessed, and which she
turned to such advantage as to make her society,
even up to this day, courted by those who look upon
wealth as the great source of distinction, and who
are willing to disbelieve any stories that they may
accidentally hear of her previous history.

THE LATE LORD HENRY SEYMOUR.—I knew Lord
Henry perhaps better than any other Englishman,
having lived with him on terms of great intimacy.

He was famous for his racing stud and good taste in his carriages and riding horses. It was said, by persons who were little acquainted with him, that he was fond of masquerades, fighting, and was also the terror of pugilists, from his great strength and science in boxing; on the contrary, he was a gentle, retiring, and humane man, and never was known to have been present at a masquerade, or any place of the sort. But it unfortunately happened that a man named "Franconi," of the Circus,—a low-born and vulgar fellow,—resembled him in looks and stature, and having been mistaken for my noble friend, gave himself out as Lord Seymour, in those dens of infamy where the noble lord was unknown.

Lord Henry Seymour was a man of fine taste, and fond of the arts, and, at his death, his paintings, library, and plate fetched a considerable sum at public auction. During his lifetime he patronised young artists: often advancing them money, and assisting them in every possible way. He was the founder of the French Jockey Club, and, in conjunction with the late Duke de Gramont (better known in England as the Count de Guiche), made racing in France what it now is: that is, they placed the turf upon a respectable footing. Lord Henry established a school of arms and gymnasium in his hotel on the Boulevard des Italiens, which became the most celebrated in Europe. He himself was an adept in the art of fencing, and his skill was considered by the professors to be incomparable.

Lord Henry's kindness of heart and unostentatious generosity were his noblest qualities. One morning, whilst we were breakfasting in his library, a friend entered, and, with a sad countenance, informed him that he had that morning been visiting an old friend of his, a man of good birth, who, with his wife and children, were absolutely starving, and that they were reduced to sleep upon straw. Lord Henry, touched by this painful information, asked where those poor people were to be found, and being told, he said not a word more, but ordered his carriage and went out. The next morning the same gentleman made his appearance, and said, "I call to tell you, Seymour, that I am just come from my poor friend, who, I am happy to say, has received relief in the shape of furniture, bedding, linen, and food, from some kind person, who also left a considerable sum of money to purchase wearing apparel for the family."

Seymour never moved a muscle of his face, and we were wondering from whence the relief came, when a fine-looking fellow entered, bowing in the most respectful manner, and addressed his lordship in the following terms :—" My lord, I am obliged to confess that I have taken some trouble to discover the name of our benefactor, and from all I have been able to learn, it cannot be any other than your lordship ; I therefore deem it my duty, on behalf of my wife, children and self, to return you my heartfelt thanks for this unexampled act of charity towards a perfect stranger." The poor fellow shed tears in thus addressing his lordship, who kindly gave him his hand, and promised to be his friend for the future ; which promise he fulfilled, by procuring him a place under the Government, that enabled him to live happily and bring up his family with honour and comfort.

FRANCE AND THE FRENCH.—I will not permit this
little volume to make its appearance in English
society, without a few words about a people with
whom I have mingled for nearly forty years. When
I first came to France, few of my countrypeople travelled, save those belonging to the rich and aristocratic classes; it was not, therefore, surprising that
those whose interest it might have been, on both
sides of the Channel, to create a bad feeling between
England and France, found little difficulty in doing
so. An Englishman was taught to hate the French
as well as to observe the Ten Commandments; and
a Frenchman, on the other hand, was educated with
the idea that his only enemy on the face of the
earth was an Englishman.

I regard this stimulated hostile feeling between
two nations which must ever influence the welfare
of the human race more than any others, as one of
the greatest calamities that could curse humanity.
We have only to read history from the days of
Agincourt up to our later struggles with Napoleon I.,
to come to the conclusion that the two bravest and
the most intelligent nations on the face of the earth
have, from DYNASTIC ambition, and a want of the
people knowing each other, been ever engaged in
inflicting mutual disasters, which have impeded for
centuries the progress, civilisation, and prosperity of
both; whilst the want of a proper understanding
between the two countries has materially aided in
retarding other nations in obtaining that political
emancipation necessary to the happiness of mankind.

I have lived through a period characterised by
sanguinary wars and huge national debts, and have

remained in this world long enough to calculate their results. I am afraid we must often be content with that empty glory which lives only in the pages of history. A battle fought fifty years ago appears very often of no more utility than the splendid tomb of a necropolis. Events and objects for which men by thousands were brought together in deadly combat, assume, a few years afterwards, mighty small proportions; and those who have taken part in deadly struggles, at a later period marvel at the enthusiasm which then animated them. I am no believer in that era of happiness which some divines imagine to be so near at hand; nor do I imagine that the next two or three hundred years will witness the sword turned into the reaping-hook of peaceful industry; but what I do believe in, and what I hope for, is that nations will know each other better than they did of old. It will be more difficult for sovereigns and governments to bring about wars between neighbouring nations now, than it was before the existence of that intercommunication which in our day has been created by the press, the railway, and the electric telegraph.

I have lived long enough to find hundreds of my countrymen participating in a real knowledge of the French, and believing with me that they are a brave, intelligent, and generous nation. Nearly half a century of experience amongst them has taught me that there is much to learn and much that is worthy of imitation in France. The social habits of the French, and their easy mode of communication, always gain the admiration, and often invite the attachment of foreigners. They are less prejudiced than we islanders, and are much more citizens of the world than ourselves. I have received an immense amount of courtesy in France; and if there be less of solid friendship—which, however, in England is based too often on a similarity of birth, position, and wealth—in France, you have, at least, a greater chance than in England of making a friend of a man who neither looks to your ancestors nor your amount of riches before he proffers you the most sincere intimacy, and, if necessary, disinterested aid, purely on the ground of your own merit and character.

Many of the better qualities of the French are not discoverable by the superficial traveller, any more than the sterling qualities of the Englishman are appreciated by the foreigner who makes a brief sojourn in Great Britain. Slowly, but, I believe, surely, the agreeable knowledge that I possess of the French is becoming more universal; and I cannot but imagine that such a correct appreciation will be fraught with the most valuable political as well as social results.

Intelligent Englishmen have lived long enough to appreciate the genius of Napoleon I., whose mode of governing France has been applied by Napoleon III., with a success which prejudice even has been compelled to acknowledge. But I remember a period when probably not a dozen Englishmen could have been found to speak of the first emperor with the most ordinary common sense. I will, however, record one honourable exception to the rule. The late Lord Dudley and Ward, an eccentric, but able man, was at Vienna, in the midst of a large party, who were all more or less abusing or depreciating the fallen hero, whose very name

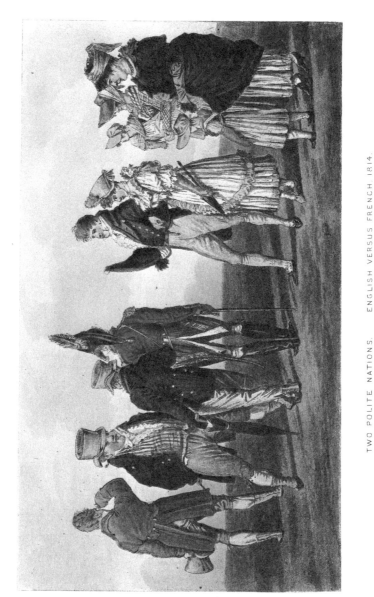

TWO POLITE NATIONS.   ENGLISH VERSUS FRENCH 1814.

had so long created fear and hatred amongst them. It was naturally supposed that the Englishman who was silently listening to this conversation must of course, as the natural enemy of France, approve of all that had been said. Prince Metternich turned at last to his guest, and said, "*Et vous*, my lord, *que pensez-vous de Napoléon?*" "*Je pense*," replied Lord Dudley, "*qu'il a rendu la gloire passée douteuse, et la renommée future impossible.*"

As an old soldier and an admirer of the Duke of Wellington, I cannot altogether admit the entire justice of the observation; yet, spoken by an Englishman to the enemies of the exiled emperor, it was a gallant homage paid to fallen greatness.

The great man who now wields the destinies of France possesses many of the remarkable qualities of the founder of his dynasty: his energetic will, his extensive and varied knowledge, his aptitude for government, his undaunted bravery, and that peculiar tact which leads him to say the right thing at the right time. To these rare gifts he joins the most princely generosity, and a kind and gentle heart: he has never been known to forsake a friend, or leave unrewarded any proofs of devotion shown to him in his days of exile. He is adored by the vast majority of the French nation, and even his political opponents, if accidentally brought under the influence of his particularly winning and gracious manner, are, in spite of themselves, charmed and softened. There can be no doubt that Napoleon III. enjoys a well-merited popularity, and that there is throughout all classes a deep and earnest confidence that the honour and glory of France are safe in his hands.

It is just this mighty power, founded on the love

and trust of his people, which is the surest pledge that peace will be maintained between our country and France. Napoleon III. does not require to court popularity by pandering to the anti-English prejudices still retained by a small minority of his subjects; and, unlike the representatives of less popular dynasties, he can afford to show that he is not only the beloved and mighty ruler of the French nation, but also the firm ally and faithful friend of England.

THREE HEROIC BROTHERS.—Among my souvenirs of 1815 there is one that has always struck me as particularly touching in the annals of French gallantry and heroism, and which shows what men we had to contend with in Spain, Portugal, and Belgium. There were three brothers named Angelet, whose heroic deeds have not, to the best of my knowledge, been recorded in any of the Memoirs of that time, and who all died or were mortally wounded on the bloody field of Waterloo.

The eldest brother started for the army as a conscript; he soon after rose to the rank of sergeant, and for many acts of daring he was raised to the rank of an officer in a regiment of the line. When in Spain he was made prisoner by the guerillas, and as he was on the point of being massacred, his life was saved by an English officer; but he was imprisoned on the Spanish pontoons, where he suffered great hardships. He contrived, however, with singular daring and dexterity, to make his escape.

Angelet went through the Russian campaign as captain in the Imperial Guard, was named major in the 141st Regiment in 1813, and took a glorious part in the battle of Lutzen, where he was dangerously wounded by a cannon-ball in the leg. After his recovery, he returned to the Imperial Guard with the rank of lieutenant-colonel, and was engaged in all the battles of 1814. On the return of the Bourbons, he was named colonel of the grenadiers of the Garde Royale ; but, on the escape of Napoleon from Elba, he immediately joined his glorious chief. After many heroic deeds at Waterloo, he received five wounds, and died at Brussels, after lingering in great agony for two months. His last moments were soothed by the presence of a beautiful young girl, to whom he was engaged to be married when he left Paris to conquer or to die.

The second brother, St. Amand Angelet, was educated at the École Militaire, was present at almost every battle in Spain, and for his gallant deeds obtained the cross of the Legion of Honour (which was not then as easily won as it is now-a-days), and the rank of captain. He received a wound in the leg at Orthes, and returned to Paris in 1814 to have it cured ; though he was always obliged to go on crutches.

St. Amand was named to the regiment commanded by his brother, and had to endure all the insolence that Napoleon's brave soldiers were forced at that time to undergo from the titled young *blanc becs* set over them by the Bourbons. St. Amand had for his *chef de bataillon* a young *émigré* of eighteen, who had never seen a shot fired, was perfectly ignorant of all military science, and excelled only in the art of tormenting his inferiors in grade. On the return of the Emperor Napoleon in 1815, St.

Amand Angelet compelled this insolent aristocrat to eat his *croix de lys* (the order of the Bourbons), in order that it might meet with the most ignominious destiny.

Angelet, who was a very handsome and agreeable man, and very much the fashion, was one day in a *salon* of the Faubourg St. Germain openly expressing his joy at the Emperor's return, when a great lady who was present jeered him on his inability, on account of his wounds, to do more than speak in favour of his hero. St. Amand, stung to the quick, and devoured by martial ardour and that passionate devotion for his chief which was the characteristic of every man in the French army, started immediately for the frontier, and made the campaign of 1815 on his crutches: he was killed in the early part of the day at Waterloo.

The third brother, who was mild and gentle as a woman in face and manner, also fell bravely fighting in the last charge of that bloody day. After the battle, Doctor D * * *, an intimate friend of the Angelet family, went to announce to the bereaved mother, who was also a widow, the death of her two younger sons. The eldest was still lingering at Brussels. "I do not wish him to recover," said the weeping woman, "for then I should be forced to live for his sake, whereas when he goes I may follow and join all those I have loved upon earth." She died in the course of the year of a broken heart— that malady which slays more than are numbered in the lists of men.

FRENCH HISTORIANS OF WATERLOO.—As I advance in years, I find myself often wandering

back to the scenes of my youth, and living over
again the stirring events of my early days; and
I confess to feeling a patriotic pride when I call
to remembrance the glorious field of Waterloo—
that "battle of giants" which decided the fate of
the world.   Many eloquent pages have been written
on that stirring topic, and varied have been the
accounts of that tremendous conflict; our present
brave allies to this very day continue to assert that
they were not beaten, but were victims of a mistaken order, an act of treachery, or an evil destiny,
—in short, that they succumbed to anything but
the genius of Wellington, the energy of Blucher,
and the dauntless courage of the English and
Prussian armies.   I must say that I cannot understand how French writers imagine that they lessen
the humiliation of defeat by attempting to decry
or diminish the fame and prowess of the victor;
or why M. Thiers and others, in their accounts of
Waterloo, make so many vain attempts to prove
that we ought to have lost the battle.

The Napoleon of M. Thiers's romance of Waterloo,
—it is certainly not a history,—his Napoleon, I say,
is not Napoleon as he was, but an ideal hero, omni-
scient and unerring.   Ney and the other French
generals are represented as brave blunderers, who
could neither give, obey, nor execute an order; Wellington as a genius of the second-rate order, slow
and unenterprising, and the English soldiers as fellows stubborn enough, but incapable of any aggres-
sive movement—heavy, beef-fed knaves, standing up
like logs, to be sabred, shot, and stuck by the active
and intelligent veterans of the Garde Imperiale.

M. Thiers has been liberal to us in one respect.

He has endowed several of our regiments with a very strong development of the vital principle. Many of our battalions, which, according to this great historian, had been entirely cut to pieces by the charges of French cavalry, nevertheless come to life again towards the end of M. Thiers's account of the engagement, and join with the utmost ardour in the last charge against the retreating French.

All this is quite unworthy of a great writer and statesman like M. Thiers, who has had every means of knowing the truth ; and I, for one, cannot refrain from entering my protest against the innumerable errors, false assertions, and convenient suppressions contained in the twentieth volume of his history. The fame of Wellington, as one of the great captains of the age, is world-wide, and, written as it is on fifty fields of battle, needs no defence from me ; but, when I hear the British soldier pooh-poohed and decried by M. Thiers, " who never set a squadron in the field, nor the division of a battle knew," I am moved to say a few words more on this stirring subject.

In spite of " Les Victoires et Conquêtes de l'Armée Française," I maintain that the British infantry is the finest in the world. I never saw anything to equal our old Peninsular regiments, not only for stubborn endurance, but for dash, pluck, intelligence, and skill in manœuvring. Nothing could beat them ; and if we had had the army of veterans with which we crossed the Bidassoa, on the field of Waterloo, we should have attacked the French instead of waiting their onset. But we had only 12,000 of our old Peninsular infantry, the rest were raw troops ; and though many did their best, they were hardly a match for the French army, which was a very efficient one, and almost entirely composed of veterans.

When I call to mind how ill rewarded our noble soldiers were for their heroic deeds, my heart bleeds for them. "Under the cold shade of aristocracy," men who in France would have been promoted for their valour to the highest grades of the army, lived and died, twenty or thirty years after the battle, with the rank of lieutenant or captain. As to the private soldiers, their stubborn endurance, their desperate courage, their indomitable pluck, were but ill-rewarded by a shilling or two a day, and a refuge in Chelsea or Kilmainham Hospital.

NAPOLEON AT WATERLOO.—The recent works of M. Thiers and Colonel Charras, Quinet's defence of Marshal Ney, and Victor Hugo's romance of "Les Misérables," have directed public attention with renewed interest to the battle of Waterloo, and the various episodes connected with it. I have therefore ventured, in addition to the slight remarks made in previous pages, to add a few further reminiscences of that eventful day. Though I took but a humble part in this great contest, yet I had opportunities of seeing and hearing much, both during and after the battle. My anecdotes are derived either from personal experience and observation, from the conversation of those to whom they refer, or from the common talk of the army at the time; and many of these anecdotes may be new to my readers.

But before I begin to retrace those scenes and episodes (which I fear will be in a very imperfect

and desultory manner) I must state that, while my
admiration for the great Duke and my gallant comrades is unbounded, yet I repudiate any share in
the vulgar John Bull exultation which glories in
having "licked the confounded French." Though
I cannot agree with their writers in attributing their
defeat to ill-luck, yet I am willing to admit that
the tide of success had turned against Napoleon ;
that he was not altogether what he had been, when
at Austerlitz and Wagram he carried all before him.
Then, flushed with victory, he was animated with
the certainty of success, which in itself was an
earnest of triumph. But all was changed when the
mighty conqueror came to play his last stake on the
field of Waterloo. He knew defeat was possible, for
he had been vanquished ; and, though his prestige
was immense, yet the Garde Imperiale, and the
other veterans of his noble army, who in former
days had only thought of victory when commanded
by him, now whispered together of dying with
him.

Even the bravest of soldiers, or the most desperate
of gamblers, plays his last stake with some degree
of emotion and hesitation, knowing that all depends
on the throw ; and Napoleon, feeling that (humanly
speaking) he held in his hand the fate of empires,
and his own, knew that if he lost the day, all was
over with him in this world. He was then not
quite his former self; and he certainly committed
several errors about the middle of the day, and
showed considerable hesitation as to the orders to
be given. The chief mistake he made, in my
humble opinion, was this : he did not support the
brilliant charges of his cavalry, and the tremendous

fire of his numerous and well-served artillery, by the general advance of his infantry, until it was too late and his cavalry were annihilated.

AFTER QUATRE BRAS.—I mentioned in a previous page that on my arrival to join my regiment, I was immediately sent to the village of Waterloo, with a detachment, under Captain Clements, brother of Lord Leitrim, to take charge of some hundreds of French prisoners. They had been taken at Quatre Bras, and were confined in a barn and the court-yard of a large farm-house. As ill-luck would have it, Clements did not place sentinels on the other side of the wall, which overlooked the plain leading to the forest of Soignies; the consequence was, that with the aid of a large waggon, which had been left in the yard, several of the prisoners scaled the wall, and made their escape. As soon as it was night, some more poor fellows attempted to follow their example; but this time the alarm was given, and our men fired and killed or wounded a dozen of them.

This firing at so late an hour brought several officers of the staff from the neighbouring houses to ascertain the cause, and among them came my poor friend Chambers, who kindly invited me to Sir Thomas Picton's quarters to supper. I accompanied him thither, and after groping our way into the house, for it was very dark, we passed the door of a room in which Sir Thomas himself was lying. I heard him groan, from the pain of the wound he had received at Quatre Bras, but did not of course venture to disturb him, and we passed on into a small hall, where I got some cold meat and wine.

THE BATTLE OF WATERLOO.—At daylight, on the 18th, we were agreeably surprised to see a detachment of the 3d Guards, commanded by Captain Wigston and Ensign George Anson, the lamented General who died in India, who had been sent to relieve us. I took the opportunity of giving Anson, then a fine lad of seventeen, a silver watch, made by Barwise, which his mother, Lady Anson, had requested me to take over to him. Bob Clements and I then proceeded to join our regiment.

The road was ankle-deep in mud and slough; and we had not proceeded a quarter of a mile when we heard the trampling of horses' feet, and on looking round perceived a large cavalcade of officers coming at full speed. In a moment we recognised the Duke himself at their head. He was accompanied by the Duke of Richmond, and his son, Lord William Lennox. The entire staff of the army was close at hand: the Prince of Orange, Count Pozzo di Borgo, Baron Vincent, the Spanish General Alava, Prince Castel Cicala, with their several aides-de-camp; Felton Harvey, Fitzroy Somerset, and Delancy were the last that appeared. They all seemed as gay and unconcerned as if they were riding to meet the hounds in some quiet English county.

In about half-an-hour we joined our comrades in camp, who were endeavouring to dry their accoutrements by the morning sun, after a night of rain and discomfort in their bivouac. I was now greeted by many of my old friends (whom I had not had time to speak to the day before, when I was sent off to the village of Waterloo) with loud cries of "How are you, old fellow? Take a glass of wine and a bit of ham? it will perhaps be your last breakfast." Then

Burges called out, "Come here, Gronow, and tell us some London news."

He had made himself a sort of gipsy-tent, with the aid of some blankets, a sergeant's halberd, and a couple of muskets. My dear old friend was sitting upon a knapsack, with Colonel Stuart (who afterwards lost his arm), eating cold pie and drinking champagne, which his servant had just brought from Brussels. I was not sorry to partake of his hospitality, and after talking together some time, we were aroused by the drums beating to arms. We fell in, and the muster-roll having been called, the piling of arms followed; but we were not allowed to leave our places.

The position taken up by the British army was an excellent one: it was a sort of ridge, very favourable for artillery, and from which all the movements of the French could be discerned. In case of any disaster, Wellington had several roads in his rear by which a masterly retreat could have been effected through the forest on Brussels; but our glorious commander thought little about retreating: on the contrary, he set all his energies to work, and determined to win the day.

Our brigade was under the orders of General Maitland, and our division was commanded by Sir George Cooke. We occupied the right centre of the British line, and had the château of Hougoumont at about a quarter of a mile's distance on our right. Picton was on the extreme left at La Haye Sainte, with his division of two British and one Hanoverian brigades. Hougoumont was garrisoned by the 2d and 3d regiments of the Guards, a battalion of Germans, and two battalions of artillery, who occupied the château and gardens. Between each regiment was a battery of guns, and nearly the whole of the cavalry was to the left of Sir Thomas Picton's division.

About half-past eleven the bands of several French regiments were distinctly heard, and soon after the French artillery opened fire. The rapid beating of the *pas de charge*, which I had often heard in Spain — and which few men, however brave they may be, can listen to without a somewhat unpleasant sensation—announced that the enemy's columns were fast approaching. On our side the most profound silence prevailed, whilst the French, on the contrary, raised loud shouts, and we heard the cry of " *Vive l'Empereur !* " from one end of their line to the other.

The battle commenced by the French throwing out clouds of skirmishers from Hougoumont to La Haye Sainte. Jérôme Bonaparte's division, supported by those of Foy and Bachelu, attacked Hougoumont, the wood and garden of which were taken and retaken several times ; but, after prodigies of valour performed on both sides, remained in the hands of the French : who, however, sustained immense loss, and the château still belonged to the invincible English Guards.

Whilst the battle was raging in the wood and orchard, eighty French guns, mostly twelve-pounders, opened upon us, and caused a heavy loss in our ranks. At the same moment, we could perceive from our elevated position that the enemy were attacking La Haye Sainte in great force. At about two o'clock, Ney, with the first corps formed in four columns, advanced *en échelon* the left wing for-

COMRADES IN ARMS

SIR THOMAS GRAHAM   LORD HILL   SIR THOMAS PICTON   MARQUIS OF ANGLESEA
(LORD LYNDOCK)

ward. They completely defeated and put to flight
a Dutch-Belgian brigade, and then attacked Picton's
division. He, however, made a desperate resistance,
and charged them several times, though they were
four times his number. It was then that noble
soldier was killed by a musket-ball. Things looked
ill there; when the Duke ordered up Adam's
brigade, which regained the ground, and pushed
eagerly forward.

At the same time Lord Uxbridge commanded the
cavalry to charge. This order was admirably executed by Somerset on one side, and by Ponsonby on
the other, and was for a time completely successful. The French infantry brigades of Quiot, Don-
zelot, and Marcoguet were rolled up and almost
annihilated; twenty guns were dismantled or spiked,
and many hundred prisoners taken; several squad-
rons of cuirassiers were also charged and put to the
rout. Unfortunately our cavalry went too far without proper supports, and were charged and driven
back by Milhaud's heavy cavalry and Jacquinot's
lancers, and had to take refuge behind our own
lines. Ney now received orders to attack La Haye
Sainte, which was taken about four o'clock. At
the same hour Bulow's first columns made their
appearance, and attacked D'Erlon and Lobau.

The Guards had what in modern battues is called
a hot corner of it, and the greatest "gluttons" (and
we had many such) must have allowed, when night
came on, that they had had fighting enough. I
confess that I am to this day astonished that any
of us remained alive. From eleven o'clock till
seven we were pounded with shot and shell at long
and short range, were incessantly potted at by

tirailleurs who kept up a most biting fire, constantly charged by immense masses of cavalry who seemed determined to go in and win, preceded as their visits were by a terrific fire of artillery; and, last of all, we were attacked by "*la Vieille Garde*" itself. But here we came to the end of our long and fiery ordeal. The French veterans, conspicuous by their high bearskin caps and lofty stature, on breasting the ridge behind which we were at that time, were met by a fearful fire of artillery and musketry, which swept away whole masses of those valiant soldiers; and, while in disorder, they were charged by us with complete success, and driven in utter rout and discomfiture down the ravine. The Prussians having now arrived in force on the French right, a general advance of the whole line was ordered, and the day was won.

During the battle our squares presented a shocking sight. Inside we were nearly suffocated by the smoke and smell from burnt cartridges. It was impossible to move a yard without treading upon a wounded comrade, or upon the bodies of the dead; and the loud groans of the wounded and dying were most appalling.

At four o'clock our square was a perfect hospital, being full of dead, dying, and mutilated soldiers. The charges of cavalry were in appearance very formidable, but in reality a great relief, as the artillery could no longer fire on us; the very earth shook under the enormous mass of men and horses. I never shall forget the strange noise our bullets made against the breastplates of Kellermann's and Milhaud's cuirassiers, six or seven thousand in number, who attacked us with great fury. I can only compare it, with a somewhat homely simile, to the noise of a violent hail-storm beating upon panes of glass.

The artillery did great execution, but our musketry did not at first seem to kill many men; though it brought down a large number of horses, and created indescribable confusion. The horses of the first rank of cuirassiers, in spite of all the efforts of their riders, came to a stand-still, shaking and covered with foam, at about twenty yards' distance from our squares, and generally resisted all attempts to force them to charge the line of serried steel. On one occasion, two gallant French officers forced their way into a gap momentarily created by the discharge of artillery: one was killed by Staples, the other by Adair. Nothing could be more gallant than the behaviour of those veterans, many of whom had distinguished themselves on half the battle-fields of Europe.

In the midst of our terrible fire, their officers were seen as if on parade, keeping order in their ranks, and encouraging them. Unable to renew the charge, but unwilling to retreat, they brandished their swords with loud cries of " *Vive l'Empereur!* " and allowed themselves to be mowed down by hundreds rather than yield. Our men, who shot them down, could not help admiring the gallant bearing and heroic resignation of their enemies.

COLONEL COLQUITT.—During the terrible fire of artillery which preceded the repeated charges of the cuirassiers against our squares many shells fell amongst us. We were lying down, when a shell fell between Captain (afterwards Colonel) Colquitt and another officer. In an instant Colquitt jumped up, caught up the shell as if it had been a cricket ball, and flung it over the heads of both officers and men, thus saving the lives of many brave fellows.

CAPTAIN CHAMBERS, PICTON'S FAVOURITE AIDE-DE-CAMP.—In looking back to former days, I recollect with pride the friendship which existed between Chambers and myself. I owe my presence at the battle of Waterloo to him; for by him I was introduced to Sir Thomas Picton, and it was by his advice that I joined my regiment the day before the battle. After Picton's death, poor Chambers, in carrying orders to Sir James Kempt to retake at all hazards the farm of La Haye Sainte, advanced at the head of the attacking column, and was in the act of receiving the sword of a French officer who had surrendered to him, when he received a musket ball through the lungs, which killed him on the spot. When the Duke of York heard of his death, H.R.H. exclaimed, "In him we have lost one of our most promising officers."

CAPTAIN ROBERT ADAIR, OF THE 1ST GUARDS.—No language can express the admiration felt by all who witnessed the heroic exploits of poor Adair. During the charges of the French cavalry, which were always preceded by a tremendous fire of artillery at point-blank distance, we lost many men. The cuirassiers and heavy dragoons approached so close, that it was feared they would enter by the gap which had been made in our square. Adair rushed forward, placed himself in the open space, and with one blow of his sword killed a French officer who had actually got amongst our men. After many exploits, showing a coolness and a courage rarely equalled, and never surpassed, Adair was struck towards the end of the day by a cannon ball, which shattered his thigh near the hip. His sufferings during the amputation were dreadful; the shot had torn away the flesh of the thigh, and the bones were sticking up near the hip in splinters. The surgeon, Mr. Gilder, had much difficulty in using his knife, having blunted it, and all his other instruments, by amputations in the earlier part of the battle. Poor Adair during the operation had sufficient pluck to make one last ghastly joke, saying, " Take your time, Mr. Carver." He soon afterwards died from loss of blood.

Ensign Somerville Burges, of the 1st Foot Guards, was a younger son of Sir James Bland Burges (his elder brother was killed at Burgos). He enjoyed soldiering in the real sense of the word, and sought glory on every field of battle. He entered the Guards before he attained the age of seventeen, and his buoyant spirits and athletic frame fitted him for a military life. I breakfasted with him on the morning of the battle. After many acts of great personal courage he was wounded by a cannon ball which shattered his leg in a frightful manner. Amputation was the consequence; and after the surgeon had dressed the wounds, he hailed some soldiers to carry Burges to the cart, upon which the latter declined being carried, saying, " I will hop into it; " and he succeeded in performing this extraordinary feat without further injury to the wounded stump. This heroic soldier, owing to the regulations then in force, was put on the shelf for the remainder of his life.

PERCIVAL, OF THE 1ST GUARDS.—The wound
which Captain Percival received was one of the most
painful it ever fell to a soldier's lot to bear. He received a ball which carried away all his teeth and
both his jaws, and left nothing on the mouth but the
skin of the cheeks. Percival recovered sufficiently
to join our regiment in the Tower, three years subsequent to the battle of Waterloo. He had to be
fed with porridge and a few spoonfuls of broth; but
notwithstanding all the care to preserve his life, he
sunk from inanition, and died very shortly after, his
body presenting the appearance of a skeleton.

SIR COLIN HALKETT.—Sir C. Halkett's wound,
which was also from a musket ball through the
jaws, was not so dangerous; for it was said by
Forbes the surgeon, that the General must have
been in the act of ordering his men to charge, with
his mouth open, when he was struck.

CAPTAIN CURZON.—Among the many episodes of
a battle-field, there is none so touching as the last
moments of a brave soldier. Captain Curzon, son
of Lord Scarsdale, was on the staff, and received a
mortal wound towards the end of the battle, and
lay bleeding to death by the side of his favourite
charger, one of whose legs had been shattered by a
cannon ball. As Lord March was passing by, Curzon had just strength to call to him, "Get me help,
my dear March, for I fear it is all over with me."
Lord March hastened to look for a surgeon, and
found one belonging to the first battalion of our
regiment, who went to the poor fellow's assistance;
but, alas! life was extinct before the doctor arrived.

The doctor, in relating this event to us afterwards, said, "I found poor Curzon dead, leaning his head upon the neck of his favourite horse, which seemed to be aware of the death of his master, so quiet did it remain, as if afraid to disturb his last sleep. As I approached, it neighed feebly, and looked at me as if it wanted relief from the pain of its shattered limb, so I told a soldier to shoot it through the head to put it out of its pain. The horse as well as its master were both old acquaintances of mine, and I was quite upset by the sight of them lying dead together." This tribute of sympathy and feeling was the more remarkable as coming from the doctor, who was one of the hardest and roughest diamonds I ever remember to have known; but on this occasion something moved him, and he had tears in his eyes at he related the incident.

CAPTAIN, AFTERWARDS COLONEL KELLY, OF THE LIFE GUARDS, AND OUR CAVALRY CHARGES.—This chivalrous man, of undaunted courage and very powerful frame, in the deadly encounter with the cuirassiers of the Imperial Guard, performed prodigies of valour.

In the gallant and, for a time, successful charge of the Household Brigade, he greatly distinguished himself; and when our gallant fellows, after sustaining a terrible fire of artillery, were attacked by an overwhelming force of French cavalry, and were forced to retreat behind our squares, Kelly was seen cutting his way through a host of enemies. Shaw, the famous prize-fighter, a private in his regiment, came to his assistance, and these two heroes fought side by side, killing or disabling many

of their antagonists, till poor Shaw, after receiving
several wounds, was killed from a thrust through
the body by a French colonel of cuirassiers, who in
his turn received a blow from Kelly's sword, which
cut through his helmet and stretched him lifeless
upon the ground.

I recollect questioning my friend Kelly about
this celebrated charge, at our mess at Windsor in
1816, when he said that he owed his life to the excellence of his charger, which was well bred, very
well broke, and of immense power. He thought
that with an ordinary horse he would have been
killed a hundred times in the numerous encounters
which he had to sustain.

CHARGE OF THE HEAVY BRIGADE.—In the charge
of the Royals, Scots Greys, and Inniskillings on
the one side, and the 1st and 2d Life Guards,
Blues, and 1st Dragoon Guards on the other, the
Scots Greys and Blues were ordered to act as supports. This their excessive ardour prevented them
from doing, and they charged with the others. On
their return the want of supports was grievously
felt. Colonel Ferrier of the 1st Life Guards, Lieutenant-Colonel Fitzgerald of the 2d Life Guards,
and Colonel Fuller of the 1st Dragoon Guards were
killed ; Major Packe of the Blues was killed by a
sword-thrust from a French sergeant; and Clement
Hill, who afterwards commanded that regiment,
received a lance-thrust which nearly pinned him to
his saddle.

LIEUTENANT TATHWELL: ILL-TREATMENT OF A
PRISONER BY THE FRENCH. — Lieutenant Tathwell

of the Blues was taken prisoner, and as he was being conducted to the rear of the French army, a wounded French officer, who was being carried by four soldiers, ordered Tathwell to be brought up to him, and inflicted several kicks upon the unfortunate prisoner. Tathwell's captors seemed very much shocked at this infamous treatment, so different to the usual behaviour of the French, but did not dare to remonstrate.

Sir W. Ponsonby, Lord E. Somerset, Sir John Elley, and Sir Horace Seymour.—Sir William Ponsonby, after heading several splendid charges, on the retreat and on refusing to surrender, was killed by a sergeant of a regiment of dragoons, of which I forget the number. He had got into some deep boggy ground, and was riding a very inferior horse, which was completely blown, and whose sluggishness cost him his life.

Lord Edward Somerset, who commanded the Household Brigade, had a very narrow escape. His horse was killed, and he had only just time to creep through a thick hedge and leap on another horse before the enemy were upon him. Sir John Elley, colonel of the Blues, and Horace Seymour, who was on the staff, two of the most powerful men in the army, performed deeds worthy of the Paladins of the olden time. Horse and man went down before them, as they swept onward in their headlong course, and neither helmet nor cuirass could stand against swords wielded by such strong arms.

The Honourable George Damer and Colonel Muter.—I remember, when at Brighton, hearing

Colonel George Damer relate the following anecdote,
which will give an idea of the losses sustained by
our cavalry at Waterloo. Damer was on the staff,
and, towards the close of the day, was sent to order
the Union Brigade to advance with the rest of the
army. After a long search, he at last came upon all
that remained of the brave fellows that composed
the brigade. They were reduced to about two hundred and fifty men ; many of them wounded, with
heads and hands bandaged, were standing by their
horses, who were panting and blowing, and looked
completely done up. At their head stood the gallant
Colonel Muter of the Inniskillings, upon whom the
command of the brigade had fallen after Ponsonby's
death. This grim veteran had his helmet beaten in,
and his arm, which had been badly wounded, was in
a sling. When Damer came up, and said, "Now,
gentlemen, you are to advance with the rest of the
army," he said he should never forget the look that
Muter cast upon him. The gallant Scot, however,
said nothing, but got his men together, and they all
broke into a sort of canter, and, guided by Damer,
came upon some French infantry, who were still
defending themselves with a kind of desperation.
As Muter gave the order to charge, the French fired
a volley and hit Damer in the knee, who heard
Muter grumble out in his Scotch phraseology, as he
dashed amongst the French, "I think you ha' it
nu', sir."

HOUGOUMONT.—I could distinctly see, at the commencement of the battle, the Young Guard advance
to attack Hougoumont, when a tremendous fire of
artillery was opened upon them, which had the

appearance of creating some confusion and disorder in their ranks. On they went, however, and in a moment got into the orchard. Then such a fire opened on both sides, and such a smoke ensued, that, like Homer's heroes, they were hidden by a cloud, and I could see no more. I had, besides, plenty to occupy my own attention immediately afterwards.

About four o'clock, Saltoun and Charley Ellis, who had commanded the light companies of the battalions of Guards, joined us with the wreck of those detachments, after their gallant defence of Hougoumont. I well remember General Maitland saying to Saltoun, "Your defence saved the army: nothing could be more gallant. Every man of you deserves promotion." Saltoun replied that it was "touch and go—a matter of life and death—for all within the walls had sworn that they would never surrender;" and Gurthorpe the adjutant added, "Our officers were determined never to yield, and the men were resolved to stand by them to the last."

MEETING OF WELLINGTON AND BLUCHER.—After our final charge, and the retreat of the French army, we arrived and bivouacked about nine o'clock in the orchard of the farm of La Belle Alliance, about a hundred yards from the farmhouse where Napoleon had remained for some hours. We were presently disturbed by the sound of trumpets; I immediately hurried off, in company with several other officers, and found that the sound proceeded from a Prussian cavalry regiment with Blucher at its head. The Duke of Wellington, who had given rendezvous to Blucher at this spot, then rode up, and the two victorious Generals shook hands in the most cordial and hearty manner. After a short conversation, our chief rode off to Brussels, while Blucher and the Prussians joined their own army, which, under General Gneisenau, was already in hot pursuit of the French. After this I entered the farmhouse where Napoleon had passed part of the day. The furniture had to all appearance been destroyed, but I found an immense fire made of a wooden bedstead and the legs of chairs, which appeared by the embers to have been burning for a considerable length of time.

SUFFERINGS OF THE WOUNDED.—On the following morning, we had not advanced for many minutes before we met some of our gallant companions in arms who had been wounded. They were lying in waggons of the country, and had been abandoned by the drivers. Some of these poor fellows belonged to our regiment, and, on passing close to one of the waggons, a man cried out, "For God's sake, Mr. Gronow, give us some water or we shall go mad." I did not hesitate for a moment, but jumped into the cart, and gave the poor fellow all the water my flask contained. The other wounded soldiers then entreated me to fill it with some muddy water which they had descried in a neighbouring ditch, half filled by the rain of the preceding day. As I thought a flask would be of little use among so many, I took off my shako, and having first stopped up with my belcher handkerchief a hole which a musket ball had made in the top of it, filled it with water several times for these poor fellows, who were

all too severely wounded to have got it for themselves, and who drank it off with tears of delight.

EXCESSES OF THE PRUSSIANS.—We perceived, on
entering France, that our allies the Prussians had
committed fearful atrocities on the defenceless inhabitants of the villages and farms which lay in
their line of march. Before we left La Belle
Alliance, I had already seen the brutality of some
of the Prussian infantry, who hacked and cut up,
in a most savage manner, all the cows and pigs
which were in the farmyards; placing upon their
bayonets the still quivering flesh, and roasting it
on the coals. On our line of march, whenever
we arrived at towns or villages through which the
Prussians had passed, we found that every article of
furniture in the houses had been destroyed in the
most wanton manner: looking-glasses, mahogany
bedsteads, pictures, beds and mattresses, had been
hacked, cut, half-burned, and scattered about in
every direction; and, on the slightest remonstrance
of the wretched inhabitants, they were beaten in a
most shameful manner, and sometimes shot. It is
true that the Prussians owed the French a long debt
of vengeance for all the atrocities committed by the
French at Berlin; particularly by Davoust's corps
after the battle of Jena.

PÉRONNE LA PUCELLE.—The fourth or fifth day
after Waterloo, we arrived before Péronne la Pucelle,
(the Virgin town), as the inhabitants delighted to
call it; for they boasted that it had never been taken
by an enemy. The Duke of Wellington suddenly
made his appearance in our bivouac, and gave orders

that we should, at all risks, take Péronne before night. We accordingly prepared for action, and commenced proceedings by battering the gates with a strong fire of artillery. The guns of the Virgin fortress returned the compliment, and the first shot from the town fell under the belly of the Duke's horse; but, beyond knocking the gravel and stones about in all directions, did no injury.

The garrison consisted of fifteen hundred National Guards, who had sworn never to surrender to mortal man; but when these ardent volunteers saw our red-coats coming in with a rush, and with a grim determination to take no denial, they wisely laid down their arms and capitulated. Our loss, on this occasion, amounted to nine killed and thirty wounded. Lord Saltoun had a narrow escape; a ball struck him on his breeches-pocket, where half-a-dozen five-franc pieces broke the force of the blow: Saltoun, though not very Buonapartist in his opinions, re-tained the mark of the Emperor's effigy on his thigh for some time; and though not returned as wounded, suffered great pain for several days after.

VÆ VICTIS.—On the Guards arriving at St. Pont Maixans, a town situated at about forty miles from Paris, I was sent by the adjutant to look out for quarters for myself and servant. In the neighbour-hood of a small wood, I perceived a mill, and near it a river, and on looking a little further, saw a large farmhouse; this I entered, but could not discover any living being. My servant, who had gone up-stairs, however, informed me, that the farmer was lying in bed dreadfully wounded from numerous sabre cuts. I approached his bed, and he appeared more dead than alive; but on my questioning him, he said the Prussians had been there the night before, had violated and carried off his three daughters, had taken away his cart-horses and cattle, and because he had no money to give them, they had tied him to his bed and cut him with their swords across the shin-bones, and left him fainting from pain and loss of blood. After further inquiries, he told me that he thought some of the Prussians were still in the cellar; upon which, I ordered my batman to load his musket, struck a light, and with a lantern proceeded to the cellar, where we found a Prussian soldier drunk, and lying in a pool of wine which had escaped from the casks he and his comrades had tapped. Upon seeing us, he, with an oath in German, made a thrust at my batman with his sabre, which was parried; in an instant we bound the ruffian, and brought him at the point of the bayonet into the presence of the poor farmer, who recognised him as one of the men who had outraged his unfortunate daughters, and who had afterwards wounded him. We carried our prisoner to the provost-sergeant, who, in his turn, took him to the Prussian head-quarters, where he was instantly shot.

NAPOLEON'S MISTAKEN OPINION OF THE ENGLISH ARMY.—When we were in Paris we heard that Napoleon, on making his first observation with his glass, surrounded by his Generals, on the morning of the 18th, had said, with an air of exultation on finding that we had not retreated as he expected, "*Je les tiens donc ces Anglais;*" but was answered by General Foy, "*Sire, l'infanterie anglaise en duel*

c'est le diable." We also heard that Soult, on re-
monstrating upon the uselessness of charging our
squares with cavalry, had been severely reprimanded,
and had undergone the biting and sarcastic remark from the Emperor, "*Vous croyez Wellington
un grand homme, Général, parce qu'il vous a
battu.*"

SIR FREDERICK PONSONBY.—This gallant and excellent cavalry officer, who greatly distinguished
himself at Talavera, and many other actions in
Spain, was the son of Lord Besborough, and a distant cousin of Sir William Ponsonby who was killed.
He commanded the 12th Light Dragoons, which
formed part of Vandeleur's brigade, and made a
brilliant charge right through a French brigade of
Marcognet's division, and rolled up part of Jacquinot's Lancers, who were in pursuit of the rem-
nant of the Union Brigade. In this most gallant
affair he was struck from his horse by several sabre
cuts, run through the body by a lancer as he lay
upon the ground, and trampled on by large bodies
of cavalry. Ponsonby always considered that he
owed his life to a French field-officer who had
brought up some troops to the spot where he lay,
had given him a draught of brandy from his flask,
and directed one of his men to wrap him in a cloak,
and place a knapsack under his head.

It is pleasant to think that Ponsonby became
acquainted, many years afterwards, with his pre-
server. The Baron de Laussat, formerly deputy for
his department, the Basses Pyrenées, and a gentleman universally respected and beloved by all who
knew him, was at this time a major in the dragoons

of the Imperial Guard. After he had quitted the army he travelled in the East for some years, and on his return, when at Malta, was introduced to Sir F. Ponsonby, then a Major-General and Governor of the island. In the course of conversation, the battle of Waterloo was discussed; and on Ponsonby recounting his many narrow escapes, and the kind treatment he had received from the French officer, M. de Laussat said, "Was he not in such-and-such a uniform?" "He was," said Sir F. "And did he not say so-and-so to you, and was not the cloak of such-and-such a colour?" "I remember it perfectly," was the answer. Several other details were entered into, which I now forget, but which left no doubt upon Ponsonby's mind that he saw before him the man to whom he owed his life. "I was with the famous Colonel Sourd," added Laussat, "and I only knew that I had rendered what assistance I could to an English officer of rank, who seemed in a very hopeless state; and I am delighted to think that my care was not bestowed in vain."

NARROW ESCAPES—RECEPTION IN LONDON.— When we were lying down in square to present a rather less fair mark to the French artillery, which had got very near us, and had caused immense loss in our ranks, a cannon ball struck the ground close to Algernon Greville and myself, without injuring either of us. At the end of the day, I found that a grape-shot had gone through the top of my shako, and one of my coat-tails had been shot off. I got leave to go to England to join my battalion after we had been in Paris about a fortnight; and I never shall forget the reception I met with as I dashed

up in a chaise and four to the door of Fenton's
Hotel in St. James's Street. Very few men from
the army had yet arrived in London, and a mob of
about a thousand people gathered round the door
as I got out in my old, weather-beaten uniform,
shaking hands with me, and uttering loud cheers.
I also recollect the capital English dinner old James,
the well-known waiter, had provided to celebrate
my return. "*Ce sont les beaux jours de la vie,*" few
and far between in our chequered existence, and
I confess that my memory wanders back to them
with pleasure, and some regret to think that they
can never more return.

CONDUCT OF THE ENGLISH AND PRUSSIAN ARMIES
DURING THE OCCUPATION OF PARIS.—The Duke of
Wellington's conduct to the Parisians was kind and
considerate. He contented himself with occuping
the Bois de Boulogne, the two faubourgs of La Vil-
lette and La Chapelle St. Denis. Blucher was not
so moderate in his conduct towards the French.
His troops were billeted in every house ; he obliged
the inhabitants to feed and clothe them ; and he issued
an order (which I well recollect seeing) commanding the authorities to supply each soldier with a
bedstead containing a bolster, a woollen mattress,
two new blankets, and a pair of linen sheets. The
rations per day, for each man, were two pounds of
bread of good quality, one pound of butcher's meat,
a bottle of wine, a quarter of a pound of butter,
ditto rice, a glass of brandy, and some tobacco.
The Prussian cavalry were not forgotten : each
horse required ten pounds of oats, six of hay, ditto
of straw, to be furnished early each day. Blucher's

PART OF THE ALLIES ENTERING PARIS, 1814.—THE RUSSIAN CONTINGENT: COSSACKS & PLUNDER.

Generals occupied all the best hotels in the Faubourg St. Germain ; General Thielman that of Marshal Ney, where he forcibly took possession of the plate, carriages, and horses. Other Prussian Generals acted in a similar manner.

The Russian and Austrian armies, with the two Emperors, entered Paris soon after our arrival. The Emperors imitated Blucher in some respects ; they refused to quarter their soldiers in the large and wholesome barracks which were in readiness to receive them : no; they preferred billeting them with peaceable merchants and tradespeople, whom they plundered and bullied in the most outrageous manner. Wellington, all this while, showed great moderation ; and his army paid for everything they required. Blucher, on the other hand, threatened to take possession of the Bank of France and the Government offices : which threat was not carried into execution, owing to the wise and timely inter-position of the Duke.

One day, I recollect, Paris was in a state of amazement and stupefaction. Muffling, the com-mander-in-chief in Paris of the Prussians, installed at the Hôtel de Ville, demanded from the French prefect a very large sum of money, and sent an officer and a hundred soldiers to enforce his de-mand. The prefect had not the money : the con-sequence was, he was marched off to the Hôtel de Ville, where General Muffling kept him prisoner, intending, the following morning, to send him to Berlin as a hostage until the money was paid into the Prussian treasury.

DR. KEATE IN PARIS.—Every one has heard

of the famous Dr. Busby, head-master of Westminster, who, while showing Charles II. over the
school, apologised to that merry monarch for keeping his hat on in the presence of royalty; "For,"
said he, "it would not do for my boys to suppose
that there existed in the world a greater man than
Dr. Busby." He was notorious for his Spartan discipline, and constantly acted up to the old adage of
not sparing the rod and spoiling the boy. He was
once invited, during a residence at Deal, by an old
Westminster—who, from being a very idle, well-
flogged boy, had, after a course of distinguished
service, being named to the command of a fine frigate
in the Downs—to visit him on board his ship. The
Doctor accepted the invitation; and, after he had
got up the ship's side, the captain piped all hands
for punishment, and said to the astonished Doctor,
"You d——d old scoundrel, I am delighted to have
the opportunity of paying you off at last. Here,
boatswain, give him three dozen."

The old pupils of Dr. Keate in Paris, soon after
Waterloo, many of whom had suffered at least
as much at his hands as the rancorous sea-captain
had at Dr. Busby's, received their former pedagogue
in a far different manner. He had been seen,
to our great astonishment, eating an ice at Tortoni's
on the Boulevards, and we determined to give him
a dinner at Beauvilliers', the best dining-place in
Paris, and far superior to anything of the kind in the
present day.

The inviters were, Lord Sunderland (the late
Duke of Marlborough), Lord James Stuart, Crosbie
(the private secretary of the Ambassador), Cartwright
Tierney, De Ros, Baring Wall, myself, and two or

three whose names I forget. We had ordered a most excellent dinner, and I never witnessed a more jovial banquet. The Doctor evinced his appreciation of the dinner and wines in a manner most gratifying to his hosts; ate as if he had never eaten before, and paid his addresses, in large bumpers, to every description of wine; and, towards the end of the dinner, expressed his delight at finding that his old friends and pupils had not forgotten him; concluding "a neat and appropriate speech" with "Floreat Etona."

After drinking his health, as the bottle passed gaily round, we took the opportunity of giving him a little innocent "chaff," reminding him of his heavy hand and arbitrary manner of proceeding. We told him how two of the masters, Drury and Knapp, contrived, without his knowledge, to go up to London every Saturday to dine with Arnold and Kean at Drury Lane. We spoke of Sumner's flirtation with the fair Martha at Spiers's; of Mike Fitzgerald tripping up Plumptree the master on his way to six-o'clock school; of Cornwall's fight with the bargee; of Lumley's poaching in Windsor Park; of our constant suppers at the Christopher; of our getting out at night; of our tandem-driving; and many other little episodes, to show that his Argus eyes were not always open. The Doctor took our jokes in good part, and in his turn told us that, if he had a regret, it was that he had not flogged us a good deal more; but he felt certain that the discipline had done us a great deal of good: he then concluded by paying us all compliments in a few well-turned phrases. We heartily cheered his address, and parted on excellent terms, highly gratified with our evening's entertainment.

Keate was a very short, thickset man, with a red face and a stentorian voice. The very sight of the cocked hat he always wore, placed front-ways on his head, like that of the Emperor Napoleon, struck terror into the hearts of all offenders. However, in spite of his severity, he was generally liked by the boys at Eton, and was a thoroughly honourable and upright man. He had been in his youth a capital fighter, was an excellent scholar, and an admirable writer of Latin verse. A well-known copy of verses on the Greek drama, written by him, are considered the finest Alcaics since the days of Horace. Every old Etonian of his time must have felt hurt that the Whig government should not have thought fit to name Keate provost of Eton, in the room of Dr. Goodall; and we all thought it very hard that he should have left the school without any recognition or acknowledgment of his long and arduous services.

SHAVING IN A MINUTE, AND COLONEL ELLISON. —About twelve o'clock, on the second day after the battle of Waterloo, when on our march to Paris, we were ordered to come to a halt. Every officer and soldier immediately set to work to get rid of the superabundance of beard which had been suffered to grow for several days. During this not very agreeable duty, a shout was heard from Lord Saltoun, who called us to witness a bet he had made with Bob Ellison, that he, Ellison, could not shave off his beard in one minute.

Preparations were made, Ellison taking care to

bathe his face for a considerable time in water. He then commenced operations, and in less than a minute, and without the aid of a looking-glass, actually won his bet (a considerable one), to the astonishment, and, I must add, the satisfaction of his comrades. This feat appeared to us all perfectly impossible to accomplish, as his face was covered with the stubble of a week's growth of hair, so dark that it had procured for him in the regiment the sobriquet of Black Bob.

Ellison was one of our best officers. After joining the brigade at Cadiz, he was present in every action in the Peninsula, and was with the light companies at Hougoumont. He greatly distinguished himself there; and on one occasion, when he was forced to retreat from the orchard to the château, he would have been bayoneted by the French, had not the men, with whom he was a great favourite, charged back, and saved his life. Ellison led the storming party at Péronne, and commanded the second battalion of his regiment in Canada. He was colonel of his old battalion in 1843; when, at a brigade field-day in Hyde Park, on the occasion of a general salute, as he gave the word " Present arms," he dropped down dead from his horse, while the old corps, in which he had passed nearly forty years, were presenting arms to him.

All who knew him will bear witness with me to his many amiable and excellent qualities. In his younger days he was remarkably good-looking, and he had still preserved his handsome face and kindly, expressive eye. Though quick and clever, no one ever heard him say a malevolent or ill-natured thing. If there was a good turn to be done, or a friendly word to be spoken, Black Bob was first and foremost; and in looking back on the old friends and comrades of bygone days, I feel there is not one I could name who was more deservedly popular or more generally regretted than Colonel Ellison.

THE DUKE AND MR. CREEVEY.—The late Mr. Creevey, the well-known Whig M.P., stated in my presence, at a dinner at Lord Darnley's, in Berkeley Square, in 1816, that he was at the Duke of Wellington's quarters at Brussels the night of the battle of Waterloo. It was late when the Duke entered, and, perceiving Mr. Creevey, shook him by the hand, and said, "I have won the greatest battle of modern times, with twelve thousand of my old Peninsular troops."

Creevey remarked that he was astonished at that, and asked, "What, sir, with twelve thousand only?"

"Yes, Creevey," replied the Duke; "with twelve thousand of my old Spanish infantry. I knew I could depend upon them. They fought the battle, without flinching, against immense odds; but nearly all my staff, and some of my best friends, are killed. Good-night! I want rest, and must go to bed."

Creevey called at an early hour on the following morning, in the hope of again seeing the Duke, but he had left Brussels before daylight, to join the army.

I do not pretend to say what the Duke meant in his conversation with Mr. Creevey,—who was truth itself,—and I am equally certain that I am correctly relating what he said, for the statement made a great impression on me. He must have meant that the victory was mainly owing to the twelve thousand veterans; for, as near as I could make out,

there were on our side at Waterloo about forty-
five thousand English and Hanoverians, and twenty
thousand Dutch, Belgian, and Nassau troops.

THE DUKE'S RAZORS.—My friend, George Smythe,
the late Lord Strangford, once told me that, staying
at Walmer Castle with the Duke of Wellington, the
Duke informed him, one morning at breakfast, that
he was obliged to go up to London immediately,
as all his razors required setting, but he would be
back to dinner.   Lord Strangford very naturally
offered to lend the Duke his razors, which, luckily
for the Duke, he did not accept; for Lord S., who
was somewhat careless about his personal appearance, shaved with razors something like miniature
saws, which made one shudder to look at.   Lord S.
then offered to take the razors to Dover, but the
Duke replied—

"The man who always sharpens my razors has
sharpened them for many years : I would not trust
them with any one else.   He lives in Jermyn Street,
and there they must go.   So you see, Strangford,
every man has a weak point, and my weak point is
about the sharpening of my razors.   Perhaps you
are not aware that I shave myself, and brush my
own clothes : I regret that I cannot clean my own
boots ; for men-servants bore me, and the presence
of a crowd of idle fellows annoys me more than I
can tell you."

MADEMOISELLE MARS.—I did not see the celebrated Mlle. Mars till she was already in the sere
and yellow leaf, as far as her personal attractions were
concerned ; but I confess I have doubts as to her

ever having been handsome. Her features did not
bear any trace of past beauty, and her figure had
lost all the slightness of youth. The process of
dressing her for the stage was a long and painful
one, and was said to have been done by degrees,
beginning at early dawn; the tightening being
gradually intensified until the stage hour, when it
has been rumoured that the finale was accomplished
by the maid's foot being placed in the small of the
lady's back, and that thus the last vigorous haul
was given to the refractory stay-lace. In spite of
this suffering for form's sake, I confess that it required more powers of imagination than I possessed
to fancy that the square-built, wrinkled woman was
a beautiful young girl of seventeen : for she almost
always appeared in very youthful parts—what are
called *rôles de jeune première*.

Mlle. Mars had preserved, when I first saw her,
very fine black hair, white and even teeth, and a
voice of surpassing sweetness. Her diction was
perfect ; and she possessed, above all other actresses,
that knowledge of the stage, and that delicacy of
touch, which gave just the right inflection to each
point, and no more. In her acting there was never
the slightest straining after effect,—or rather, I
should say, the effect was produced without any
apparent effort,—and she spoke her part just as a
lady might make a witty, or piquant, or pathetic
remark in her drawing-room : every movement
was intensely studied, but seemed perfectly natural.
Her voice was mellow and varied in its tones, without
any of those sudden changes in vogue now-a-days,
which seem more like ventriloquism than acting.
There was a certain chaste reserve even in the scenes

of passionate love, and propriety observed even
in the most *risqué* passages. One was charmed,
melted, touched, rather than powerfully moved.

Mlle. Mars was a woman of superior education
and refined manners. Many persons of aristocratic
birth felt themselves honoured in being received in
her *salon*, which was the rendezvous of the *élite*
of the artistic world. There reigned that easy, courteous *bon-ton* which has almost become a tradi-
tionary legend both in England and France. The
drawing-room was a school for good manners and
good French; and the lady of the house, though
affable and kind to all, knew well how to keep her
guests in order. Mlle. Mars, though not altogether
immaculate, had never run to the excess of riot so
common to many persons of her profession in those
days, and she had preserved a tolerably fair reputation.

Amongst the very few persons supposed to be
on terms of great intimacy with this celebrated
actress was the Count de M * * *, a well-known
dandy of the Restoration. He divided his attentions
between the Duchesse de R * * * and Mlle. Mars, who
were both a long way on the shady side of forty,
and was known by the sobriquet of *l'homme du
siècle:* a name which had been bestowed on Napoleon for very different reasons. To sum up, I should
be disposed to say that Mlle. Mars had more grace
and charm than beauty, more talent and *savoir
faire* than *bonâ-fide* genius. Her most touching
personation was perhaps "Valérie," or the blind girl.

MADEMOISELLE RACHEL.—One cannot imagine a
more striking contrast than that between Mlles.

Mars and Rachel, each perfect and without a rival
in her separate department.   I confess that my own
taste was far more gratified by witnessing the performance of *La Grande Tragédienne* in some of
her parts, than it ever was by the more polished but
colder talent of Mlle. Mars; which charmed, but
did not carry you away on the wings of enthusiasm.
Rachel, in her moments of passionate declamation,
bore all before her, as in a whirlwind.   The spectators could not calmly criticise—they could only
admire and weep.

I cannot conceive anything more splendid than
Rachel's personification of " Phèdre."   She looked
the very woman consumed by her guilty passion,
pursued by an avenging deity, the prey of conflict-
ing powers struggling for mastery in that poor
wasted bosom.   The fire of unhallowed passion
seemed to burn in her dark, hollow eyes,—the
anguish and humiliation of rejected love to crush
to the earth that frail form,—the gnawing of
remorse to eat into her very heart.   Those who
have not seen Rachel in "Phèdre" can have no
conception of what she was as an actress: the
dignity and grace of her bearing in the first scenes,
contrasted with her passionate despair in the latter
part, which at last found vent, each syllable forcing
itself through her clenched teeth, as if the very
words scorched her lips.

In those parts which brought into play her powers
of fascination, such as "Adrienne Lecouvreur,"
and others, nothing could be more coquettishly
attractive, more irresistibly winning, than Rachel.
Her deep rich voice had an inexpressible charm
when softened into tenderness, and she possessed

such a peculiar talent for enveloping her meagre figure in fleecy clouds of gauze and muslin, and decking it with rows of gold ornaments and pearls, that every man at the end of the performance thought his wife or mistress too much developed in figure, whilst every woman for the moment wished she were as devoid of all protuberances as the fair tragedienne.

I have had the pleasure of frequently meeting Rachel in society, and certainly it was impossible to have seen any one more high-bred in appearance, dress, and manner. There was nothing exaggerated in her style of dress, which was always of rich materials, but in perfect taste. She generally, in order to conceal the excessive spareness of her form, wore a high gown, fitting tight round the long, slight throat, and falling in heavy folds; the lace collar being fastened by some costly ornament. Her head, which was beautifully shaped, was generally adorned only by her thick waving hair. Her eyes were very deeply set, and too jet black to be soft or pleasing; her profile was regular in its outline, but her face was long and narrow, and bore evident traces of its Jewish origin. She had very small, well-formed hands, with long, thin, taper fingers, and pink nails remarkably *bien soignés*. Her manner in a drawing-room was particularly quiet, pleasing, and ladylike. She was neither forward nor servile; never forcing herself on any one's acquaintance, and yet never accepting a position of humiliation.

I could completely understand how thoroughly English society had been taken in during her first visit to London, and how the most strait-laced dowagers had invited her, almost on a footing of intimacy, to their houses and select parties. It is true that she had not then completely thrown all appearance of propriety to the winds, as in her later career. I think I may say, without subjecting myself to any accusation of scandal or exaggeration, that no woman ever went beyond Rachel in immorality.

I have heard men say that it was just that contrast between her "company" manners, so distinguished, graceful, and dignified, and the coarse ribald tone which she assumed when at ease with her boon companions, that fascinated them. She must have studied vice as another might have studied virtue, and instead of feigning to appear better than she really was, it seemed to be her glory to show to her admirers the darkest shades of her character, and make them kneel down and worship the idol of mud they had set up.

Rachel exercised a wonderful power over numerous admirers, whom she took no pains to blind or to deceive. One day the Count D * * *, one of the most agreeable and gentlemanlike of the *élégants* of that epoch, who had been for some time in her good graces, called to see Mlle. Rachel by appointment. He was told that she was not visible; but from what he overheard, he had reason to believe that a certain illustrious prince was at that very moment shut up in her boudoir. Forced to retreat, Count D * * * met Rachel's physician, who was coming in, and poured forth such a volley of invectives as led Dr. X * * * to imagine that all was at an end, and that D * * *'s eyes were opened at last. He congratulated his friend, terminating with the truly French phrase, " *Que voulez-vous, mon cher ami? c'est une ignoble créature!* " to which D * * * echoed back with a second torrent of abuse, touching especially on the lady's physical defects.   He then shook hands with X * * *, and quickly added in an under-tone, " *Je reviendrai ce soir!* "

Rachel had some redeeming points.   She was extremely kind to her poor relations, and if a case of real distress was placed before her she would give generously and without ostentation.

SIR JAMES KEMPT AND MR. DAVIES.—General Sir James Kempt, who died at a very advanced age about ten or twelve years since, refused at different times the high posts of Commander-in-Chief in India, and Commander-in-Chief in England ; and, I have heard, even that of Governor-General.   His great abilities and bravery were only equalled by his modesty and simplicity of manners.   It is said that he began life as a clerk at Greenwood's, the army agent's, and for his good conduct was recommended for a commission in the army.

The Duke of York took a great fancy to Kempt, and put him into one of our crack fighting regiments, where, if a man was not knocked on the head, he was sure to make his way.   Kempt greatly distinguished himself, and rose rapidly to the highest honours of the profession.   When Kempt was at Greenwood's, Mr. Davies was the principal clerk of the establishment, and it happened that a brother of the latter was a tailor in Cork Street, Burlington Gardens, with a very large and lucrative trade. The tailor died suddenly, and Davies, who was his sole heir, abandoned his clerkship and succeeded

his brother in the business, so that the junior
clerk at Greenwood's house became a General, and
the senior official sunk into the ninth part of a
man.

THE CORN-LAW RIOTS AND LORD CASTLEREAGH.
—When I call to mind the dangerous state of the
country at that time, the very bad feeling of the
people towards the upper classes, the want of employment in the manufacturing districts, and the
great misery all over England from the high price
of bread,—when I recollect, at the same time, the
total absence of any sort of police, and the small
military force we possessed, I am astonished that
some fatal catastrophe did not occur in the years
immediately following the war.

Those who remember the Luddite riots, the Corn-
Law riots, the Spitalfields meetings, and other
public demonstrations of a people driven to mad-
ness by every sort of oppression, will agree with me
in thinking that those were days of great peril. I
recollect, during the Corn-Law riots in London,
having walked from St. James's Palace (where I was
on guard) to St. James's Square. I there beheld,
collected together, thousands of the lowest of the
London rabble. These ruffians, with loud shouts,
and threats of summary vengeance on the Ministers,
were at the time I arrived breaking the windows of
most of the houses in the square. The Life Guards
were patrolling in the neighbouring streets, and,
whenever they appeared, were received with volleys
of stones mingled with mud, and cries of " Down
with the Piccadilly butchers ! " The mob was evidently bent on more mischief, and I beheld one

man exciting the crowd to force the doors of the
Bishop of London's residence. As the fellow was
making a rush against it, I told him to desist, or
I would immediately run my sword through his
body. This threat had the effect of calming the
gentleman's ardour; he skulked away, and was
soon lost in the crowd.

I was afterwards returning towards King Street,
when I was accosted by Lord Castlereagh. He
thanked me for the energy I had displayed, but
recommended a little more discretion in future;
"for the mob," said he, "is not so dangerous as you
think." This remarkable man was quietly looking
on while his windows were being broken by these
ruffians. I see him before me now, dressed in a
blue coat buttoned up to the chin, a blue spenser,
kerseymere breeches, long gaiters, shoes covered by
galoshes, and a white neckcloth. He was a particularly handsome man, possessed great pluck and
energy, and on this occasion appeared perfectly
calm and unconcerned, and not in the slightest
degree ruffled by the popular excesses and the abuse
which was liberally heaped upon himself and his
colleagues in the government.

THEN AND NOW.—Perhaps it is because I am
growing old, and woman has less power to charm
than heretofore; but, whatever may be the reason, I
cannot help thinking that, in "the merry days when
I was young," or "in my hot youth, when George
the Third was king," the women of England were
more beautiful, better-bred, and more distinguished
in appearance, and, above all, in manner, than they
are now-a-days. How grand they used to look,

with their tall, stately forms, small thoroughbred
heads, and long, flowing ringlets, dreamlike fair,
and queenly as Ossian's fabled daughters! You
could not help feeling somewhat elated and self-
satisfied, if perchance one of those sidelong glances,
half-proud, half-bashful, like a petted child's, fell
upon you, leaving you silent and pensive, full of
hopes and memories. Egad! it was worth being
loved by such women as those! And if there were
then, as now, tales of sin and shame, there were
also the extenuating circumstances of strong temptation, overwhelming passion, self-sacrifice, remorse :
often the blighted heart and early grave—things
almost unknown in these days of flirtation and
frivolity.

I do not mean to say that there are not now, as
there always have been in every state of society,
beautiful and amiable women, combining good sense
and high principle; but there are too many who
seem to have taken for their ideal a something
between the dashing London horse-breaker and some
Parisian *artiste dramatique* of a third-rate theatre;
the object of whose ambition is to be mistaken for
a *femme du demi-monde*, to be insulted when they
walk out with their petticoats girt up to their knees,
showing (to do them justice) remarkably pretty
feet and legs, and to wearing wide-awake hats
over painted cheeks and brows, and walk with that
indescribable, jaunty, "devil-may-care" look which
is considered "the right thing" now-a-days,—to
make sporting bets,—to address men as Jack, Tom,
or Harry,—to ride ahead in the Park,—to call the
paterfamilias " governor," and the lady - mother
" the old party,"—to talk of the young men who

Le Bon Genre. N° 75.

Costumes Anglais.

"spoon" them, and discuss with them the merits of "Skittles" and her horses, or the last scandalous story fabricated in the bay window at White's, the very faintest allusion to which would have made their mother's hair stand on end with dismay and horror :—this is to be pleasant, and "fast," and amusing. The young lady who is weak enough to blush if addressed rather too familiarly, and so unwise as to ignore the existence of *les dames aux camélias*, is called "slow," and distanced altogether : in the London steeplechase after husbands she is "nowhere"—an outsider—a female muff. The girl of the year 1862 who is not "fast" is generally dull and *blasée*, pleased with nothing, and possesses neither the wisdom of age nor the *naïveté* of youth.

I have often heard discussions on the comparative degrees of worldliness in London and Parisian society. It has been my lot in my day to mingle much in both, and I should be inclined to bestow the palm for frivolity on our volatile neighbours the French, and adjudge to my own countrywomen that of worldliness. In Paris, the atmosphere is light, clear, and brilliant ; conversation free and easy ; and the people really love pleasure for pleasure's sake. From the dapper little *grisette* in her neat calico gown and tidy cap, who accompanies her favourite *étudiant* Léon Lionceau to the Closerie des Lilas, and winds up with cold veal, salad, and beer, at six in the morning, in her beloved's garret on the sixth storey, to the high-bred Comtesse, who, after a round of balls, " comes to champagne and a chicken at last" at the Maison Dorée with that magnificent dandy, Arthur de Crèvecœur, it is all the same mad, and, to a certain degree, successful hunt after amusement. *Vive le plaisir!* is the cry of the Parisian population. They invoke it, and it does come; they grasp the shadow of it as it flies rapidly along; and they would sell the soul (of whose existence they doubt) for that day of pleasure in which they fully believe. As far as they can manage it, they strive to make life one joyous holiday.

Now, the good Londoners do not seem as if they expected to be amused. As Froissart said of them five hundred years ago, "they take their pleasure sadly," with long faces and lugubrious voices, set to a particular whining tone. Mrs. Danby Tremayne comes up for the London season, hires a house in Lower Grosvenor Street, very dark, very dirty, very dear, and nurtures in her expansive bosom the stern determination "to go everywhere," —that is, within the range of the charmed circle yclept good society. Mrs. Danby Tremayne would be unspeakably wretched if her name, and those of all her daughters who have been presented, did not figure in the columns of the *Morning Post.* In spite of her antiquated notions concerning the propriety of deportment and modesty of speech becoming youthful maidens, she would force those shy, demure, strait-laced, red-elbowed damsels, to frisk about, talk slang, and wear wide-awakes, and praise Anonyma, if by these means she could get an invitation to * * * House, or see the faintest chance of capturing some fast young lord.

Amelia, Countess of Crinoline, who is on the wrong side of fifty, is worn to a shadow in running after what is called pleasure. She considers herself in duty bound to show her poor hollow

cheeks and skinny shoulders everywhere, lest it
should be said that she is voted an "old party"
and only asked to "rococo" drums. That worn-
out, painted old harridan, Lady Rattlesnake, whose
daughters, ay, and grand-daughters too, are all
married, and going their melancholy rounds on
their own account, takes possession of some handsome, but friendless damsel, and uses her as a
decoy to obtain invitations and an arm to lean
upon and throw her cloak over her gaunt shoulders. And woe betide the poor dependent girl if
the expected civilities are wanting, and the good-
looking young guardsman, who delights to gaze
into Isabella's bright eyes and whisper soft nonsense in her ear, should rebel at finding himself compelled to make the agreeable and give his arm to
the withered old mummy, call her carriage, &c. &c.
Should he take himself off, muttering, "This won't
pay," the ancient dowager on her way home
snubs poor Isabella, accuses her of being slow,
stupid, unattractive, and so on; and the wretched
girl, as she throws her beautiful head wearily back
on the cushions, murmurs to herself, echoing the
devil's whisper, "I have not been fast enough to
please him this evening; but to-morrow he will
hand out Lady Rattlesnake with all the ardour of
a youthful lover."

In London in bygone days a worldly man or
woman would, without scruple, cut their father or
mother did they not belong to the particular set
which they considered good society. Mr. S * * * was
once riding in the Park many years ago with the
Marquis of C * * *, then one of the kings of the

fashionable world, and some other dandies of that day, when they met a respectable-looking elderly man, who nodded somewhat familiarly to S * * *. " Who's your friend ? " drawled Lord C * * *. " That ? " replied S * * *, " oh, a very good sort of a fellow, one of my Cheshire farmers." It was his own father; a most amiable and excellent man, and who had better blood in his veins, and a larger fortune, than any of the lordlings by whom his unworthy son was surrounded. A celebrated leader of fashion, Lady X * * *, never asked her own mother, a well-born and well-conducted, but somewhat eccentric person, to any of her parties : she ignored her very existence ; and yet she was by nature a kind, well-meaning, and good-natured woman. But the world's canker had eaten into her heart.

In these days of railways and monster parties, the folly of exclusiveness has very much died away : cutting near relatives is out of fashion—it is un- necessary in the whirl and bustle of life. There is little chance of meeting those we do not seek ; and there is more self-respect among those who do not belong to the upper ten thousand. Jones does not care one straw whether young Lord Popinjay cuts him or not. He has his own circle of admirers —his own particular summer and winter toady. He is a much better-looking fellow; and while Popinjay is sending Perdita or Imogen Kettledrum enormous bouquets, and catching cold under her window, the handsome Jones is snugly ensconced in the lady's boudoir, eating pigeon-pie and mimicking the unlucky lord. Miss Jackson, if a pretty girl, a good dancer, and showy rider, will have more partners and invitations than Lady Araminta Drystick, with her ancient pedigree and aristocratic airs.

How unspeakably odious—with a few brilliant exceptions, such as Alvanley and others—were the dandies of forty years ago. They were a motley crew, with nothing remarkable about them but their insolence. They were generally not high-born, nor rich, nor very good-looking, nor clever, nor agreeable; and why they arrogated to themselves the right of setting up their own fancied superiority on a self-raised pedestal, and despising their betters, Heaven only knows. They were generally middle-aged, some even elderly men, had large appetites and weak digestions, gambled freely, and had no luck. They hated everybody, and abused everybody, and would sit together in White's bay window, or the pit boxes at the Opera, weaving tremendous crammers. They swore a good deal, never laughed, had their own particular slang, looked hazy after dinner, and had most of them been patronised at one time or other by Brummell and the Prince Regent.

These gentlemen were very fond of having a butt. Many years ago Tom Raikes filled this capacity; though he did kick out sometimes, and to some purpose. They gloried in their shame, and believed in nothing good, or noble, or elevated. Thank Heaven, that miserable race of used-up dandies has long been extinct! May England never look upon their like again!

With regard to France, I should say that the general run of French dandies now-a-days is a sorry mixture of coxcombry and snobbishness. Young France thinks he has done wonders when he has ascended the giddy height of a hideous dog-cart, with a gigantic groom fastened on behind by some mysterious adhesive process, which does not seem altogether to reassure John (all Frenchmen's grooms rejoice in this appellation; be their names Pierre or Paul, when once they put on leathers and boots they become John). Another amusement of the Parisian *élégants* which surprises Englishmen, is to drive about in solitary glory in a brougham or barouche and pair. You see fifteen-stone men, with tremendous whiskers and moustaches, who ought to be taking violent exercise on horseback or on foot, driven up and down the fashionable promenade by the lake in the Bois de Boulogne, lolling on well-stuffed rose-coloured cushions, and ogling through their eye-glasses the fair and frail damsels in gorgeous equipages who frequent this drive.

What used to be called, thirty or forty years ago, *la jeunesse dorée* may now be termed *la jeunesse Ruoltz*, a base imitation of the precious metal: and this term well explains the difference that exists between the dandies of the olden time and the wretched swells of the present day. Formerly, if young men were guilty of follies, those follies were committed with some energy, enjoyment, and zest, and that ardour and *entrain* which accounts for, if it does not excuse them; but now they take their pleasure sadly, soberly, and stupidly, as if, when they ruin themselves at their clubs, at baccarat or quinze, or in giving horses and India shawls and diamonds to some fashionable Phryne, they were performing some painful but necessary duty. They are *blasés* and *ennuyés*, and, above all, *ennuyeux*. Formerly, one used to hear, in the scandalous

tittle-tattle of the day, that Monsieur X*** was
desperately in love with Mademoiselle ***; but
now, all that is ever said is that "an intrigue
is being carried on," or that "such and such a
lady has captured her prey." "And is Monsieur
X*** also very much enamoured?" I once inquired. The answer was, "*Il subit courageusement
son bonheur.*"

I heard the other day a good story of a well-
known Frenchman, M. de St. ***, having fallen in
love with the not very attractive wife of a great
financier. The various phases of his courtship were
of course related to the half-dozen intimate myrmidons who surround every Frenchman of note
in the fashionable world, and who echo back his
opinions like the chorus in a Greek tragedy. One
day this select circle see M. de St. *** arrive with
a face expressive of the deepest dismay. He sinks
into a chair apparently quite overwhelmed, and
hides his face in his handkerchief. "What has
happened?" asks the chorus. "Has she proved
faithless? are you betrayed?" What pen could
render the look of despair, which formed a ludicrous
contrast with M. de St. ***'s somewhat bacchan-
alian features, as he shrieked out, "*Mes amis, je suis
perdu! elle m'a pris au sérieux!*"

This reminds me of a truly French story, of a
man who, after a long siege, had at last obtained
the promise of a reward for his patience and perseverance; but there was one condition—he must
take his solemn oath, *sur l'âme de sa mère*, that
he would never breathe the tale of his success to
mortal ear. The Frenchman was honest, and frankly
answered, "*J'aime mieux m'en aller;*" in other

words, " What would be the use of a *bonne fortune*
if I am to keep it to myself ? "

I remember an amusing adventure happening to
my friend the Count de M * * *, then an *homme à
bonnes fortunes* with beautiful fair hair and a light
active figure, but now an elderly gentleman, somewhat bald, and very stout. He was, I am sorry to
say, paying an evening visit to a fair lady during
her husband's absence, when that gentleman unex-
pectedly returned, and the room having only one
door, which was to give ingress to the jealous husband, the gallant gay Lothario, after looking wildly
round the room for a hiding-place, took refuge in
a large old-fashioned clock-case which stood in a
corner of the room. There he ensconced himself ;
and, as his entry stopped the pendulum, he tried
with his tongue against his palate to imitate the
ticking noise of the clock ; hoping that the husband would make a short stay, and that he
would be soon released from his uncomfortable
situation.

But that gentleman, who had been privately
warned by an anonymous letter that all was not
right at home, showed no symptoms of moving from
the large arm-chair, just in front of the clock, where
he had taken up his position. My unfortunate
friend could no longer keep on the clicking noise,—
his tongue clove to the roof of his mouth,—and
he had to keep silence. The husband arose, cry-
ing out to his wife, "*Chère amie*, the clock is
stopped : I must wind it up." Before the lady
could arrest his progress, he had opened the door
and found the young Lovelace tightly wedged in.
" What are you doing there, you villain ? " shouted

the enraged husband. "*Je me promène*," replied the young man.

One more anecdote of *la jeunesse Ruoltz.* A lady of certain virtue, and uncertain age, had been courted by a young "fashionable" in a moment of *désœuvrement* in a country house. The lady was flattered, and at last fell in love, but held out for a time, when one fine day, as the gentleman was languidly pressing his suit, she exclaimed, throwing herself on his neck in an agony of tears, "*Eh bien, Raoul, je me damne pour toi!*" "*Et moi, je me sauve!*" responded the terrified Lovelace; and, seizing his hat, he rushed to the stable, mounted his horse, and was never seen or heard of again.

Talking of Lovelaces, there was a rather amusing story of my old friend, Dan M'Kinnon of the Guards, to whom I have already alluded. He was very good-looking, and a great favourite with the fair sex; and, at the time of which I speak, many, many years ago, he was beloved by Miss C * * *; and ill-natured people said that they "loved not wisely, but too well." Unfortunately people don't fall simultaneously out of love as they do into it, and, as generally occurs, the lady proved the most faithful of the pair. When Miss C * * * could no longer doubt that she was forsaken, and that some more fortunate rival had taken her place, she wrote a letter full of despair and reproaches, with threats of suicide, commanding M'Kinnon to send her back the lock of hair which she had given him in happier days, &c. The barbarian gave no written answer to this passionate appeal, but sent his orderly to the lady (who was a person of high birth and aristocratic connections), with a large packet or portfolio containing innumerable locks of hair, from grey to flaxen, from raven to red, with a message that she was to choose from among them her own property. Miss C * * *'s answer was to dash the whole collection into the fire.

SUMNER, AND OTHER ETON MASTERS.—When I was a boy at Eton, now, alas! many, many years ago, by far the most popular tutor was Dr. Sumner, whose loss as Archbishop of Canterbury we have lately had to deplore. This most able and excellent man went by the name of "Crumpety Sumner," whether from some fancied resemblance in his fine open countenance to that farinaceous esculent, or from some episode of his more youthful days, I was never able to discover; but I can safely say that no one was more universally beloved throughout the precincts of the venerable college of Henry VI. than he was.

This respected Eton tutor, after passing through many intermediary posts of great utility and importance, became primate of England, with the applause of all who had at any time been brought within the sphere of his beneficent influence. He was at once the most learned, able, and at the same time the most modest and unpretending of men. Though he lived to a great age, his mind was vigorous to the last, and he preserved all the fire and energy which distinguished him in youth, and which was always exercised for some useful and benevolent purpose. Peace to his ashes! I feel proud to have known him, *memor actæ non alio rege puertiæ*, and regret to think that so much of his advice and example should not have brought better fruit in me.

But I had very different examples in other tutors who were contemporaries of Sumner. Two of them, Drury and Knapp, were good-natured men enough, but passionately devoted to theatricals. Instead of gratifying this taste by burning midnight oil in their chambers in the perusal of Æschylus, Sophocles, and other great masters of the Greek drama, they used to start for London after school, to get in time for the theatre, and passed their nights in jovial suppers with that great but eccentric genius, Edmund Kean. They terminated these little expeditions by driving back, with very bad headaches (for Edmund always "forswore thin potations"), in a vehicle the very sight of which would have struck horror into "Henry's holy shade," could he or it have beheld two Eton tutors in a curricle. Nothing was ever seen like it since the famous "*patres conscripti* took a boat and went to Philippi;" and I can only account for their predilection in favour of this particular vehicle, by a classical remembrance of the third line of the First Ode of Horace, "Sunt quos curriculo pulverem Olympicum." The *pulverem Olympicum* was on this occasion the Slough road.

One fine day, these jovial pedagogues, unmindful of the adage of "Maxima sit puero reverentia," took with them two of my chums, John Scott, the son of Lord Eldon, and Lord Sunderland, the late Duke of Marlborough. The curricles were again brought into play, and they arrived in a few hours at the Hummums, a famous hotel in Covent Garden, where Kean had ordered dinner.

With such an example as the great actor, it is
no wonder that they drank pretty freely; and, as
every one did in those jovial days, they sallied out
after dinner in search of adventures. They created
such a disturbance, that, after several chivalrous
encounters with the watchmen, they were taken to
Bow Street, and had to be bailed out of durance
vile by the secretary of the all-powerful Chancellor,
who had been apprised of their mishap. This incident created much scandal. The two tutors were
threatened with the loss of their places, and clerical
degradation; but Lord Eldon, who was no enemy
to a bottle of port, threw over them the mantle of
his protection, and they got off without incurring
the punishment they so richly deserved.

COUNT MONTROND.—This well-known personage
belonged to a good family, and had already taken
his place in the best French society before the first
Revolution. He was an inveterate gambler, rarely
lost, and lived like a man possessed of a large
fortune. When very young, at the court of Marie
Antoinette, a certain Monsieur de Champagne, an
officer of the Guards, who was playing at cards
with him, said, "*Monsieur, vous trichez.*" Montrond
answered, with the *sang-froid* which distinguished
him through life under every circumstance, "*C'est
possible; mais je n'aime pas qu'on me le dise,*" and
threw the cards in Champagne's face.

They fought next morning with swords, and
Montrond was run through the body. He was confined to his bed for two months, but when he got
well again, called out Monsieur de Champagne, and,
although he received another wound, succeeded in

killing his adversary. This duel set him up in the world as a dangerous man to meddle with, and saved him from many insults, to which his very suspicious luck at play would have exposed him. Talleyrand said, *à propos* of this, "*Il vit sur son mort.*"

Montrond was thrown into prison during the reign of terror. For many days he expected every morning to be his last; and he used to relate that he had observed that those who showed themselves much at the windows, or talked to the sentry through the bars, were generally called for the next morning to be guillotined. He in consequence kept himself very much in the background, and remained at last with only one companion, an old lady, in his cell. One morning he heard so great a noise in the street, that he, with his usual caution, persuaded his companion to speak to the sentry, who said, "Robespierre is dead—you will soon be free!"

He was released very shortly afterwards, and became intimate with Barras, and other leading men of that time. He shortly afterwards formed that intimacy with Prince Talleyrand which lasted through life. On one occasion the prince, who was at that time minister for foreign affairs under Napoleon, gave Montrond some information which enabled him to gain twenty thousand pounds on the Bourse. When this lucky *coup* had been achieved, Talleyrand said to him, "My dear Montrond, now you have got a large sum of money, you must think of investing it. Where will you place it?" "Place it! why, in my desk, to be sure."

Montrond was always very improvident, and spent during his life enormous sums of money. He was always much disliked by the Emperor Napo-

leon I., partly, it was said, from his being supposed
to be an admirer of one of the imperial princesses,
and partly owing to some kind friend having repeated *bons mots* made upon majesty itself: for
his bitter and sarcastic wit spared no one.　In
spite of this dislike, strange to say, he was selected
by Fouché, in 1815, during the Hundred Days,
when all other negotiations had failed, to undertake
a mission as confidential as it was difficult.　He
was to start for Vienna under an assumed name,
giving himself out to be a learned botanist, and try
to win over Prince Talleyrand, pacify Prince Metternich, and, if possible, persuade the Empress Marie
Louise to return to Paris.

After being honoured with a private interview
by the Emperor Napoleon, he started, and, on his
arrival at Vienna, saw Talleyrand and Metternich,
but soon found that there was no hope of bringing
matters to a satisfactory solution.　He afterwards
obtained access to the gardens of Schœnbrunn,
where Marie Louise was then residing.　She was
passionately fond of flowers, and Montrond, under
his assumed character, was able to accost her during
her walks, and deliver the message with which he
had been charged.　He soon found, as he told his
friends on his return, "that a woman so devoted to
tulips would not care much for her husband's laurels,"
and that she was, in fact, completely estranged from
the emperor.

I knew Montrond well, but several years later;
he had then no trace of having been the *charmant
garçon* tradition represents him.　He was rather
above the middle height, and what the English
novelists call *embonpoint,* and had the appearance

WELL KNOWN BOND STREET LOUNGERS. 1820.

THE EARL OF SEFTON   THE DUKE OF DEVONSHIRE   POODLE BYNG.   LORD MANNERS.   THE DUKE OF BEAUFORT

of a *vieux bonhomme*. He was perfectly bald, had
blue eyes, very small features, and a florid complexion. There was a peculiar twinkle in his eye,
which boded no good to the victim he had selected
for his prey.

His countenance, as beheld by a casual observer,
bore the stamp of an almost Pickwickian bene-
volence; but, on a closer inspection, there lurked
behind this mask of mild philanthropy the stinging
wit of Voltaire, mingled with the biting sarcasm of
Rogers or Sir Philip Francis. Montrond had none
of the lively gestures or grimaces with which most
foreigners adorn their conversation: his manner
was singularly quiet. He was not a great talker,
nor did he swagger, speak about himself, or laugh
at his own *bons mots*. He was demure, sleek, sly,
and dangerous. He would receive with a paternal
air the silly quizzing of some feeble jester, but then
would come the twinkle of that little pale blue eye,
and then the poor moth or butterfly was ground
to pieces on the wheel of his sharp sarcastic wit.
But to return to his history. On his first visit to
England Byron is supposed to allude to him as the

"'Preux chevalier de la Ruse'
Whom France and fortune lately deign'd to waft here,
Whose chiefly harmless talent was to amuse ;
But the clubs found it rather serious laughter,
Because, such was his magic power to please,
The cards seem'd charm'd, too, by his repartees."

In the London clubs he went by the name of
Old French, and managed to win very large sums
of money off Lord Sefton (the only specimen I ever
saw of a gigantic hunchback), who, with all his wit
and cleverness, lost very largely on all occasions, as

well as off the late Lord Foley, the Duke of York, and many others.

"Who the deuce is this Montrond?" said the Duke of York, one day to Arthur Upton.

"They say, sir," replied Upton, "that he is the most agreeable scoundrel and the greatest reprobate in France."

"Is he, by Jove!" said H.R.H.; "then let us ask him to dinner immediately."

The invitation was sent and accepted, and Montrond, as usual, made himself very agreeable, and became a constant guest at the dinner-table of H.R.H.; and, unfortunately, at his whist-table also, by which the duke was a loser of many thousand pounds. Montrond lived in the best society both at Paris and in London, and was on terms, if not of intimacy, at all events of familiarity, with many of the greatest people in Europe. In the latter years of his life he resided in the Place Vendôme, in an apartment now occupied by Mr. Brooke Greville, and was in the receipt of a pension of two thousand pounds a year from Louis Philippe; with some of whose secrets he was acquainted, and with whom he had been mixed up in various political intrigues, before the citizen-king came to the throne. He was universally considered to be one of the wittiest men of the age: but all his *bons mots* were in French, and the greater part of them lose by translation; so I hope my readers will excuse me if I give them in the original.

His death was a very wretched one. Left alone to the tender mercies of a well-known *lorette* of those days, Desirée R * * *, as he lay upon his bed, between fits of pain and drowsiness, he could see his fair friend picking from his shelves the choicest specimens of his old Sèvres china, or other articles of *virtu*. Turning to his doctor, he said, with a gleam of his old fun—

"*Qu'elle est attachante, cette femme là!*"

Shortly before his death he received the visit of Count Charles de M * * *, a well-known dandy of that time, whom he liked to call one of his pupils, but who, fortunately, only resembled him in two points—natural wit, and rather extravagant habits. He turned on the boon companion of his happier days a glance of hopeless regret, and said—

"My good friend, I have not got a shilling; I have no appetite; I can't drink; Desirée's only occupation is to carry off my best china. '*Je vous demande un peu si c'est là Montrond?*'"

There is a moral in this tale, but perhaps this is not the book in which to note it down; so I will let my readers find it out for themselves.

The following are some of Montrond's best sayings; the two first have been falsely attributed to Talleyrand:—"*La parole a été donnée à l'homme pour l'aider à cacher sa pensée.*" "*Défiez-vous des premiers mouvements; ils sont presque toujours bons.*" "*S'il vous arrive quelque chose d'heureux, ne manquez pas d'aller le dire à vos amis, afin de leur faire de la peine.*"

Emile de Girardin, the famous political writer, a natural son of Alexandre de Girardin, becoming celebrated, Montrond said to the father, "*Dépêchez-vous de le reconnaître, ou bientôt il ne vous reconnaîtra pas.*"

A French general, Count F * * *, well known in English circles, who had the misfortune to be bald-headed, said that he wished to make a present to a lady, and to give her something rare. "Give her a lock of your hair," remarked Montrond.

The Bailli de Ferrette was always dressed in knee-breeches, with a cocked hat and a court sword, the slender proportions of which greatly resembled those of his legs. "Do tell me, my dear Bailli," said Montrond, one day, "have you got three legs or three swords?"

In General Malet's conspiracy, the Duke de Rovigo, then minister of police, was seized by the conspirators and taken to prison. His wife, very much alarmed at seeing her husband carried off, jumped out of bed in a very simple costume. Montrond said, "*Le ministre a été faible; mais sa femme s'est bien montrée.*"

A friend, who was about to marry the natural daughter of the Duke de * * *, was expatiating at great length on the virtues, good qualities, and talents of his future wife, but without making any allusion to her birth. "*A t'entendre,*" observed Montrond, "*on dirait que tu épouses une fille sur-naturelle.*"

A very thin lady, with whom he had a violent quarrel, saying, "*Qu'elle lui ferait voir du pays,*" Montrond, calmly surveying her from head to foot, replied, "*Madame, ce sera du plat pays.*"

SIR PEPPER ARDEN, FATHER OF LORD ALVANLEY. —This distinguished lawyer was of a violent and irascible temperament. Upon one occasion a Frenchman, accompanied by his interpreter, entered one of our law courts, when Sir Pepper, with a stentorian voice, and in a great rage, was har-

anguing the jury in a most unbecoming manner.
The Frenchman, not understanding English, inquired what the lawyer's name was, saying he
never saw or witnessed a more violent and irascible
advocate. The interpreter translated literally Sir
Pepper's name from English into French, and designated him as " *Le Chevalier Poivre Ardent.*"
"*Parbleu! il est très bien nommé,*" replied the
Frenchman.

JOHN KEMBLE.—In the autumn of 1821, I met
Mr. and Mrs. Kemble at Lausanne, at a dinner given
by Lady Caroline Capel (mother of the present
Earl of Essex); and a few weeks later I saw
them again at Milan, where, as we lived at the
same hotel, I had the pleasure of passing much
time in their company. The first evening we went
together to the "Scala," I remember the great
tragedian exclaiming, as he surveyed the proportions of that magnificent theatre, "How like old
Drury!"

The opera pleased him well enough; but with the
ballet he was quite delighted, and highly amused;
for the dancers, by order of the police, were obliged
to wear sky-blue pantaloons which reached down to
their knees, but were so tight that the outline of
the figure was more apparent, and the effect produced more indelicate, than if the usual gauze in-
expressibles had been used. Kemble, after a hearty
laugh, inveighed, in no measured terms, against the
imperial government, saying—

"What bullies and savages these Austrians are!
They interfere with the unfortunate Italians in
everything, even in their amusements, and make

even the dancing-girls put on the breeches of their Hungarian infantry."

I wish I could remember some of the numerous anecdotes of this remarkable man, who, without being actually witty, had a vein of rich dry humour ; which, contrasting with his grave classical face, deep sepulchral voice, and serious manner, had a very ludicrous effect.

John Kemble had the honour of giving the Prince of Wales some lessons in elocution. According to the vitiated pronunciation of the day, the Prince, instead of saying " oblige," would say " obleege," upon which Kemble, with much disgust depicted upon his countenance, said—

" Sir, may I beseech your Royal Highness to open your royal jaws, and say ' oblige ' ? "

Conway was a mediocre actor, but a very handsome man, and a great favourite with the fair sex. On some one asking Kemble if Conway was a good actor, the only answer they could get from Kemble was, " Mr. Conway, sir, is a very tall young man." " But what do you think of him ? " " I think Mr. Conway is a very tall young man."

One day he was saying, before Lord Blessington, who was an amateur actor of no mean capacity, that the worst professional player was better than the best amateur performer. Lord Blessington, somewhat nettled by this observation, asked John Kemble if he meant to say that Conway acted better than he did?

" Conway," replied Kemble, in his most sepulchral voice, " is a very strong exception."

Like the Sheridans, the Kembles were a most remarkable family—John and his sister, Mrs. Sid-

dons, taking the lead ; then came Mrs. Twiss, Fanny
(now Mrs. Butler), the tragedian and authoress,
Adelaide (now Mrs. Sartoris), with her splendid
musical talent, and their father, Charles Kemble,
who, had he not been John's brother, would have
been reckoned the first of English actors ; and I
believe that several young scions of the same stock,
distinguished in their several professions, might be
added to the list.

There is not only the stamp of genius and talent
of a high order in this gifted family, but also a certain nobility of mind and feeling. We might say
of one of them, " He or she comes of a good stock,"
and expect from them a kind word, a generous
impulse, a self-denying action. No mean thought
could take its birth in those broad, grand foreheads,
expressive of the majestic calmness of strength and
power ; and those full, firm, kind lips could not give
vent to petty, spiteful, or malicious words. They
were of the men and women one meets sometimes
in good old England ; not of the common clay, but
cast in the Titanic mould. Would there were more
such in our days of mediocrity !

REVOLUTION OF 1848.—The character of the two
great outbreaks of popular feeling in 1830 and 1848
was widely different. The first had a far grander
aspect, from the simple fact that, under the elder
branch of the Bourbons, there were real grievances
to redress. It was absolutely necessary to arrest the
wide-spreading encroachments of the priesthood,
and to crush the infatuated pride of aristocracy,
which would have ignored the reforming work of
1789. The Revolution of 1830 was the expression

of a strong genuine feeling, the death-struggle between blind superstition and that latent love for
truth and liberty which cannot be trampled out of
the human breast.   But that of 1848 was of a very
different kind.

There still hangs a kind of mystery over the
exact origin of the outbreak.   Dark hints have been
thrown out of treachery on the part of at least one
of the leading Generals at that time.   Many have
supposed that there existed, in the bosom of the
royal family of France itself, a plot to bring about
the abdication of Louis Philippe, in favour of his
grandson, the Count de Paris, under the regency of
the Duchess of Orleans.   It is thought that M.
Thiers was the leading spirit of this plan, and that
all the princes, except the Duke de Nemours, agreed
to, or secretly approved of, this combination ; and it
is supposed that, in their anxiety to bring about this
scheme, they allowed the revolutionary movement
to gain ground, and wilfully ignored the republican
feeling—which really existed in France before the
French knew what a republic was.   I do not pretend
to vouch for the truth of these suppositions, but undoubtedly some of the events that occurred gave a
colouring to them.

Various untoward circumstances, during 1847, had
combined to excite the people and bring matters to
a crisis.   Among these may be noted the disgraceful trials in which some of the ministers had been
implicated, and the murder of the poor Duchess de
Praslin.   It was very much to be regretted that the
perpetrator of this fearful crime did not expiate his
guilt on the scaffold, and was allowed to commit
suicide in his prison.   Nay, more, to this day the

people firmly believe that a convict who had died in prison was buried in the murderer's stead; and that the aristocratic criminal was suffered to escape, and still lives, under an assumed name, in Scotland. Very exciting works had been published. That splendid fable, *L'Histoire des Girondins*, by Lamartine, had electrified the masses; while the popular novels of Eugène Sue had demoralised them, and inspired them with hatred against the more fortunate classes of society. There had been a bad harvest; and the French invariably render their government responsible for such disasters. The death of Madame Adelaide, the king's much-loved sister, and wise counsellor, having put a stop to all official gaieties, had also produced a bad effect on the commercial interests of Paris.

I cannot but think that royalty has no right to indulge in the outward expression of private grief, when the welfare of a large capital is at stake. A poor actor who has just heard of the death of his wife or child, must needs paint his cheeks, still wet with the tears of natural affection, and come before the public with a breaking heart, to smile and jest for their amusement. Surely a monarch has also his obligations and duties; and if he takes the pay, and other pleasant parts of the kingly office, he should also bear his burthen, and fulfil his duties. Thus, he would secure far more efficaciously the sympathy of his people than if he were trying to force them to suffer with him.

Madame Adelaide was a clever, hard-headed, some say hard-hearted, woman of the world, and there can be no doubt that she exercised considerable influence over her royal brother. Her appearance was extremely *bourgeois*, and without dignity. In speaking of their aunt, the princes used to say, "*Notre tante est bonne femme au fond, mais un peu épicière.*" But it was just perhaps her want of refinement and royal dignity which adapted Madame Adelaide to the tone and councils of the citizen monarchy. However this may be, it was generally remarked that the king's mental faculties had been much impaired since his sister's death, which event took place in the early part of the winter preceding his fall; that he was no longer the wise, prudent, energetic man of former days; and that his whole conduct during the last months of his reign was marked by vacillation of purpose, and a strange irritability of temper, as if he felt that he was going all wrong, but was hurried on by that blind fatality which drags monarchs down from their tottering thrones.

The extreme unpopularity of the ministers was another cause of Louis Philippe's downfall. M. Guizot, the *austère intrigant*, as he had been cleverly designated, was himself of Spartan probity, and proud of his comparative poverty; but at the same time he permitted, or at all events did not prevent, the peculations and speculations on the Bourse, founded on official news, of those employed under him. Neither was he likely, by his manner, or his language, to conciliate his numerous enemies.

I never can forget his attitude in the Chamber of Deputies during the period immediately preceding the fall of Louis Philippe. He seemed, with his fine head thrown proudly back, his eagle glance, his hard-flashing eye, his biting sarcasm, and disdainful eloquence, to hurl defiance at his adversaries, and to dare them to the combat; just as a matador strives to irritate the bull he is going to fight by dashing a scarlet flag in his face: and, Heaven knows, the French require no stirring up, or egging on, to increase their natural pugnaciousness and irritability. Instead of answering the accusations of his political opponents, Guizot insulted them; and, firm in the consciousness of his own personal integrity, he covered the petty larcenies of his myrmidons, or the wholesale robberies of his colleagues, with the mantle of his stern morality.

I am *kein Freund*, as the Germans say, to any class of courtiers; but I think the most hateful of all this hateful class were the Doctrinaires in office. They seemed to glory in the antipathy they inspired. Cold, dry, grasping, stingy, insolent, and mean, they cared only for their master, inasmuch as he could minister to their ambition. There can, I think, be no doubt that the *morgue* and *maladresse* of his supporters had much to do with the fall of Louis Philippe; and though they talked a good deal of all they would have done to back him up, had he been wise enough to employ the military means placed at his disposal, I firmly believe, that not one among the whole set would have sacrificed a thousand-franc note to keep the constitutional king on his throne. They played high—a royal crown for their stake; and when it was cast down into the mire by the triumphant mob, they vanished: to return when all was quiet, and make *de l'opposition* in the gilded saloons of their sumptuous Parisian houses.

To complete the series of unlucky circumstances,

the two most popular princes of the royal family were absent in Algeria. The favour with which they were regarded by the lower orders was greatly increased by the rumour that they had fallen into disgrace with the king and his government on account of their liberal opinions. The Duke de Nemours, a brave and kind-hearted prince, did all he could to support his sister-in-law on her visit to the Chamber of Deputies ; but he was paralysed by the conviction of his own unpopularity. He accomplished a difficult and dangerous duty without the *élan* which turns the soldier into a hero. He supported the duchess, but was unable to utter one of those stirring appeals which electrify an audience, and, like a whirlwind, carry all before them : the duke, pale, serious, collected, was too resigned to be able to obtain a victory over the passions of an enthusiastic multitude. If the Duchess of Orleans, who was a woman full of energy and eloquence, had been allowed to speak, she would have won the day ; but her voice was drowned in the cries of the infuriated mob.

On the eve of the day which was to see Louis Philippe hurled from his throne, I remember walking down the Boulevards, which were crowded with people. It has been generally remarked, that revolutionary movements in France never take place during very cold weather, and the last week of February 1848 was singularly mild and warm. It seemed to me, during my promenade, that there was about the assembled masses that peculiar aspect of sullen defiance which characterises the Paris mobs before an outbreak.

I had had some experience in these matters, owing

to my long residence in France, and I felt quite certain that the persons assembled at various points, and in divers groups, were combining their plans, and that we might look out for squalls. The only soldiers one saw on that day, the 23d, were the municipal guards; for the troops of the line were confined to their barracks. Unfortunately, the municipal guards did not show much forbearance in their treatment of the people, invariably answering their vociferations by a charge. It would have been far wiser, in my opinion, not to have irritated the mob by these half-measures, which could be productive of no beneficial result. When the troops were called out, instead of being made to act immediately, they were allowed to stand all day and all night in the streets, weary, unoccupied, and without provisions, to endure the jeering of the *gamins* and the cajoling of the workmen, or rather *émeutiers* disguised as workmen and carrying arms under their blouses. This long inaction, coupled with physical exhaustion, brought about their fraternising with the mob, which lost the Orleans dynasty one of the finest thrones in the world.

I lived at this period in the Place de la Madeleine, and could observe from my windows the increasing numbers of the populace, and the insolence of their bearing. As I went to my club at the Café de Paris, I saw a battalion of the 14th Regiment of the line, stationed in the garden of the Foreign Office, which was then on the Boulevards.

The king, at the time I mention, had at last consented to dismiss his ministers, and to replace them by members of the Liberal party. There was great joy at this news, and even a commencement of illu-

minations in consequence. At the club where I was
dining, the friends of the monarchy were rejoicing
at the prospect of matters being satisfactorily arranged; when, just as we were all congratulating
ourselves on the peaceful termination of the *émeute*,
a terrific yell burst upon our ears. Its cause was
soon explained. On rushing to the windows, we
beheld a large cart full of dead and dying persons,
followed by an immense concourse of men and
women in the highest state of excitement, flinging
their arms up towards heaven, and shouting out,
"*Aux armes!*"   "*Vengeons nos frères!*"   We soon
learnt what had occurred.

A large and peaceable crowd had collected before
the Foreign Office, the garden of which looked upon
the Boulevard des Capucines, and were gazing with
Parisian delight at the illumination, when it is supposed that the republican party, enraged at seeing
peace restored by the announcement of a change of
ministry, determined to strike a murderous blow at
the tottering monarchy, and—with that utter disre-
gard of human life, which characterises Frenchmen
when they have a political end in view—put forward
an agent (Lagrange), who fired a pistol-shot at the
officer commanding the battalion. The soldiers
immediately responded by a volley of musketry
upon the unsuspecting people, and strewed the
Boulevard with dead and wounded. Many of the
corpses were placed by the revolutionary party upon
a cart to excite the passions of the people, and
followed by vast crowds shouting vengeance.

From my club window that evening, I witnessed
another extraordinary sight. An infuriated mob
broke into the shop of a gunmaker opposite, and

robbed him of every weapon he possessed : guns, pistols, swords, sabres, carbines, were slung round the shoulders, or fastened round the waists of men and boys, who were all singing the forbidden " *Marseillaise*," and the " *Chant de Départ*," and shouting seditious cries. In a few hours, barricades were raised, as if by magic, on every point of Paris, ready for the conflict that commenced at break of day.

I went out early on the following morning, and visited the Place de la Concorde, where several regiments of cavalry had bivouacked ; and owing to the blundering and mismanagement of the military authorities,—who all seemed to have taken leave of their senses,—the troops had remained all night, the men without any food, and the horses with neither corn nor hay. From the Place de la Concorde, I directed my steps to the Boulevard Montmartre, by the Palais Royal, and the Rue Vivienne.

I spoke to several persons, all of whom appeared disgusted at the unaccountable apathy shown by the Government. As I passed along the Boulevard Bonne Nouvelle, I witnessed a strange scene : a regiment of the line, who, if they had been well led, would have put to flight all the mob of Paris, were actually in the hands of the *émeutiers*, who had persuaded the soldiers to give up their muskets. A General rode up and addressed the crowd, saying that the soldiers would never more fire on their brethren. Upon which there was a tremendous shout of applause.

I then endeavoured to make my way to the Chamber of Deputies, but could not reach it owing to the denseness of the crowd. I met a member of my club, Emmanuel Arago, son of the great

astronomer. Having always been a republican, and
opposed to Louis Philippe's government, he was
radiant with joy; and after leaving me, he placed
himself at the head of sixty or seventy of the armed
mob, and forced his way into the Chamber. At the
moment when the regency of the Duchess of Orleans
would probably have been proclaimed, Emmanuel
Arago's friends made their way into the tribunes,
and levelled their muskets at the heads of Sauzet,
the President, and other members of the Chamber,
who were about to speak in favour of the regency
of the Duchess of Orleans. The President and the
Deputies left their seats; Arago and his friends
raised an immense shout of " *Vive la République !* "
Lamartine, then Ledru-Rollin, Crémieux, and other
Deputies of extreme opinions, were listened to with
attention; and they undertook to establish a Pro-
visional Government, and to adjourn to the Hôtel
de Ville.

In this extraordinary manner, and almost I may
say by chance, the Orleans dynasty ceased to reign
over the French people; and Louis Philippe—long
reputed the Nestor of monarchs, the wisest sovereign
in Europe—was driven from the throne, as he constantly exclaimed during his flight—" *Absolument
comme Charles X. !—Absolument comme Charles X. !* "

ROGERS AND LUTTRELL.—I saw a good deal of
the poet Rogers during his frequent visits to Paris ;
and often visited him in his apartments, which
were always on the fourth or fifth storey of the hotel
or private house in which he lived. He was rich,
and by no means avaricious, and chose those lofty
chambers partly from a poetic wish to see the sun

rise with greater brilliancy, and partly from a fancy that the exercise he was obliged to take in going up and down stairs, would prove beneficial to his liver.

I could relate many unpublished anecdotes of Rogers, but they lose their piquancy when one attempts to narrate them. There was so much in his appearance, in that cadaverous, unchanging countenance, in the peculiar low drawling voice, and rather tremulous accents in which he spoke. His intonations were very much those one fancies a ghost would use if forced by some magic spell to give utterance to sounds. The mild venom of every word was a remarkable trait in his conversation. One might have compared the old poet to one of those velvety caterpillars that crawl gently and quietly over the skin, but leave an irritating blister behind. To those, like myself, who were *sans* consequence, and with whom he feared no rivalry, he was very good-natured and amiable, and a most pleasant companion, with a fund of curious anecdote about everything and everybody. But woe betide those in great prosperity and renown ; they had, like the Roman emperor, in Rogers the personification of the slave who bade them "remember they were mortal."

At an evening party many years since at Lady Jersey's, every one was praising the Duke of B * * *, who had just come in, and who had lately attained his majority. There was a perfect chorus of admiration, to this effect : "Everything is in his favour —he has good looks, considerable abilities, and a hundred thousand a year." Rogers, who had been carefully examining the "young ruler," listened to these encomiums for some time in silence, and at last remarked, with an air of great exultation, and in his most venomous manner, "Thank God, he has got bad teeth!"

His well-known epigram on Mr. Ward, afterwards Lord Dudley—

> "They say that Ward's no heart, but I deny it;
> He has a heart, and gets his speeches by it"—

was provoked by a remark made at table by Mr. Ward. On Rogers observing that his carriage had broken down, and that he had been obliged to come in a hackney-coach, Mr. Ward grumbled out in a very audible whisper, "In a hearse, I should think;" alluding to the poet's corpse-like appearance. This remark Rogers never forgave; and I have no doubt pored for days over his retaliatory impromptu, for he had no facility in composition: Sydney Smith used to say that if Rogers was writing a dozen verses, the street was strewn with straw, the knocker tied up, and the answer to the tender inquiries of his anxious friends was, that Mr. Rogers was as well as could be expected.

It used to be very amusing in London to see Rogers with his *fidus Achates*, Luttrell. They were inseparable, though rival wits, and constantly saying bitter things of each other. Luttrell was the natural son of Lord Carhampton, Commander-in-Chief in Ireland, and in his youth known as the famous Colonel Luttrell of Junius. I consider him to have been the most agreeable man I ever met. He was far more brilliant in conversation than Rogers; and his animated, bustling manner formed an agreeable contrast with the spiteful calmness of his corpse-like companion. He was extremely irritable and even passionate; and in his moments of anger he would splutter and stutter like a maniac in his anxiety to give utterance to the flow of thoughts which crowded his mind, and I might almost say, his mouth.

On one occasion the late Lady Holland took him a drive in her carriage over a rough road, and as she was very nervous, she insisted on being driven at a foot's pace. This ordeal lasted some hours, and when he was at last released, poor Luttrell, perfectly exasperated, rushed into the nearest club-house, and exclaimed, clenching his teeth and hands, " The very funerals passed us ! "

The last time I saw him was at Paris, in June 1849, when I remember meeting him at a very pleasant dinner at the Frères Provençaux. Lord Pembroke, Lockwood, Auriol, Lord Hertford, and one or two others, were present, and though Luttrell was then above eighty years of age, we thought him quite delightful. He had lost none of the fire and eagerness of youth, but took the greatest interest in everything that was going on in Paris at that most exciting period, and I had for several days the great pleasure of acting as his cicerone.

Strange to say, on his return to England he married a second time, but died shortly afterwards. He was the author of *Advice to Julia,* and other poems ; but nothing that he ever wrote gave an idea of the amusing variety of his conversation, and his brilliant wit and humour. He was the last of the " Conversationists."

THE PIG-FACED LADY.—Among the many absurd reports and ridiculous stories current in former days,

I know of none more absurd or more ridiculous than the general belief of everybody in London, during the winter of 1814, in the existence of a lady with a pig's face. This interesting specimen of porcine physiognomy was said to be the daughter of a great lady residing in Grosvenor Square.

It was rumoured that during the illuminations which took place to celebrate the peace, when a great crowd had assembled in Piccadilly and St. James's Street, and when carriages could not move on very rapidly, *horresco referens!* an enormous pig's snout had been seen protruding from a fashionable-looking bonnet in one of the landaus which were passing. The mob cried out, "The pig-faced lady!—the pig-faced lady! Stop the carriage—stop the carriage!" The coachman, wishing to save his bacon, whipped his horses, and drove through the crowd at a tremendous pace; but it was said that the coach had been seen to set down its monstrous load in Grosvenor Square.

Another report was also current. Sir William Elliot, a youthful baronet, calling one day to pay his respects to the great lady in Grosvenor Square, was ushered into a drawing-room, where he found a person fashionably dressed, who, on turning towards him, displayed a hideous pig's face. Sir William, a timid young gentleman, could not refrain from uttering a shout of horror, and rushed to the door in a manner the reverse of polite; when the infuriated lady or animal, uttering a series of grunts, rushed at the unfortunate baronet as he was retreating, and inflicted a severe wound on the back of his neck. This highly probable story concluded by stating that Sir William's wound was a severe one, and had been dressed by Hawkins the surgeon, in St. Audley Street.

I am really almost ashamed to repeat this absurd story; but many persons now alive can remember the strong belief in the existence of the pig-faced lady which prevailed in the public mind at the time of which I speak. The shops were full of caricatures of the pig-faced lady, in a poke bonnet and large veil, with "A pig in a poke" written underneath the print. Another sketch represented Sir William Elliot's misadventure, and was entitled, "Beware the pig-sty!"

BALZAC AND EUGÈNE SUE.—It has been my good fortune, during the many years I have lived in Paris, to meet some remarkable characters, among whom I should wish particularly to name, the celebrated novelists Balzac, Eugène Sue, and Dumas.

Balzac had nothing in his outward man that could in any way respond to the ideal his readers were likely to form of the enthusiastic admirer of beauty and elegance in all its forms and phases: the wonderful master-mind, which had so vividly drawn the pictures of his heroes and heroines, that one had ended by imagining one had lived in the charmed circle; had borrowed money from Gobseck, and the Père Goriot; flirted with Madame de Beauséant; followed the "Fille aux Yeux d'Or" in the mazes of the Tuileries gardens; been cheated by De Trailles; or patronised by De Marsay.

The great enchanter was one of the oiliest and commonest-looking mortals I ever beheld; being short and corpulent, with a broad florid face, a cascade of double chins, and straight greasy hair. The only striking feature in that Friar Tuck countenance was his eye; dark, flashing, wicked, full of sarcasm and unholy fire.

Balzac had that unwashed appearance which seems generally to belong to French *literati*, and dressed in the worst possible taste, wore sparkling jewels on a dirty shirt-front, and diamond rings on unwashed fingers. He talked little, but it was evident that nothing escaped him, and that bright eye seemed almost to read the secrets of the heart. No literary man, except perhaps Alexandre Dumas, ever ran through so much money as Balzac. The immense sums which he received for his writings were spent in the most absurd attempts at aristocratic luxury, which ended invariably in a steeple-chase between the great author and the bailiffs.

Eugène Sue was the very reverse of Balzac, both in appearance and manner. Nothing could have been more correct and scrupulously neat than his dress, which was rather dandified, but in good taste, according to the notions of twenty or thirty years ago. He wore always a very broad-brimmed hat, of glossy newness, and remarkably tight, light-coloured trousers: which, by the bye, were not particularly becoming to a man built in a stout mould; but a Frenchman who cannot diminish the rotundity of his abdomen, generally revenges himself upon his legs, which he circumscribes in the smallest possible compass, giving himself very much the appearance of what we Englishmen are taught to believe to be his national characteristic and prototype—a frog.

Eugène Sue was rather above the middle height,
strongly-built, with somewhat high shoulders. His
hair and brows were very dark, his eyes blue, long,
and rather closed, and his complexion of a livid
paleness. In general society, he did not show off,
and preferred rather being treated as a man of the
world, than as a distinguished writer. But when
he found himself among some kindred spirits,
and felt he was appreciated, his conversation was
particularly agreeable. He never had the sparkling
wit and versatility of Dumas, or the extraordinary
descriptive powers of Balzac; but he possessed
the immense advantage over his great rivals in
being veritably *un homme du monde*, living in
the very best Parisian society. He could, therefore, make the men and women in his novels act
and speak as people really do, and not like workmen in their Sunday coats, or actors in the old
melodramas.

Sue's imagination was wonderful; but one can see
that in his books he carried out his own principle,
that the beginning of the novel was three parts of
the battle. He always commenced his tales in a
manner certain to fix the attention of the reader;
but we generally find towards the close of the
numberless volumes symptoms of weariness in
the writer, which are apt to communicate themselves to the reader.

He was remarkable for the beauty of his horses;
his cab was one of the best-appointed in Paris; his
house in the Rue de la Pépinière (now an asylum)
was a perfect *bonbonnière*, and his dinners were
renowned for their excellence. He was supposed
(and to my knowledge with considerable reason)

to lead a very Sardanapalian life. Strange stories are told of his castle in Sologne, where he was waited on by a number of beautiful women, of all countries, and of all shades of colour.

In manners, Eugène Sue was particularly gentle-manlike and courteous, without servility. He held his own, but with good taste and good breeding. He had a wonderful passion for beautiful flowers, and was well skilled in botany. He had been in early life a navy surgeon, and in his distant voyages had become thoroughly versed in the names and pro-perties of rare tropical plants. He had in his house a beautiful conservatory, full of valuable exotics. His handkerchiefs were always steeped in essence of bouquet; and he had generally a tuberose or a camellia in the button-hole of his coat. Though a man utterly devoid of moral principle, Sue was charitable and kind to the poor, and obliging to his friends. At the Revolution of 1848, he went all lengths with the Red Republican party; and, after being one of the members for Paris in the National Assembly, was obliged to leave France, and passed the few remaining years of his life in Savoy, in complete seclusion.

Eugène Sue had grown very unwieldy; and, as he lived in a village at the foot of a mountain called, I think, the Solève, he had set himself, in order to grow thinner, on a course of training, which con-sisted in climbing to the top of this high hill. The weather, which was very sultry, and the over-exer-tion, brought on a fever, which carried him off in a few days. His death was attributed, among the ignorant peasantry, to poison given by the Jesuits, who had never forgiven the violent attacks he had made on their order in the ardent and eloquent pages of the *Juif Errant.*

ALEXANDRE DUMAS.—Of all the distinguished writers of the nineteenth century that have appeared in France, Alexandre Dumas is perhaps the most remarkable, from the versatility of his talent and the brilliancy of his imagination, which carries the reader along with unflagging interest through dozens of volumes. Who among us has not in fancy shared the perils of the *Trois Mousquetaires?* or followed with unabated interest the avenging course of *Monte Christo?* or believed firmly in the existence of a " Bifstek d'Ours," served up in a Swiss inn to an astonished traveller?

The reader, however heavy he may be in himself, is carried impetuously forward; and, like the stout old lady placed on a " Montagne Russe," " is forced to go the pace," whether he will or not. Bright or Cobden himself is forced to fight D'Artagnan's battles along with him; and the most benevolent Pickwick finds himself burning with anger, and glowing with martial ardour, as he peruses those admirable descriptions. There is no great depth of thought in the " Père Prodigue," as the younger Dumas wittily styled his juvenile and extravagant father. There are none of those wonderful touches of pathos, and profound study of human character, that we find in Balzac's tales,—passages any one would wish to copy into his scrap-book, or mark with a pencil as he goes along. In Dumas the touches of real feeling are rare; there are none of those aspirations after better things which throw now and then a golden light even on the sensual pages of George

Sand or Alfred de Musset. All is action—bright,
dazzling, *entrainant*; a torrent of incident carrying
all before it.

Alexandre Dumas is the son of General Alexandre
Dumas, who served with some distinction in the
republican armies of France, and was a native of
one of the French West India Islands. In appearance, he is far above the middle height, and is
almost a mulatto, with woolly curling hair, and
copper complexion. This peculiarity of appearance
has given rise to some amusing *traits d'esprit*,
which, though well known in France, may be new
to some of my English readers.

" A. Dumas fils " (the son of the writer), who has
inherited all his father's wit, with a quiet and
gentlemanlike demeanour, said the great novelist
was so fond of " show-off," that he was always
expecting him to get up behind his own carriage,
in order to make people think that he had got a
negro footman.

Another story is told on the same subject. A.
Dumas has a daughter who made a very good marriage. There were, report says, some difficulties in
the preliminary arrangements, but these were got
over ; and the mother of the bridegroom, a pro-
vincial lady of great respectability, arrived in Paris
to be present at the wedding. The church was full
of spectators ; and it so happened that among them
were several negroes. This circumstance excited
the surprise of the bridegroom's mother, who was
seated beside the bride's father. Persons from the
provinces, *les Provinciaux*, are rather disposed to
wonder at everything they see in Paris, and Madame
X***, in a weak treble, expressed her astonishment

to Alexandre Dumas at seeing so many men of colour.

"Oh, I can explain that very easily," replied the incorrigible jester: "*C'est ma famille, qui voulait assister aux noces de ma fille.*" The old lady, who, like most provincials, was a very matter-of-fact person, looked unutterable things, and was perfectly horrified at the prospect of this enormous negro connection.

Dumas, who is the most generous and kind-hearted man in the world, had been away from his house in Paris on one of his many trips to foreign lands; and, with his usual munificence, had allowed his friends the run of his house and cellar during his absence. On his return home, he gave a great breakfast to celebrate the event. His numerous guests, towards the end of the repast, expressed a wish to drink his health in champagne, and the servant went downstairs, as if to look for some, but soon returned with the dismal intelligence that it had been all drunk. Dumas slipped a few napoleons into the valet's hand, and ordered him to buy some at the neighbouring *restaurateurs;* but having some suspicion, he followed the servant, when, to his great surprise, he beheld the fellow emerging from his own cellar, from whence he had brought up his own champagne. Dumas, though the soul of good-nature, was about to turn the rascal off on the spot, when the man fell at his kind master's feet, reminded him that he had a wife and family, and implored his mercy.

"Well, I will forgive you this time," said the great writer; "*mais au moins une autre fois faites-moi crédit.*"

Dumas married an actress, from whom he separated, making her a liberal allowance, which was seldom or never paid. A friend of the lady went to expostulate on the distressed condition in which she found herself. "I will double her annuity," cried out the generous author. "You would do better," said the more matter-of-fact friend, "to pay her the allowance you make her."

The sums which the " Père Prodigue " spent on his Monte-Christo villa near St. Germain—so called from having been built at the time his novel of *Monte Christo* met with so much success,—were fabulous. He was horribly cheated by architects, builders, upholsterers, and in fact by everybody he employed; yet he did not succeed in making it a pretty house. Nothing could be more inconvenient, or in worse taste, than the way in which the rooms were laid out : the only thing that struck me as being pretty was the little dressing-room in white marble. This "Folie Dumas " did not remain long in his possession, but was sold about twelve years ago.

Dumas is one of the most amusing men I ever met, and a most wonderful talker. His wit is prodigious, his fund of anecdote inexhaustible, the strength of his lungs overpowering. To give my English readers an idea of his Herculean powers of conversation, I may remark that I was present at a dinner some twelve or fifteen years ago, where Lord Brougham and Dumas were among the company, and the loquacious and eloquent ex-chancellor could not literally get in a single word, but had to sit, for the first and last time in his life, a perfect dummy.

CIVILITY REWARDED.— We have all heard the story alluded to by Charles Lamb, in the *Essays of Elia*, of the bank clerk who was in the habit, as he proceeded daily to his office, of giving a penny to a crossing-sweeper, and how in process of time the sweeper died and left £5000, which sum had been half a century in accumulating, to the charitable *employé*. The grandfather of the present Marquis of Hertford having been very civil to an old gentleman in a stage-coach during a journey to York, the said old gentleman very kindly died shortly after, and left his lordship a large fortune.

But I know of no incident more curious than the following; the moral of which would seem to be, that we ought all to go to church early and secure a good place. Like the novel of *Waverley*, " 'tis sixty years since," when a young gentleman named Green, the son of a clergyman, wishing to hear a famous preacher, went one Sunday morning unusually early to church, and thereby secured a good place in a pew near the preacher. The church filled rapidly, and a venerable and rather infirm-looking old man, after walking up and down the various aisles, being unable to get a seat, was about to leave the church, when Green, who was a good-natured young fellow, took pity on him, as he looked very weak and ill, and offered him his seat; it was accepted with many thanks, whilst Green stood with his back against the wall during the service and sermon. On leaving the church the old gentleman again thanked him, and asked his name and address, which were given. A few days after, Mr. Green received an invitation to dinner from the stranger, who was living in Grosvenor Square. It would appear that the acquaintance thus accidentally

formed, became a fast friendship, for the old gentleman shortly afterwards died, and left the whole of
his fortune, a very considerable one, to his young
friend, with the condition that he should take the
name of Wilkinson in addition to that of Green. I
may add that the young gentleman made the most
excellent use of the fortune which he owed to his
good-nature and civility, and became the head of a
very popular and prosperous family.

A propos of pews and pew-openers, I remember, when I was staying at Deal some years back,
hearing of an incident in which a lady, who had not
the good-breeding of Mr. Green, played a somewhat
unenviable part.

The Duke of Wellington, then residing at Walmer
Castle, had walked one Sunday evening into Deal,
and entered Trinity Church. After wandering about
for some time in search of the sexton (who, as a
matter of course, was engaged elsewhere), the Duke
ensconced himself in a roomy-looking pew, in front
of the pulpit. After a short time a lady of portly
and pompous appearance, the owner of the pew,
entered. After muttering a prayer, she cast a scowl
at the intruder, which was intended to drive him
out of the place he had taken. She had not the
least idea who he was, and would probably have
given her eyes, had she known him, to have touched
the hem of the great Duke's cloth cloak, or asked
for his autograph. Seeing that the stranger bore
the brunt of her indignant glance without moving,
the lady bluntly told the Duke, as she did not know
him, that she must request he would immediately
leave her pew. His Grace obeyed, and chose another
seat. When he was leaving the church, at the end

of the service, and had at last found the sexton, who
received him with many bows and salutations, he
said—

"Tell that lady she has turned the Duke of Wellington out of her pew this evening."

PARTY AT MANCHESTER HOUSE IN 1816, AND THE
REGENT'S ETIQUETTE.—In 1816, when I was residing
in Paris, I used to have all my clothes made by
Staub, in the Rue Richelieu. He had married a
very pretty *dame de compagnie* of the celebrated
Lady Mildmay, and in consequence of this circum-
stance was patronised and made the fashion by Sir
Henry Mildmay and his friends, the dandies.

As I went out a great deal into the world, and
was every night at some ball or party, I found that
knee-breeches were only worn by a few old fogies;
trousers and shoes being the usual costume of all
the young men of the day. I returned to London
with Hervey Aston, towards the end of the year,
and we put up at Fenton's in St. James's Street.

I mention the following somewhat trivial circumstance to give some notion of the absurd severity in
matters of dress and etiquette of Brummell's worthy
pupil, the Prince Regent. A few days after my
arrival, I received an invitation to a party at Manchester House, from Lady Hertford, "to have the
honour of meeting the Prince."

I went there dressed *à la Française*, and quite
correctly, as I imagined, with white neckcloth and
waistcoat, and black trousers, shoes, and silk stock-
ings. The Prince had dined there, and I found him
in the octagon-room, surrounded by all the great
ladies of the Court. After making my bow, and re-

tiring to the further part of the room, I sat down by the beautiful Lady Heathcote, and had been engaged in conversation with her for some time, when Horace Seymour tapped me on the shoulder and said, "The 'great man,'" meaning the Prince, "is very much surprised that you should have ventured to appear in his presence without knee-breeches. He considers it as a want of proper respect for him."

This very disagreeable hint drove me away from Manchester House in a moment, in no very pleasant mood, as may be imagined; and I much fear that I went to bed devoting my royal master to all the infernal gods.

In the morning, being on guard, I mentioned what had occurred, with some chagrin, to my colonel, Lord Frederick Bentinck, who good-naturedly told me not to take the matter to heart, as it was really of no consequence; and he added—"Depend upon it, Gronow, the Prince, who is a lover of novelty, will wear trousers himself before the year is out, and then you may laugh at him."

Lord Frederick proved a true prophet, for in less than a month I had the satisfaction of seeing "the finest gentleman in Europe" at a ball at Lady Cholmondeley's, dressed exactly as I had been at Lady Hertford's, when I incurred his displeasure, in black trousers and shoes; and Lord Fife, who was in attendance upon the Prince, congratulated me upon the fact that his royal master had deigned to take example by the young Welshman.

THE BRITISH EMBASSY—LORD AND LADY GRAN-VILLE.—The announcement of the lamented death of Lady Granville in the papers the other day, brought to my mind vivid recollections of the palmy days of the British Embassy, and all the blooming happy faces that used to be constantly congregated there; but who are now grown old and careworn, or are lying in the grave, forgotten by those who loved them best, whilst others, fair, young, and happy, reign in their stead. England was never represented more worthily, or with greater magnificence, than by Lord and Lady Granville; though the high post of ambassador to Paris has been occupied by some of the greatest and proudest of our countrymen. The royal pomp of the proud Buckingham, the skill and courage of Stair, the cunning and energy of old Horace Walpole, the splendid prodigality of Lord Albemarle, the firm attitude and dignified bearing of Lord Whitworth, and the master-mind of the Great Duke, have all been displayed upon this most important field of action.

Lord Granville had been ambassador at St. Petersburg in early life, and greatly distinguished himself as an able diplomatist on a most delicate and important mission. He was the *beau-idéal* of a high-bred English nobleman. He was considerably above the middle height, with a figure remarkable for symmetry and grace, which he preserved to an advanced age. His features were regular, and his countenance expressive of mildness and good-nature. He was one of those men who, once seen, leave an impression on the memory: he belonged to a race of gentlemen of the olden time, that seems almost extinct in our present free-and-easy days.

Lady Granville, though she did not possess the

outward advantages of her husband, was considered
his superior in conversational powers, and possessed,
in a high degree, the charm of voice and manner
which belongs to the Cavendish family. She rather
affected a remarkable simplicity in her dress, was
generally attired in black, and would receive her
guests in the plainest of caps, and wrapped up in a
shawl. But, in spite of the homeliness of her costume, figure, and features, there was something in
the *tout ensemble* which spoke of noble blood and
ancient lineage; and her manner of receiving was
perfect. Unlike most of our countrywomen, she was
not subject to fits of caprice; she was perfectly independent, and could afford to form her own opinion,
and act upon it; and if there was a kind and
generous action to be performed, she was sure not
to miss the opportunity of doing it. Through good
report and evil report, she would cleave to those
who had once won her affectionate regard, and without any appearance of patronising, she knew how to
throw the mantle of her loving protection round
those who needed it. At the same time, there was
nothing *banal* in her manner or character. She
had none of that excess of constrained politeness,
which is, in reality, the height of incivility, but was
courteous to all; by her perfect breeding, she constrained the presuming British Gogs and Magogs to
keep at a respectful distance, without ever saying
an unkind word, or showing any symptom of being
ruffled or discomposed.

It was rather amusing, when Lady Granville
first came to Paris, to see some of the *grandes
dames* of the Faubourg St. Germain feeling their
way, and trying whether they could not dictate to

and domineer over the quiet-looking English lady,
who had more wit, and fun, and humour, and cleverness than a dozen of them put together. These
arbiters of fashion soon discovered that they had
found more than their match in Lady Granville,
and that she would have her own list of guests,
choose her own cap and shawl, and settle her arm-
chairs and sofas in her own way, without taking the
advice of a jury of noble matrons, who had hitherto
considered themselves infallible.

The magnificent hospitality of Lord and Lady
Granville, and the great liberality with which the
Embassy was conducted in their time, were the constant theme of conversation and remark. Large
dinners of the most *recherché* kind were constantly given. Small and intimate receptions were
held every Monday, and large ones every Friday;
whilst *déjeûners* and balls on a most magnificent
scale electrified the whole of Parisian society.

When Lord and Lady Granville left Paris there
was a general mourning in the gay world. Their
place in Parisian society has never been filled up,
and they themselves, personally, have never been
forgotten.

HOBY, THE BOOTMAKER, OF ST. JAMES'S STREET.—
Hoby was not only the greatest and most fashionable bootmaker in London, but, in spite of the old
adage, "*ne sutor ultra crepidam*," he employed his
spare time with considerable success as a Methodist
preacher at Islington. He was said to have in his
employment three hundred workmen; and he was
so great a man in his own estimation that he was
apt to take rather an insolent tone with his cus-

tomers. He was, however, tolerated as a sort of privileged person, and his impertinence was not only overlooked, but was considered as rather a good joke. He was a pompous fellow, with a considerable vein of sarcastic humour.

I remember Horace Churchill (afterwards killed in India with the rank of major-general), who was then an ensign in the Guards, entering Hoby's shop in a great passion, saying that his boots were so ill made that he should never employ Hoby for the future. Hoby, putting on a pathetic cast of countenance, called to his shopman—

"John, close the shutters. It is all over with us. I must shut up shop; Ensign Churchill withdraws his custom from me."

Churchill's fury can be better imagined than described.

On another occasion the late Sir John Shelley came into Hoby's shop to complain that his top-boots had split in several places. Hoby quietly said,

"How did that happen, Sir John?"

"Why, in walking to my stable."

"Walking to your stable!" said Hoby, with a sneer. "I made the boots for riding, not walking."

Hoby was bootmaker to the Duke of Kent; and as he was calling on H.R.H. to try on some boots, the news arrived that Lord Wellington had gained a great victory over the French army at Vittoria. The Duke was kind enough to mention the glorious news to Hoby, who coolly said—

"If Lord Wellington had had any other bootmaker than myself, he never would have had his great and constant successes; for my boots and prayers bring his lordship out of all his difficulties."

One may well say that there is nothing like leather; for Hoby died worth a hundred and twenty thousand pounds.

Hoby was bootmaker to George III., the Prince of Wales, the royal dukes, and many officers in the army and navy. His shop was situated at the top of St. James's Street, at the corner of Piccadilly, next to the old Guards' Club. He was bootmaker to the Duke of Wellington from his boyhood, and received innumerable orders in the Duke's handwriting, both from the Peninsula and France, which he always religiously preserved. Hoby was the first man who drove about London in a tilbury. It was painted black, and drawn by a beautiful black cob. This vehicle was built by the inventor, Mr. Tilbury, whose manufactory was, fifty years back, in a street leading from South Audley Street into Park Street.

HAIRDRESSING FIFTY YEARS SINCE, AND VAILS TO SERVANTS.—Nobody in the present day can conceive the inconvenience of our military costume when I first entered the Guards in 1813, or the annoyance to which we were subjected at being constantly obliged to seek the assistance of a *coiffeur* to powder our hair. Our commanding officers were very severe with respect to our dress and powdering; and I remember, when on guard, incurring the heavy displeasure of the late Duke of Cambridge for not having a sufficient quantity of powder on my head, and therefore presenting a somewhat piebald appearance. I received a strong reprimand from H.R.H., and he threatened even to place me under arrest should I ever appear again on guard in what he was pleased to call so

slovenly and disgraceful a condition. The hair-
dresser was not only required at early dawn,
before our field-days or parades, but again in the
evening, if we dined out, or went to parties or
balls.

The most fashionable *coiffeur* was Rowland, or
Rouland, a French *émigré*. His charge for cutting hair was five shillings; and his shop was next
door to the Thatched-House Tavern in St. James's
Street. He was the inventor of the famous Macas-
sar oil, and made a large fortune. He came to
London with the Bourbons on the breaking out of
the French Revolution, and followed them back to
France in 1814. When he died, he left a daughter,
Madame Colombin, the well-known pastry-cook in
the Rue de Luxembourg.

There was another custom in my young days
which has luckily fallen into disuse. If one dined
at any of the great houses in London, it was considered absolutely necessary to give a guinea to the
butler on leaving the house. One hundred and
thirty years ago this very bad habit (as I always
considered it) prevailed to an even greater extent;
for Pope the poet, whenever he dined with the
Duke of Montagu, finding that he had to give five
guineas to the numerous servants at Montagu
House, told the Duke that he could not dine with
him in future unless his grace sent him five guineas
to distribute among his myrmidons. The Duke, an
easy, good-natured man, used ever after, on sending
an invitation to the great poet, to enclose at the
same time an order for the tribute-money: he preferred doing this to breaking through a custom
which had grown to be looked upon by servants as

a right, and the abolition of which they would have considered as a heavy grievance.

TWISLETON FIENNES, THE LATE LORD SAYE AND SELE.—Twisleton Fiennes was a very eccentric man, and the greatest epicure of his day. His dinners were worthy of the days of Vitellius or Heliogabalus. Every country, every sea, was searched and ransacked to find some new delicacy for our British Sybarite. I remember, at one of his breakfasts, an omelette being served which was composed entirely of golden pheasants' eggs! He had a very strong constitution, and would drink absinthe and curaçoa in quantities which were perfectly awful to behold. These stimulants produced no effect upon his brain; but his health gradually gave way under the excesses of all kinds in which he indulged. He was a kind, liberal, and good-natured man, but a very odd fellow. I never shall forget the astonishment of a servant I had recommended to him. On entering his service, John made his appearance as Fiennes was going out to dinner, and asked his new master if he had any orders. He received the following answer,—"Place two bottles of sherry by my bed-side, and call me the day after to-morrow."

BURIED ALIVE.—In the retreat of the French army from Moscow, the brave General d'Ornano, a Corsican, second husband of the beautiful Comtesse Walewska, and a distant relation of the Buonaparte family, received a severe wound from the bursting of a shell, which killed his horse and several soldiers who were near him. The General's aide-de-camp, on looking round, observed d'Ornano lying on his back, to all appearance dead, with the blood flowing from his mouth. A surgeon soon arrived, and declared that life was extinct. The aide-de-camp and a few soldiers commenced digging a grave ; but the ground was so hard, owing to the terrible cold which prevailed, that they could not make it deep enough to cover the body, and, being pressed for time, they collected snow instead of earth, arranged the supposed corpse in decent order, and covered it with snow. After this had been done, the aide-de-camp reported to the Emperor Napoleon, who was not far off, the loss the army had sustained in the death of General d'Ornano. He was only twenty-six years of age, and the youngest officer of his rank in the army.

The Emperor, who was very fond of the General, was deeply grieved, and exclaimed—

"Poor fellow ! he was one of my best cavalry officers !" and, turning to one of his orderlies, desired him to go immediately and find out all about the wound which had caused his death. The officer, in order to satisfy himself on this point, had the supposed corpse taken out of the snow, and, on looking at the wound, observed that the body was still warm, and the General consequently could not be dead. Furs and flannels were, at the officer's suggestion, heaped upon the corpse, which was then placed upon a stretcher, and taken to headquarters ; after much care and perseverance, he was restored to life, to the great joy of the Emperor, and the whole army. General d'Ornano is now a marshal of France, and governor of the Invalides, and related the above anecdote to one of my friends last summer.

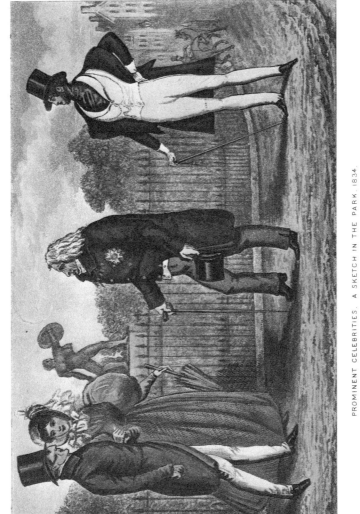

PROMINENT CELEBRITIES.   A SKETCH IN THE PARK 1834.

THE DUKE OF WELLINGTON   MRS ARBUTHNOT.   PRINCE TALLEYRAND   COUNT D'ORSAY.

COUNT D'ORSAY.—In speaking of this gifted and accomplished man, I shall strictly confine myself, as I have done in other instances, to his public character, and not enter into the details of his private life ; which are, perhaps, better left in the shade. I first saw him at an evening party given in 1816, by his grandmother, the well-known Madame Crawford, in the Rue d'Anjou Saint Honoré. He was then sixteen years old, and he appeared to be a general favourite, owing to his remarkable beauty and pleasing manners. His father and mother were both present, and did me the honour to invite me to their house in the Rue du Mont Blanc, now called the Rue de la Chaussée d'Antin. They occupied the apartment in which the celebrated composer Rossini now lives. D'Orsay's father, justly surnamed " Le Beau d'Orsay," was one of the handsomest men in the French army ; he was one of Napoleon's generals, and distinguished himself in Spain, particularly at the battle of Salamanca.

I believe, and I like to think, that had Count d'Orsay fallen into good hands, he might have been a great many things that he was not. Unfortunate circumstances, which entangled him as with a fatal web from his early youth, dragged him downwards and led him step by step to his ruin. On these peculiar circumstances, I shall not dwell. They are known to all, and cannot be palliated. But he was a grand creature in spite of all this ; beautiful as the Apollo Belvidere in his outward form, full of health, life, spirits, wit, and gaiety, radiant and joyous, the admired of all admirers :—such was D'Orsay when I first knew him. If the Count had been born with a fortune of a hundred thousand pounds a year, he would have been a great man. He loved money, not for money's sake, but for what it could procure. He was generous even to ostentation, and he had a real pleasure in giving even what he himself had borrowed. He was born with princely tastes and ideas, and would have heartily despised a man who could have sat down contented in a simple dwelling-place, with a bad cook and a small competence.

He possessed in a great degree the faculty of pleasing those whom he wished to attract. His smile was bright and genial, his manner full of charm, his conversation original and amusing, and his artistic taste undeniable. It might have been objected that this taste was somewhat too gaudy; but the brilliant tints with which he liked to surround himself suited his style of beauty, his dress, and manner. When I used to see him driving in his tilbury some thirty years ago, I fancied that he looked like some gorgeous dragon-fly skimming through the air; and though all was dazzling and showy, yet there was a kind of harmony which precluded any idea or accusation of bad taste. All his imitators fell between the Scylla and Charybdis of tigerism and charlatanism; but he escaped those quicksands, though, perhaps, somewhat narrowly, and in spite of a gaudy and almost eccentric style of dress.

Many of his *bons mots* and clever sayings have been cited by his numerous friends and admirers; but perhaps there was more humour and *à propos* in the majority of them than actual wit. There was also much in his charming manner, and the very successful mixture of French and English which he had adopted in conversation. I call to mind a story of him not generally known. When he first came to England as a very young man, and was about twenty-two years of age, he was invited to dine at Holland House, where he was seated next to Lady Holland herself, who supposed that the handsome stranger was a shy young man, awe-struck by her majestic selfishness. Owing to a considerable abdominal development, her ladyship was continually letting her napkin slip from her lap to the ground, and as often as she did so, she smiled blandly, but authoritatively, on the French Count, and asked him to pick it up. He politely complied several times, but, at last, tired of this exercise, he said, to her great surprise, "*Ne ferais-je pas mieux, Madame, de m'asseoir sous la table, afin de pouvoir vous passer la serviette plus rapidement?*"

On another occasion, the well-known Tom Raikes, whose letters and memoirs have been lately published, and who was a tall, large man, very much marked with the small-pox, having one day written an anonymous letter to D'Orsay, containing some piece of impertinence or other, had closed it with a wafer, and stamped it with something resembling the top of a thimble. The Count soon discovered who was the writer, and in a room full of company thus addressed him—"Ha! ha! my good Raikes, the next time you write an anonymous letter, you must not seal it with your nose!"

I cannot conclude without giving some description of the personal appearance of one who reigned pre-eminent in the fashionable circles of London and Paris. He was rather above six feet in height, and when I first knew him, he might have served as a model for a statuary. His neck was long, his

shoulders broad, and his waist narrow, and though
he was, perhaps, somewhat underlimbed, nothing
could surpass the beauty of his feet and ankles.
His dark chestnut hair hung naturally in long
waving curls; his forehead was high and wide, his
features regular, and his complexion glowed with
radiant health. His eyes were large and of a light
hazel colour, he had full lips and very white teeth,
but a little apart; which sometimes gave to the
generally amiable expression of his countenance a
rather cruel and sneering look, such as one sees in
the heads of some of the old Roman emperors. He
was wonderfully strong and active, and excelled in
manly exercises. He was a fine horseman, a good
swordsman, and a fair shot. I knew him intimately,
and saw a great deal of him. He had an amusing
naïveté in speaking of his own personal advantages.

I remember on one occasion, when about to fight
a duel, he said to his second, Monsieur D * * *, who
was making the preliminary arrangements, "You
know, my dear friend, I am not on a par with my
antagonist: he is a very ugly fellow, and if I wound
him in the face, he won't look much the worse for it;
but on my side it ought to be agreed that he should
not aim higher than my chest, for if my face should
be spoiled, '*ce serait vraiment dommage.*'" He said
this with such a beaming smile, and looked so handsome and happy, that his friend, Monsieur D * * *,
fully agreed with him.

Though his tastes, pursuits, and habits were
thoroughly manly, yet he took as much care of his
beauty as a woman might have done. He was in
the habit of taking perfumed baths, and his friends

remember the enormous gold dressing-case, which it required two men to carry, and which used to be the companion of all his excursions. Peace be to his ashes! it will be long before the world looks upon his like again.

THE SPAFIELDS RIOTS.—The years 1816 and 1817 were a most dangerous period. The spirit of the people of England, exasperated by heavy taxation, the high price of bread, and many iniquitous laws and restrictions now happily done away with by successive liberal administrations, was of the worst possible nature. In the riots and meetings of those troublous times, the mob really meant mischief; and had they been accustomed to the use of arms, and well drilled, they might have committed as great excesses as the ruffians of 1793 in France.

On the 15th November 1816, a monster meeting was held in Spafields, to petition the Prince Regent. Early in the morning of that day, I was sent with a company of the Guards to occupy the prison of Spafields, and to act, if necessary, in aid and support of the civil power. On our arrival, we found that a troop of horse artillery, with their guns, had already taken up their position within the yard. We lost no time in making loopholes in the walls, in the event of an attack from without, and made ready for action. The mob, which was not very numerous on our arrival, had by this time increased to an enormous multitude. Sixty or seventy thousand persons must have been present. Their principal leaders appeared to be Major Cartwright, Gale Jones, and the notorious Henry Hunt, the blacking-maker. The major was an old, grey-headed,

vulgar-looking man. Hunt was a large, powerfully made fellow, who might have been taken for
a butcher : he always wore a white hat, which was,
I never knew why, in those days supposed to be an
emblem of very advanced liberal, or even republican
opinions. These two demagogues, and two or three
more of the leaders of the mob, got into a cart, that
had been brought up as a sort of tribune or rostrum,
from which they harangued the people. More violent
and treasonable discourses it was impossible to make;
and the huge multitude rent the air with their shouts
of applause.

After a time, a magistrate and some constables
appeared, and summoned the people to disperse ;
and, at the same moment, a messenger arrived from
the prison, who whispered in Hunt's ear that if the
mob committed any outrage, or made any disturbance, and did not quietly disperse, they would be
dealt with by the soldiers, who had orders above
all to pick off the ringleaders, should any attack be
made upon the prison. This intelligence, conveyed
to the gentlemen in the cart by one of their friends,
produced a very marked effect. In a very short
time they got down, as they seemed to consider
themselves in rather an exposed position, declared
the meeting at an end, and hurried off, leaving the
crowd to follow them; which they shortly afterwards did.

Several years after this event, at the time of the
Reform Bill, Hunt was elected member of Parliament for Preston, beating Mr. Stanley, the present
Earl of Derby, and I was elected for the immaculate
borough of Stafford. I well recollect, but cannot
describe, the amazement of the blacking-man when

I told him one evening, in the smoking-room of the House of Commons, that if any attack had been made upon the prison at Spafields, I had given my men orders to pick off Major Cartwright, himself, and one or two more who were in the cart. Hunt was perfectly astonished. He became very red, and his eyes seemed to flash fire.

"What sir! do you mean to say you would have been capable of such an act of barbarity?"

"Yes," said I; "and I almost regret you did not give us the opportunity, for your aim that day was to create a revolution, and you would have richly deserved the fate which you so narrowly escaped by the cowardice or lukewarmness of your followers."

MAD AS A HATTER.—Towards the close of the year 1848, it was my good fortune, during a residence of some weeks at Brighton, to see a good deal of my old acquaintance, Lord Alvanley. Though he was then very ill, and suffering great pain, I never knew him in better spirits, more full of brilliant flashes of wit and amusing anecdotes.

On one occasion I happened to call at his house with my old commanding-officer, Arthur Upton, when in the course of a conversation on France, he asked my opinion on the revolution, and of Prince Louis Napoleon's chance of being named President of the Republic. Alvanley informed us that he had not very long before passed some days with the Prince at Colonel Dawson Damer's country seat, and he observed that he had never met with a more agreeable person; that the Prince was very communicative, and would sit up smoking ciga-

rettes till two or three o'clock in the morning; and
that upon one occasion, in a long political discus-
sion, he had said, among other things—

"It is fated that ere long I shall become Emperor
of France, avenge the defeat of Waterloo, and drive
the Austrians out of Italy; and the time for this is
not far distant."

On the following morning, Lord Alvanley related
what he had heard to Colonel Damer, who observed—

"Prince Louis is a charming person—so gentlemanlike and pleasing in manner, so accomplished
and well-informed. He has a thousand good and
agreeable qualities, but on the subject of politics,
my dear Alvanley, he is as mad as a hatter!"

HARRINGTON HOUSE AND LORD PETERSHAM.—
When our army returned to England in 1814, my
young friend, Augustus Stanhope, took me one afternoon to Harrington House, in Stableyard, St. James's,
where I was introduced to Lord and Lady Harrington, and all the Stanhopes. On entering a long
gallery, I found the whole family engaged in their
sempiternal occupation of tea-drinking. Neither in
Nankin, Pekin, nor Canton was the teapot more
assiduously and constantly replenished than at this
hospitable mansion. I was made free of the corporation, if I may use the phrase, by a cup being
handed to me; and I must say that I never tasted
any tea so good before or since.

As an example of the undeviating tea-table habits
of the house of Harrington, General Lincoln Stanhope once told me, that after an absence of several
years in India, he made his reappearance at Harrington House, and found the family, as he had left

them on his departure, drinking tea in the long gallery. On his presenting himself, his father's only observation and speech of welcome to him was, " Hallo, Linky, my dear boy ! delighted to see you. Have a cup of tea ? "

I was then taken to Lord Petersham's apartments, where we found his lordship, one of the chief dandies of the day, employed in making a particular sort of blacking, which he said would eventually supersede every other. The room into which we were ushered was more like a shop than a gentleman's sitting-room : all round the walls were shelves, upon which were placed tea-canisters, containing Congou, Pekoe, Souchong, Bohea, Gunpowder, Russian, and many other teas, all the best of the kind ; on the other side of the room were beautiful jars, with names, in gilt letters, of innumerable kinds of snuff, and all the necessary apparatus for moistening and mixing. Lord Petersham's mixture is still well known to all tobacconists. Other shelves and many of the tables were covered with a great number of magnificent snuff-boxes ; for Lord Petersham had perhaps the finest collection in England, and was supposed to have a fresh box for every day in the year. I heard him, on the occasion of a delightful old light-blue Sèvres box he was using being admired, say, in his lisping way—" Yes, it is a nice summer box, but would not do for winter wear."

In this museum there were also innumerable canes of very great value. The Viscount was likewise a great Mæcenas among the tailors, and a particular kind of great-coat, when I was a young man, was called a Petersham.

In person, Lord Petersham was tall and handsome, and possessed a particularly winning smile. He very much resembled the pictures of Henry IV. of France, and frequently wore a dress not unlike that of the celebrated monarch. His carriages were unique of their kind: they were entirely brown, with brown horses and harness. The groom, a tall youth, was dressed in a long brown coat reaching to his heels, and a glazed hat with a large cockade. It is said that Lord Petersham's devotion to brown was caused by his having been desperately in love with a very beautiful widow bearing that name.

In addition to his other eccentricities, Lord Petersham never ventured out of doors till six P.M. His manners were decidedly affected, and he spoke with a kind of lisp; but in spite of his little foibles, Lord Petersham was a thorough gentleman, and was beloved by all who knew him.

TOWNSHEND, THE BOW-STREET OFFICER.—Townshend, the famous Bow-Street officer, when I knew him, was a little fat man with a flaxen wig, kerseymere breeches, a blue straight-cut coat, and a broad-brimmed white hat. To the most daring courage he added great dexterity and cunning; and was said, *in propriâ personâ*, to have taken more thieves than all the other Bow-Street officers put together. He frequently accompanied mail-coaches when the Government required large sums of money to be conveyed to distant parts of the country.

Upon one occasion, when Townshend was to act as escort to a carriage going to Reading, he took with him the famous Joe Manton, the gunmaker, who was always ready for a lark, and was as brave as steel. Soon after reaching Hounslow three footpads stopped the coach, and Joe Manton was preparing to try the effect of one of his deadly barrels upon them, when Townshend cried out—" Stop, Joe, don't fire!—let me talk to the gentlemen." The moment the robbers heard Townshend's voice they took to their heels; but he had been able to identify them, and a few months afterwards they were taken, tried, and, upon Townshend's evidence, sent to Botany Bay.

The short, corpulent police-officer was, for his daring exploits and general good conduct, selected by the Home Office to attend at drawing-rooms, levees, and all state occasions; and he became a kind of personage, and was much noticed by the Royal Family and the great people of the day: every one went up to speak to Townshend. He was eccentric and amusing, and somewhat inclined to take advantage of the familiarity with which he was treated; but he was a sort of privileged person, and could say what he liked.

On one occasion the Duke of Clarence recommended Townshend to publish his memoirs, which he thought would be very interesting. Townshend, who had become somewhat deaf, seemed rather surprised, but said he would obey H.R.H.'s commands. A few weeks afterwards, Townshend was on duty at Carlton House, when the Duke asked him if he had fulfilled his promise. His answer was—

" O sir, you've got me into a devil of a scrape! I had begun to write my *amours*, as you desired, when Mrs. Townshend caught me in the act of writing them, and swore she'd be revenged; for you know, your Royal Highness, I was obliged to divulge many secrets about women, for which she'll never forgive me."

When the Duke of Clarence became king, and was going down to prorogue Parliament, the Master of the Horse had not got the state carriage ready in time; and the King, in a fit of anger against Lord Albemarle, swore he would order a hackney-coach and go to the House in that humble vehicle. Upon which Townshend, to the amazement of every one, cried out from behind a screen—

"Well said, sir; I think your Majesty is d——d right." The King, very much surprised and amused, called out—

"Is that you, Townshend?"

"Yes, sir; I am here to see that your Majesty has fair play!"

At one of Queen Charlotte's drawing-rooms—I think the last before her death, which was held at old Buckingham House—an immense crowd assembled, and in going up the stairs much confusion arose among the ladies; for as no order was kept, and every one wished to get first into the presence of royalty, much rushing and squeezing took place, loud shrieks were heard, and several ladies fainted.

I was on guard on that day, and doing what I could to preserve order, when Townshend called out to me to conduct a foreign lady, who had fallen and nearly fainted on the staircase, to the top of the landing-place. I did so, and brought her into the presence of the Queen; when a gentleman, in very good English, thanked me for the courtesy I had shown to his wife, the Duchess of Orleans (afterwards Queen Marie Amélie).

MADEMOISELLE DUTHÉ. — This celebrated courtesan, whose fame in the days of the grandfathers of
the present generation equalled the renown of the
Laises or Phrynes of ancient Greece, or that of the
Imperias and Marozias of the Rome of the Middle
Ages, lived with great splendour and magnificence
in Paris before the first French Revolution. The
old Lord Egremont, a man of immense wealth, who
had then lately come of age, and the Count d'Artois,
afterwards Charles X., were rivals in her affections,
and vied with each other in the most reckless prodigality. Her splendid mansion, and her carriages,
which were covered with gold, and drawn by eight
cream-coloured horses, were the admiration of all
Paris. When the Revolution broke out in France,
this fair and frail beauty took example from her
betters, and emigrated to England.

Mademoiselle Duthé was the idol of the young
men of fashion ; and from the pictures of her at
this time, she must have been surpassingly beautiful.
Her principal admirers in England were Bob Byng,
brother of old Byng, for so many years member
for Middlesex, Perregaux, the rich banker, who had
emigrated, and Mr. Lee. The younger brother of
the latter gentleman acted the part of master of the
ceremonies to the fair Frenchwoman, gave her his
arm in all the public promenades, and escorted her to
the play and opera on all occasions. The elder Lee,
her favoured inamorato, though dotingly fond of her,
would never appear with her in public.

The Duke of Queensberry, so well known by
the name of old Q, and who was a great friend
of Mademoiselle Duthé (as he was of all persons
eminent in that lady's profession), asked her the

meaning of her conduct with respect to the two
brothers. She replied, with unblushing effrontery,
"The younger Lee is '*mon Lit de parade;*' the
elder, '*mon Lit de repos.*'"

On the restoration of the Bourbons, Mademoiselle
Duthé, in possession of a considerable fortune, but
no longer beautiful and young, returned to Paris,
and resided at a fine house in the Rue Marbœuf, in
the Champs Elysées. One of the famous gilt carriages given her by Lord Egremont again figured
in the public promenades; but, instead of being
admired, was much laughed at, as the style and
shape were quite out of fashion. At her death it
was sold to the elder Franconi, for theatrical performances.

Mademoiselle Duthé, in addition to a beautiful
face, was supposed to have the finest figure in the
world. A picture of her is extant, which I have
seen. It was painted by one of the first artists in
France. She is represented in all the glory of her
youth and beauty, at full length, reclining on a
couch, very much in the costume of our mother
Eve. She is said to have been full of wit and
cleverness, and possessed a fund of curious anecdotes about everything and everybody.

Mr. Lee, whose fortune was much injured by her
extravagance, bade her farewell in a single Latin
line, which he told her her friend the Duke of
Queensberry, of whom he was rather jealous, would
translate; it was, "*Non possum te cum vivere, nec
sine te.*"

A STRANGE RENCONTRE.—In the spring of 1815
—I think it was in the month of March—when the

Duke of York was returning from the theatre, accompanied by Mrs. Johnstone, the actress, his carriage broke down in the Strand, opposite to the Government engraver's, Mr. Sylvester's; who, perceiving a crowd assembled, went out, and knowing the lady, offered her and the royal Duke refuge until the servant brought a coach for them.

Mrs. Sylvester, hearing the noise in the street, left her drawing-room, where there was a small evening concert, to see what had happened, when, to her surprise, she recognised her friend Mrs. Johnstone. After some whispering between them, and after some hesitation, the Duke of York said—

"With the permission of Mrs. Sylvester, we will go upstairs."

Accordingly they proceeded to the drawing-room, where, to the Duke's astonishment, he was received by his brother, the Duke of Sussex, who was listening to the singing of his friend, the famous Mrs. Billington. The two royal brothers had not for some time before been on speaking terms; but this sudden rencontre was the means of reconciling them, and they ever after had a most affectionate and brotherly regard for one another.

Mrs. Sylvester, *née* Price, was a lady of an ancient Welsh family, the niece of the celebrated Dr. Price, the great calculator. She was handsome and accomplished. I had the honour to know her, and it was from her lips I received the above rather curious anecdote.

ADMIRAL SIR RICHARD STRACHAN.—This brave sailor was famous for many daring actions and gallant feats of arms ; but will perhaps be best known to posterity by the celebrated verses on the Walcheren expedition :—

> "Sir Richard, longing to be at 'em,
> Was waiting for the Earl of Chatham ;
> The Earl of Chatham, *all forlorn*,
> Was waiting for Sir Richard Strachan !"

In the piping times of peace, when there was no longer any hostile fleet to watch, or stray French squadron to capture, the veteran turned his whole attention to the worship and admiration of the fair sex ; and displayed the same ardour in the pursuit of a pretty girl or handsome matron, as he had formerly shown in the chase of a fine frigate or tight little schooner. His field of action, which had once been the Channel, the North Sea, or the Mediterranean, was now confined to Bond Street, Piccadilly, or the squares and parks. He always rode a grey horse ; and the "Old Admiral" was as well known to the Londoners of his day as the Iron Duke was to every one in town some twenty or thirty years ago.

In his sixty-first year, Sir Richard fell desperately in love with a young girl, daughter of a man who kept a china shop in South Audley Street; and, though married and the father of a large family, he persecuted this young beauty with his attentions from morning till night. He would pass and repass the house where her father lived at least a hundred times a day, and send her gigantic bouquets and presents without number.

These proceedings created much scandal in the neighbourhood, and the father of the girl was determined to put a stop to the admiral's wicked design to run off with his daughter. It had been proposed by Sir Richard to the fair Sophy R * * * that she was to meet him at nine P.M. opposite Fladong's Hotel, where a carriage and four would be in readiness. She appeared to agree to this proposal; but the admiral, on arriving at the place of rendezvous, found, instead of the girl, her father and brother armed with bludgeons, with which they belaboured him to their hearts' content. The old Lovelace defended himself as best he could till the watchmen in the neighbourhood came to the rescue, and took all parties to Marlborough Street, where they remained in durance vile during the night.

The following morning, they were brought before the magistrate, who was proceeding to interrogate them, when Admiral Lord Gardner entered to swear an affidavit: and perceiving Sir Richard in a miserable plight, and surrounded by a motley crew, exclaimed, in true melodramatic style—"What do I see! Dicky Strachan a prisoner, and his colours struck! impossible—impossible!"

The magistrate begged an explanation of what had occurred on the previous night, when Sir Richard stated that he had been attacked and severely beaten by two men with bludgeons; but he refused to swear that the persons present were the culprits, for the night was dark, and he could not identify them. In short, though he had been so badly treated, the gallant veteran would not say a word against the father and brother of his beloved Sophy. The father, however, carried his point, for the admiral ceased cruising in the " china " seas, and the gallant grey and his rider were never again seen in the neighbourhood of South Audley Street.

THE BONAPARTE FAMILY.—It was my good fortune, during a winter at Rome, to come into contact with several members of this illustrious family, then in exile. I have had the honour of being introduced to Madame Mère (as the mother of the great Napoleon was called); and have often met La Reine Hortense, mother of Napoleon III. (she was then styled Duchesse de St. Leu), in her promenades on the Monte Pincio, or the gardens of the various palaces open to the public.

I have also seen at Rome Jérôme Bonaparte, ex-king of Wesphalia, with his devoted wife, a daughter of the King of Wurtemberg: she remained faithful and true to her exiled husband, when no stone was left unturned in the political world to make her withdraw her allegiance from him. Le Roi Jérôme, as he was generally called, was at the time of which I write a very handsome man, bearing a striking resemblance to his brother the Emperor Napoleon. He had the same deep-set eye, the square, massive jaw, the broad, thoughtful brow, the pallid complexion, the delicately-formed white hand, but he was a good deal taller and slighter.

The ex-queen was a true German in appearance, fat, fair, and forty, with that good-natured *ménagère* look which is a characteristic of the Teutonic race. Under that calm housewife-like exterior, you would never have supposed her to be the enduring, heroic wife and mother. If report speaks true, her early married life with her handsome but fickle spouse had not been a happy one; and many thought that the neglected wife and injured queen might not be sorry to revenge herself when the tables turned in 1815. But those who thus judged, little knew that noble-hearted princess, who, in the days of adversity, clung yet more faithfully to the husband of her youth; and if she failed to make Le Roi Jérôme a constant husband, there can be no doubt that she won his esteem and affection.

The palace occupied by the ex-king and queen was one of the finest in Rome. Strangers were permitted to visit it, and gazed with a melancholy interest on the various relics of departed greatness which the splendid apartments contained. I remember being particularly struck by some exquisite likenesses of the Princess Pauline Borghese, whose perfect beauty, both of face and figure, has gone down to posterity, thanks to Canova's immortal statue of her! Some of her old admirers, who are still alive, affirm that the only woman whose beauty can be compared to the Princess Pauline's is the Countess Castiglione, and that the one is as vain and capricious as was the other.

Madame Mère was the very living image of the statue Canova made of her. Her features were classical, her eyes large and expressive, and her bearing full of imperial dignity and grace. There was no pride in her manner, but you saw the consciousness of greatness—the stately calm as of the reflected light from her son's glory.

Whatever La Reine Hortense might have been in youth, when I saw her she was no longer handsome; and, to say the honest truth, I must confess that I have my doubts as to her ever having been remarkable for personal attractions. But the charm of her manners, and the grace of every movement, were indisputable facts: and I think she has transmitted to her son, Napoleon III., much of that

peculiar fascination which has subjugated and gained
over to him so many hostile spirits.

The Duchesse de St. Leu was universally allowed
to be one of the most accomplished and amiable
women of her day. Her voice, though not very
powerful, was extremely sweet, and her musical taste
and science were remarkable : she drew beautifully
also, and possessed an album filled with likenesses
taken by herself. Her conversation was pleasant
and piquant, without the slightest mixture of male-
volence or ill-nature ; her tact was exquisite ; and
her generosity unequalled. During the whole time
of her prosperity, it may be safely said that she
never made a single enemy ; and she bore her adversity with a dignity and unrepining simplicity
beyond all praise. She well deserved the almost
idolatrous devotion and reverence with which her
son cherishes the memory of his most amiable and
excellent mother.

Louis, the ex-king of Holland, I once saw at
Florence, and he struck me as being a heavy and
unintellectual-looking man. Joseph, the ex-king of
Spain, must, in his youth, have been very handsome ;
but he had a listless and weak expression of countenance, which accorded well with his character.
As to the Emperor himself, he was pointed out to
me, at a distance, on the field of Waterloo ; but
beyond a white horse and a dark coat, I could see
nothing, and I never had another opportunity of
beholding him.

All anecdotes of this great man are interesting,
and I heard a few details respecting him in 1820,
from an intimate friend of mine, the late Count
B * * *, who was one of his household for many

years, and which I do not remember to have seen
published. The Emperor, said the Count, though
at times very magnificent, and knowing (as his
nephew does) how to reward services done to the
country, was a man of much order in all his domestic arrangements, and would not allow certain sums,
which he had laid down and allotted for special purposes, to be exceeded upon any account. He knew
to a penny what was spent every day in his household. He gave one hundred francs for his own
food, which was very simple, and allowed the Grand
Maréchal of the palace, General Bertrand, twenty
francs a head for the persons who dined habitually
at his table, and forty francs for those whom the
Emperor invited to dinner. Napoleon generally
dined alone, except on Sundays, when some of the
most favoured members of his family were admitted
to his table. A roast fowl was kept continually
ready for his dinner, as the great man rarely dined
at the same hour, and when he ordered dinner, expected it to be served immediately. His beverage
was Chambertin and water.

With his abstemious habits, and a mind and body
in constant activity, he did not merit the infliction
of growing fat, which he suffered from during the
last years of his life.

The Emperor allowed no one to approach him too
familiarly, and ought, therefore, to have treated his
inferiors with deference ; but good-breeding was not
the Emperor's *forte*, and he was accustomed to see
his playful pinches received by his courtiers (and no
prince ever had more servile ones) as the highest
earthly favour. One day he so far forgot himself
as to try the unpleasant caress of ear-pinching on

Dr. Hallé, one of the luminaries of medical science. The doctor, more surprised than flattered at this pungent mark of imperial favour, observed, with dignity—

"*Sire, vous me faites beaucoup de mal.*" This remark, made respectfully but firmly, prevented a repetition of this unpleasant liberty.

One of the great ladies of the Faubourg St. Germain, whose son held a place in the imperial household, was obliged once or twice a year to put in an appearance, and make her courtesy to the Emperor and Empress. Napoleon, on one of these occasions, after fixing his eagle glance upon the lady, said, in an irritated voice—

"*Je sais que vous ne m'aimez pas.*"

The lady, with much presence of mind, replied, "*Sire, je ne suis encore qu'à l'admiration.*"

Napoleon I. had not the courtesy and perfect breeding of the present Emperor. He took a spiteful pleasure in embarrassing women by disagreeable questions and remarks in public; and the kind and gentle Josephine had often much to do in healing the wounds her husband had made. However, it sometimes happened that the rude question or remark made in public was followed up by some private message of quite another nature. It has been supposed by many that the hatred with which Napoleon hunted down the beautiful Madame Récamier, took its first origin in the admiration her beauty had inspired, and his displeasure at seeing his addresses rejected. Just as the famous Madame de Staël's anger against him, the "*spretæ injuria formæ,*" originated in the disdain with which he met her marked advances.

THE EMPEROR NAPOLEON I. AT THE HEAD OF HIS STAFF.

But, in spite of these spots on the sun, one may say of Napoleon I. what Bolingbroke said of the Duke of Marlborough, " He was so great a man, that I have forgotten all his faults."

PARIS AFTER THE PEACE.—In 1815 and the following years there were gathered together in Paris all the flower of English society—men of fashion and distinction, beautiful matrons and their still lovelier daughters. A history of all that occurred in those days would afford amusing materials for the pen of the novelist, and tickle agreeably the ears of scandal-loving people. I shall, however, content myself with recording some of my own *souvenirs*.

Lord Castlereagh was the pre-eminent star of the autumn of 1815,—"the observed of all observers." He was here, there, and everywhere. Indeed, the mass of business he had to transact was so immense, and the fatigue he had to undergo so great, that he was compelled to spend several hours each day in a bath; his nights being generally passed without sleep. His bath was always taken at the Bains Chinois, at the corner of the Rue de la Michodière. He was there shampooed by the celebrated Fleury, and recruited his exhausted faculties by dozing for an hour or two. His favourite promenade was the gallery of the Palais Royal. In his walks he was almost always alone, and used to dress very simply, never wearing any orders or decorations. On the other hand, Lady Castlereagh astonished the French by the magnificence of her diamonds. At the balls and parties she used to be followed about by envious women, affecting to admire, but looking daggers all the while. On one occasion I heard a French lady exclaim, "England is renowned for beautiful women ; but when they are ugly, '*elles ne le sont pas à demi.*'" But this remark was as false as it was ill-natured, for Lady Castlereagh was rather handsome than otherwise.

The magnificent saloons of the *noblesse* in the Faubourg St. Germain, and the gorgeous *hôtels* of the ambassadors and ministers of the Allied Powers, were thronged with fair ladies of all nations. Madame Edmond de Périgord, who died lately as Duchesse de Sagan, was remarkable for her wit and beauty. She was all-powerful with her uncle, Prince Talleyrand, and was a sort of queen in the diplomatic world. The Vicomtesse de Noailles was the Lady Jersey of the world of fashion, and though her face was not pretty, she, by her graceful *tournure*, skilful *toilette*, and clever conversation, drew after her a host of admirers. I might also name the Princesse de Beauveau and her daughters, the Comtesse d'Audenarde, with her splendid figure, Madame de Vaudreuil, with her handsome face and beautiful hands, the handsome Madame de Gourieff, the two Countesses Potoska, and, though last, not least in my recollection, the lovely Princess Bagration, with her fair hair and delicately-formed figure. The Princess never wore anything but white India muslin, clinging to her form and revealing it in all its perfection.

Among the English beauties were Lady Conyngham, and her daughter, Lady Elizabeth ; Lady Oxford, and her three daughters ; Lady Sydney Smith, and her two beautiful relatives, the Misses Rumbold : one of whom, when already in the " sere and yellow leaf" of old‑maidism, married Baron

Le Bon Genre, N.º 68.

Costumes Anglais.

Delmar, a rich banker, and, puffed up with *par-venu* pride, ruled over Parisian society with a rod of iron.

The Duke of Devonshire, then young, graceful, and distinguished, was hunted down by mothers and daughters with an activity, zeal, and perseverance—and, I am sorry to add, a vulgarity—which those only can conceive who have beheld the British huntress in full cry after a duke. It was amusing to see how the ambitious matrons watched every movement, and how furious they became if any other girl was more favoured than their own daughters by the attention of the monarch of the Peak. The young ladies, on their side, would not engage themselves with any one until all hope of the Duke asking them to dance was at an end. But as soon as he had selected a partner, the same young ladies would go in search of those whom they had rejected, and endeavour to get opposite or somewhere near him.

I remember seeing a serious quarrel between two great ladies, who were only prevented from coming to extremities by the timely intervention of our ambassadress, Lady Elizabeth Stuart. There were at this time many men of rank and fortune among our countrymen—Lords Surrey, Sunderland, Grosvenor, Clare ; Messrs. Beaumont, Leigh, Montague, Standish, &c. Some of these were particular in their attentions to Lady Elizabeth Conyngham, but her mother, who was bent on securing a ducal coronet for her handsome daughter, discouraged all attempts that were made in less high quarters. Rumour had even then whispered that, owing to family secrets of a very peculiar nature, the Duke of Devonshire had entered into a solemn engagement never to marry; and though I have reason to believe that this was entirely false, it is certain that he lived and died a bachelor. Besides this, he was always considered by those who knew him well to be very unlikely to fall in love with any one.

While the Duke was being made up to in this very marked manner, Lord Sunderland (the late Duke of Marlborough) fell desperately in love with Lady E*** C***, and proposed to her. Lady C*** refused him, giving as a pretext her daughter's extreme youth; but in reality, hoping against hope, that the besieged Duke of Devonshire would surrender and propose. But whilst the worthy Marchioness was indulging in these matrimonial dreams, "the favourite bolted," and a few years after, Lady E*** C*** married Lord Strathaven (now Marquis of Huntly), a very handsome man, and was till her lamented death universally beloved and esteemed by all who knew her.

About this time (but I may sometimes make a mistake in the exact date of my *souvenirs*) the Duke of Gloucester arrived in Paris. He made himself conspicuous in aiding the elopement of Mr. (afterwards Sir Charles) Shakerly with Mademoiselle d'Avaray, daughter of the Duke d'Avaray, an intimate friend of Louis XVIII. The young lady was only seventeen years of age, and very handsome. It was the only case I remember of a young French lady running away from her father's house, and the sensation created by such an extraordinary occurrence was very great. The marriage, as runaway marriages usually are, was a very unhappy one; and the quarrels of the ill-matched couple were so violent that the police had to interfere. Unfortunately the fair lady having once eloped, thought she might try the same experiment a second time, and one cold winter's night she decamped from a ball at the Austrian ambassador's, with a black-haired Spanish Don, the Marquis d'Errara.

THE OPERA IN PARIS IN 1815. — The English flocked to the opera, and occupied some of the best boxes. The *corps de ballet* was at that time very efficient, and possessed some of the handsomest women and best dancers in Europe. This reminds me of an amusing incident. General D * * *, a fine old veteran of the empire, and an *habitué* of the *coulisses* at the time I speak of, asked me a few years since to accompany him to the opera, which, from a prolonged absence from Paris, he had not visited for many years. When we arrived, after taking a good survey with his glass, he observed, "I find they now call the young ladies we used to call *figurantes, des rats de l'opéra;* I am curious to see them again." At this moment a whole army of young sylphides, more or less pretty, came fluttering across the stage. My friend looked at them attentively with his *lorgnette,* and at last exclaimed, with a sigh, " *Mais je ne reconnais plus ces rats-là."* " *Je crois bien, mon Général,"* said I, " *les vôtres n'auraient plus de dents pour grignoter leur prochain."*
Amongst the most remarkable dancers, were the inimitable Bigottini, Legros, Fanny Bias, Lacroix, Brocard, Noblet, Martin, Baron, and the short *trapue* Madame Montessu, with her large head, thick legs, and powerful *pointes.* It was a curious

sight to behold ambassadors and great state func-
tionaries assembled in the *foyer de danse*, paying
court to the *danseuses*. The most conspicuous of
these gentlemen were the Dukes de la Rochefoucauld, de Gramont, Fitzjames, and Maillé; all
attired in knee-breeches and opera hats, and with
buckles in their shoes, and frills and ruffles of the
costliest kind. After the opera, these same personages retired to the *Salon des Étrangers*, where
they generally spent an hour or two collecting all
the gossip they could hear, in order to divert the
king. There was not a scandalous story that was
not retailed by those gentlemen for their master's
recreation.

Among our countrymen who had the *entrée* to
the *foyer* or green-room, Lord Fife made himself
the most conspicuous by his unremitting attentions
to Mlle. Noblet, whom he never quitted for an
instant. He would carry her shawl, hold her fan,
run after her with her scent-bottle in his hand,
admire the diamond necklace some one else had
given her, or gaze in ecstasy on her pirouettes. On
his return to London, the old *roué* would amuse
George IV. with a minute description of the lady's
legs, and her skill in using them. Horses' legs are
frequently the cause of the ruin of numbers of our
aristocracy, but in the case of Lord Fife, the beautiful shape of the supporters of Mlle. Noblet had such
an effect upon the *perfervidum ingenium Scoti*,
that he from first to last spent nearly £80,000 on
this fair daughter of Terpsichore.

Another original much talked of about this time
was Sir John Burke, who married a Miss Ball
Hughes. He was known by the name of "The

Delegate Dandy," from having been sent on a mission to the Pope from the Irish Catholics. He was a great frequenter of the *coulisses* and the gaming-houses, where he would be seen nightly, rushing about from room to room, chattering the vilest French with unblushing effrontery; or making such a disturbance as to draw down on his head curses both loud and deep from the gamblers, which, however, he received with perfect equanimity and good-humour.

THE COUNTESS OF ALDBOROUGH.—From the first years I remember Paris, I became acquainted with Lady Aldborough, who had already acquired a kind of rather unenviable celebrity in the *beau monde*, for her *bons mots* and anecdotes of a peculiar kind. She spent many years of her long life in Paris, where she kept open house, and gave agreeable dinners, made up of pleasant men and good-looking women, not remarkable for any false modesty or affected prudery. Her sayings were quoted all over Europe, and she enjoyed a considerable share of popularity among a certain set, who admitted that her death (which occurred about twenty years ago) left a blank in Parisian society.

It behoves me in general to deal gently with the private characters of those who have gone to their last homes, but Lady Aldborough had no prejudices, and, far from being ashamed of the irregularities of her early life, continued in her old age to glory over them, and to speak of her past exploits with as much zest and ardour as some old veteran might recount his campaigns. Like the respectable old lady in Béranger's poem, she seemed to say—

" Combien je regrette
Mon bras si dodu,
Ma jambe bien faite,
Et le temps perdu ! "

Lady Aldborough's language was plain and un-varnished, and many hardened men of the world have been known to blush and look aghast when this free-spoken old lady has attacked them at her dinner-table with sundry searching questions respecting their tastes and habits; in the presence perhaps of their wives and daughters, who could not easily avoid hearing the stage whisper in which her remarks were conveyed to the ears of the unwilling listeners.

With a kind of cynical *naïveté*, Lady Aldborough has often said she was perfectly aware that many persons objected to her style of conversation, but that, unfortunately, all the wit and humour for which she was celebrated lay in that kind of jesting which the over-particular considered offensive.

In appearance she did not give one (at least in her later years) the impression of having been as handsome as her full-length portrait by Cosway would have led one to suppose. She was rather under the middle height, but well formed; and to the last preserved a slight figure and a neat foot and ankle. Her features were regular in outline, but somewhat sharp; and the expression of her countenance was stern, hard, and restless. Her voice had none of those mellifluous tones so appreciated by Byron; it was harsh and loud, partly, perhaps, owing to her deafness; her manner was abrupt and unequal; and her wit, which was undeniable, fluctuated between levity and sarcasm.

She did not possess the French art of wrapping up a joke of doubtful propriety : her witticisms wore no mask, and left her hearer very little chance of appearing not to understand them. When an attempt has been made by a luckless wife to feign innocence in the presence of a jealous husband, the old lady would tap her victim sharply on the hand with her fan, saying, with a sardonic smile, and in her clear voice, audible from one end of the room to the other—

"You understand very well what I mean, my dear."

Lady Aldborough had a very peculiar style of dress, which she continued to adopt till the latest period of her life. She wore habitually, when going out in the evening, a long white veil, which was fastened to her wig, and hung down to her feet ; white satin shoes with diamond buckles, very short sleeves and petticoats, and an extremely *décolleté* gown.

Every one arrived at middle age has heard of innumerable *bons mots* attributed to Lady Aldborough ; but, in newspaper phrase, they are generally "unfit for publication." It may, to a certain degree, be her excuse that the mode of speaking in the olden time was far plainer and coarser than anything which would be tolerated now-a-days ; and even ladies of very good reputation were guilty of using queer language, and, as Pope says, of "calling a spade a spade."

En résumé, Lady Aldborough was a woman of good sense, and capable, if called upon seriously, of giving her opinion on important matters, and with great judgment and feeling. I have known of her

doing many kind things to old friends, who had got
into awkward scrapes ; and if she spent a good deal
of money on herself, she was very charitable, and
always ready to extend a helping hand to the poor
and needy.

ELECTIONEERING IN 1832 — GRIMSBY. — In 1832,
I was residing in Chesterfield Street, in a house
that had once belonged to Brummell, when Parliament was dissolved.   A few days after this great
event, which threw all England into a state of excitement, I received a visit from the old Lord Yarborough, to ask me if I would stand for Grimsby.
After some hesitation, I consented to do so, and his
lordship therefore promised me his utmost support
and interest—but with one proviso, that I would
give him my word not to bribe.   I agreed to his
conditions, and started the following morning for
Lincolnshire.   On arriving at Grimsby, I found
that Henry Hobhouse and myself would have a
very sharp contest, and that the Tory candidates,
Captain Harris, of the navy, and Mr. John Shelley,
were already in the field.   I immediately commenced my canvass, which continued for several
days, and was apparently very successful.   When
the polling commenced, I thought myself sure of
being elected, when, on the second day, an apparently respectable man, and one of my best supporters, came to me and said — " There are four
persons of great influence to whom you must give
£100 apiece.   If you don't come in, I will engage
to return the amount to you myself; and if you
refuse to give the money, you are quite sure to be
beaten."

I told this gentleman that I had promised Lord Yarborough upon my honour not to use bribery, and therefore could not break my word. "Then the consequences be upon your own head," said my friend; who was, no doubt, himself one of the four influential persons who wished to see my money. However, what he said was perfectly true, for the numbers at the close of the poll were—

Harris,	.	.	.	.	200
Shelley,	.	.	.	.	192
Gronow,	.	.	.	.	187
Hobhouse,	.	.	.	.	173

Mr. Shelley, who was then a rather timid young gentleman, and who is now the radical M.P. for Westminster, had been told by some facetious friend, that if I got beat, I firmly intended to shoot him. He, in consequence, treated me, when on the hustings, with such marked and studied politeness as delighted the wicked wag and all his friends who had been let into the secret of this foolish hoax. The Tory party did not long enjoy their triumph, for a petition was presented, which cost Lord Yarborough many thousand pounds, but unseated Harris and Shelley. A new election took place, but I had had enough of Grimsby, and did not present myself: two Liberals were, however, returned; and the four influential gentlemen received, I have no doubt, their £100 apiece.

STAFFORD IN 1832.—Having discovered, by experience at Grimsby, the ill success of purity of election principles, I went down to Stafford on the dissolution in 1832, determined to leave no means

untried to secure my return. On the morning after
my arrival at the Star Inn, which became the headquarters of myself and friends, several hundred
electors assembled, in military array, under my
windows, and on my appearance received me with
three cheers. One of the leaders of this worthy
band of brothers—who, to do them justice, were
no hypocrites, but came immediately to business—
then spoke out thus:

"Now, Gronow, my old boy, we like what we
have heard about you, your principles, and all that
sort of thing; we will therefore all vote for you
if"—— Here every man in the crowd struck his
breeches-pocket several times with his open hand.
After this expressive pantomime, the speaker continued, "You know what we mean, old fellow? If
not—you understand—you won't do for Stafford."

His comrades loudly cheered their leader; and I
then made them a speech of some length, setting
forth the principles upon which I presented myself
to their notice, and solicited their suffrages; concluding by significantly assuring them that they
should all have reason to be well satisfied with
me.

I had plenty of money in those days, and was
determined that no one should outbid me for the
support of these worthy and independent gentlemen, so I set to work to bribe every man, woman,
and child in the ancient borough of Stafford. I
engaged numerous agents, opened all the public-
houses which were not already taken by my opponents, gave suppers every night to my supporters,
kissed all their wives and children, drank their
health in every sort of abominable mixture, and

secured my return against great local interest; for, at the close of the poll, the numbers were—

Chetwynd, .	.	.	.	.	392
Gronow,	.	.	.	.	253
Blount,	.	.	.	.	230

I sat during the whole of the first Reform Parliament for Stafford, but was beaten at the next general election by the long purse of Mr. Holyoake, now Sir Francis Goodricke, Bart.   Mr. Bonham, the whipper-in of the Tory party, told me, some years after this time, that Mr. Holyoake obtained his baronetcy from Sir Robert Peel for having succeeded in beating me on this occasion.

COUNTESS GUICCIOLI AND MADAME DODWELL.—I knew Madame Guiccioli by sight in her youthful days, when she was a celebrity, owing to her acquaintance with Lord Byron.   I was rather disappointed with her personal appearance, as, though handsome, she give one more the idea of a healthy, rosy, jolly-looking milkmaid, than a heroine of romance.

Madame Guiccioli was short in stature, and somewhat square-built; her hair was golden, her eyes were blue, her complexion and teeth beautiful in the extreme, and her face would have been much admired had she been taller.   As it was, there was a great disproportion between her colossal head and her short figure.   Her bust was also on a large scale, and very fine.   She was, like most Italian women, unaffected, kind, and matter-of-fact, but had nothing in physical appearance or intellectual gifts to account for her having inspired a romantic passion. She was " of the earth, earthy."

At the same period I was introduced to a person who for many years passed for being the handsomest woman in Europe—a Roman lady, who had married a very ugly old antiquary named Dodwell. The lovely Theresa had been offered the choice of a convent, or this ill-washed Briton. After much weeping and gnashing of her beautiful teeth, the lady, who was then only sixteen years of age, chose the latter.

Madame Dodwell was what English novelists describe as rather *petite* than otherwise, but her face was acknowledged by every painter, sculptor, and poet to be the most perfect in creation ; she had crisp, black, waving hair, the large, hazel, almond-shaped eye, full of Italian fire or Eastern languor, the classical features, the full mouth, magnificent teeth, and clear, pale, brunette complexion, so rarely met with. Perfectly illiterate, but full of wit and fun, this beautiful woman amused herself by chaining many victims to her triumphal car ; while, like a true Italian, her heart was faithful all the time to the one reigning attachment. She talked of her own beauty with as much simple composure as a man might have in dwelling on his horse or dog. With all this self-appreciation, she was perfectly unaffected, and had none of the grimaces of an acknowledged beauty, but remained calm and collected in the consciousness of her own undisputed superiority.

I was amused at a ball at the French ambassador's at Rome, at seeing her suddenly brought into contact with a new star that had risen in the firmament of fashion — the Duchesse d'I * * *, who had just arrived from Paris.

The Duchesse was some years Madame Dodwell's junior, and a formidable rival in many respects. She was very tall, and particularly brilliant in her general effect. She was dressed in the height of the then Parisian fashion, her hair *à la giraffe*, rolled in high bows, and decorated with artificial flowers. She looked magnificent; and a group of men gathered round to admire the new comer. I watched Madame Dodwell, as one of her disappointed *soupirants* came up, and rather maliciously asked her what she thought of *la belle Duchesse française*. The indifferent look the fair signora fixed upon the rival beauty was most amusing, and the only remark she made was—

" *Comment ! cette grande femme qui nous a apporté le Jardin des Plantes sur la tête !* "

THE LIGHT COMPANY'S POODLE AND SIR F. PONSONBY.—Every regiment has a pet of some sort or another. One distinguished Highland regiment possesses a deer; the Welsh Fusiliers a goat, which is the object of their peculiar affection, and which generally marches with the band. The light company of my battalion of the 1st Guards, in 1813, rejoiced in a very handsome poodle, which had, if I mistake not, been made prisoner at Vittoria. At the commencement of the battle of the 9th of December 1813, near the mayor's house, not far from Bidart, we observed the gallant Frederick Ponsonby well in front with the skirmishers, and by the side of his horse the soldiers' poodle. The colonel was encouraging our men to advance; and the poodle, in great glee, was jumping and barking at the bullets, as they flew round him like hail.   On a sudden, we observed Ponsonby struggling with a French mounted officer, whom he had already disarmed, and was endeavouring to lead off to our lines ; when the French skirmishers, whose numbers had increased, fired several shots, and wounded Ponsonby, forcing him to relinquish his prisoner and to retire. At the same time, a bullet broke one of the poor dog's legs.   For his gallant conduct in this affair, the poodle became, if possible, a still greater favourite than he was before ; and his friends, the men of the light company, took him to England, where I saw my three-legged friend for several years afterwards, the most prosperous of poodles, and the happiest of the canine race.

EXTRAVAGANCE—THE DUKE OF MARLBOROUGH, GRANDFATHER OF THE PRESENT DUKE. — Lord Blandford, afterwards fifth Duke of Marlborough, with many good and amiable qualities, was by far the most extravagant man I ever remember to have seen.   He lived in lodgings at Triphook's the bookseller in St. James's Street, whilst his father and mother resided in great state at Marlborough House. Although supporting himself upon money borrowed at an exorbitant interest, Lord Blandford would give Lee and Kennedy £500 for a curious plant or shrub ; and I well remember his paying £1800 for a fine edition of Boccaccio ; whilst his country-seat, Whiteknights, near Reading, was kept up with a splendour worthy of a royal residence.

His mother, the Duchess of Marlborough (of whom Queen Charlotte used to say, that she and

Lady Carlisle, grandmother of Lord Carlisle, were the two haughtiest and proudest women in England), had quarrelled with Lord Blandford for several years past. She persuaded the Duke to settle a large portion of the Blenheim estates, which were unentailed, upon his brother, Lord Francis Spencer, who was created Lord Churchill. Lord Blandford's allowance during his father's lifetime was insufficient for a person in his position. He was, therefore, obliged to have recourse to the Jews, who eventually ruined him. He was always very kind to me, and I lived a good deal with him and his sons when I was a young man.

I remember, in 1816, going down with him to Whiteknights; which was afterwards sold, and has since been pulled down. During our journey, Lord Blandford opened a sort of cupboard, which was fixed on one side of the coach in which we travelled, and which contained a capital luncheon, with different kinds of wine and liqueurs. Another part of this roomy vehicle, on a spring being touched, displayed a sort of *secrétaire*, with writing materials, and a large pocket-book; the latter he opened, and showed me fifty Bank of England notes for £1000 each, which he told me he had borrowed the day before from a well-known money-lender in the city, named Levy. He stated that he had given in return a post-obit on his father's death for £150,000; and added, "You see, Gronow, how the immense fortune of my family will be frittered away: but I can't help it; I must live. My father inherited £500,000 in ready money, and £70,000 a year in land; and, in all probability, when it comes to my turn to live at Blenheim, I shall have nothing left

but the annuity of £5000 a year on the Post-
Office."

Lord Blandford's prediction was verified; for when
I went to see him at Blenheim some years later,
and when he had become Duke of Marlborough,
he told me that I should find a great difference
between his magnificent way of living at Whiteknights, and his very reduced establishment at
Blenheim. He said that he had from the estate,
fish, game, venison, mutton, and poultry in abundance, and a good cellar of wine; but that he was
so involved that he could obtain credit neither in
Oxford nor in London, and that his sole revenue
(and much of that forestalled) was the annuity on
the Post-Office, which was inalienably secured to the
great Duke.

Fortunately for his successors, the vast estates of
the Marlborough family were strictly entailed, and
the present possessor has ample revenues, and is a
most worthy representative of one of the greatest
names in English history.

MALIBRAN AND GRISI.—Maria Malibran was still
in the zenith of her fame, when Giulia Grisi made
her appearance on the stage in Paris. She was not
at that period of her life the consummate actress
she afterwards became, but trusted a good deal to
the power of her personal attractions, as well as to
the singularly fine compass and sweet tones of her
beautiful voice, to insure the applause of the public.

Malibran was, on the contrary, the soul of music.
She was a grand being; that small, slight woman,
with flushed cheeks and ardent expressive eyes, consumed by the love of her art, and that one passion-

ate attachment which seemed woven into her soul, a part of her very being. I really believe that this blind idolatry for the man who afterwards became her husband, was the cause of the kind of frenzy with which she clung to her fame as an artist. She felt instinctively that she had been sought because she was celebrated, and that the applause which she elicited was the fuel which fed the flickering flame in De Bériot's heart. There can be no doubt that the dread that in losing the one, she might fail to keep the other, fastened on her heart and killed her.

Poor Malibran! Grisi's new-born fame was a canker-worm, eating into her very soul; and I truly believe not from a mean feeling of envy, but for the reason that I have assigned.

I remember hearing, some seven-and-twenty years ago, of a rather ludicrous scene which took place at L * * * House. At one of the celebrated concerts at that noble mansion, Malibran and Grisi were to sing a duet. Malibran did not make her appearance, and, after waiting a considerable time, the noble and courteous host supplied her place by an inferior artist, and Grisi had all the honours of the evening. In the midst of her triumph who should march in but the "Diva" herself, flushed with anger, her fine brow lowering, and her full lips compressed with anger. Lord L * * *, with that scrupulous urbanity which always distinguished him, advanced towards Malibran and made her a thousand apologies for having begun the concert without her, on account of the lateness of the hour. Poor Maria, by no means softened, and having caught sight of the beautiful face of her rival wreathed in triumphant smiles, saluted the astonished Marquis with a volley of abuse; to which he kept bowing politely till she had exhausted her vocabulary (a pretty large one), and had darted frantically out of the room.

Malibran was not regularly handsome, but I always thought her in her young days remarkably attractive. As she grew older, her features became coarser, and a certain bold, hard look settled on her face. Her head was well formed; her mouth, though wide, was prettily shaped, and adorned with very good teeth, and her small figure was graceful. Her voice was splendid, full of passion and pathos. Who that ever heard her in Desdemona, could forget that cry of struggling agony, "*Se il padre m'abbandona*" or the sorrowful wail of the blighted heart in the romance "*Assisa al pie d'un salice*"? She identified herself so thoroughly with the part she acted that it required some courage to face her in the last scene. She died "hard" and fought to the last; and Othello had to make a kind of steeplechase after her, and suffer many kicks and cuffs before he could, as an Irish friend of mine remarked, "bring her to rason by taking her life."

I was lucky enough to see the first representation of the *Puritani*, with that grand galaxy of singers, Lablache, Rubini, Tamburini, and Grisi; the like of whom, as a whole, will perhaps never be heard again. The bridal song, "*Son vergine vezzoza*," was one of Grisi's triumphs, and it must be allowed that it was impossible to look on a fairer sight than Giulia, with her long white veil flowing to her feet, carolling that sweet happy lay. Grisi's head and face, bust, arms, and hands, were almost faultless; her mouth and teeth were lovely beyond description; her hair was black as jet, and luxuriant

though not long, for which reason probably she
never let it fall completely down. But owing to
her rather thick waist, her large feet, and short legs,
the spell was broken when she attempted to run
across the stage in pursuit of Edgardo or Arturo.

As Grisi's beauty waned, or her voice lost some
of its rich, mellow notes, her good sense taught her
that she must study more, and act better. She set
herself conscientiously to work, and in the latter
years of her stage career gained the reputation of
being an admirable actress. She had not the pathos
of Pasta, nor the genius of Malibran, but she had
love for her art, and a desire to do the very best she
possibly could. She was neither huffy, capricious,
nor tricky; she neither feigned illness when she was
well, nor allowed a passing whim or fancy to interfere with her duty to the director or the public. A
good warm heart beat in that ample bosom, and no
one, I believe, ever heard of Giulia Grisi doing a
mean or unkind action.

LORD ALVANLEY.—From the time of good Queen
Bess, when the English language first began to
assume somewhat of its present form, idiom, and
mode of expression, to the days of our most gracious
sovereign Queen Victoria, every age has had its
punsters, humourists, and eloquent conversationists;
but I much doubt whether the year 1789 did not
produce the greatest wit of modern times, in the
person of William Lord Alvanley.

After receiving a very excellent and careful education, Alvanley entered the Coldstream Guards at
an early age, and served with distinction at Copen-
hagen and in the Peninsula; but being in posses-

sion of a large fortune, he left the army, gave himself up entirely to the pursuit of pleasure, and became one of the principal dandies of the day. With the brilliant talents which he possessed, he might have attained to the highest eminence in any line of life he had embraced.

Not only was Alvanley considered the wittiest man of his day in England, but, during his residence in France, and tours through Russia and other countries, he was universally admitted to possess, not only great wit and humour, but *l'esprit français* in its highest perfection ; and no greater compliment could be paid him by foreigners than this. He was one of the rare examples (particularly rare in the days of the dandies, who were generally sour and spiteful) of a man combining brilliant wit and re-partee with the most perfect good-nature. His manner, above all, was irresistible ; and the slight lisp, which might have been considered as a blemish, only added piquancy and zest to his sayings.

In appearance, he was about the middle height, and well and strongly built, though he latterly became somewhat corpulent. He excelled in all manly exercises, was a hard rider to hounds, and was what those who do not belong to the upper ten thousand call " a good-plucked one." His face had somewhat of the rotund form and smiling expression which characterise the jolly friars one meets with in Italy. His hair and eyes were dark, and he had a very small nose, to which, after deep potations, his copious pinches of snuff had some difficulty in finding their way, and were in consequence rather lavishly bestowed upon his florid cheek. He resided in Park Street, St. James's, and

LORD ALVANLEY.

LORD HILL.

LORD YARMOUTH.

THE LIGHT OF OTHER DAYS.

his dinners there and at Melton were considered to be the best in England. He never invited more than eight people, and insisted upon having the somewhat expensive luxury of an apricot tart on the sideboard the whole year round.

Alvanley was a good speaker; and having made some allusion to O'Connell in rather strong terms in the House of Lords, the latter very coarsely and unjustly denounced him, in a speech he made in the House of Commons, as a bloated buffoon. Alvanley thereupon called out the Liberator, who would not meet him, but excused himself by saying, "There is blood already on this hand,"—alluding to his fatal duel with D'Esterre.

Alvanley then threatened O'Connell with personal chastisement. Upon this, Morgan O'Connell, a very agreeable, gentlemanlike man, who had been in the Austrian service, and whom I knew well, said he would take his father's place. A meeting was accordingly agreed upon at Wimbledon Common. Alvanley's second was Colonel George Dawson Damer, and our late consul at Hamburgh, Colonel Hodges, acted for Morgan O'Connell. Several shots were fired without effect, and the seconds then interfered, and put a stop to any further hostilities.

On their way home in a hackney-coach, Alvanley said—"What a clumsy fellow O'Connell must be, to miss such a fat fellow as I am! He ought to practise at a haystack to get his hand in." When the carriage drove up to Alvanley's door, he gave the coachman a sovereign. Jarvey was profuse in his thanks, and said, "It's a great deal for only having taken your lordship to Wimbledon."

VOL. I.　　　　　　　　　　　　　　　　　x

"No, my good man," said Alvanley, "I give it you, not for taking me, but for bringing me back."

Everybody knows the story of Gunter the pastry-cook. He was mounted on a runaway horse with the King's hounds, and excused himself for riding against Alvanley, by saying, "O my lord, I can't hold him, he's so hot!" "Ice him, Gunter—ice him!" was the consoling rejoinder.

In the hunting-field in a northern county, Sir Charles S * * *, whose married life was not a very happy one, wore one morning at the meet a wonderful greatcoat, with enormous horn buttons. Alvanley, riding up to him, and apparently looking at the buttons with great admiration, said, "A little attention of Lady S * * * 's, I presume, Sir Charles?"

Alvanley had a delightful recklessness and *laisser aller* in everything. His manner of putting out his light at night was not a very pleasant one for his host for the time being. He always read in bed, and when he wanted to go to sleep, he either extinguished his candle by throwing it on the floor in the middle of the room, and taking a shot at it with the pillow, or else quietly placed it, when still lighted, under the bolster. At Badminton, and other country houses, his habits in this respect were so well known, that a servant was ordered to sit up in the passage to keep watch over him.

Alvanley's recklessness in money matters was almost incredible. His creditors having become at last very clamorous, that able and astute man of the world, Mr. Charles Greville, with the energetic and bustling kindness in mixing himself up in all his friends' affairs which still distinguishes him, had undertaken to settle those of Alvanley. After going

through every item of the debts, matters looked
more promising than Mr. Greville expected, and he
took his leave.   In the morning he received a note
from Alvanley, to say that he had quite forgotten
to take into account a debt of fifty-five thousand
pounds.

In his latter years Lord Alvanley was a martyr to
the gout, but preserved his wit and good-humour to
the last.   He died in 1849.

SALLY LUNN CAKES — THE ETYMOLOGY OF THE
WORD "BUN." — Some fifty years back or there-
abouts, Albinia, Countess of Buckinghamshire, lived
in her charming villa in Pimlico, surrounded by a
large and beautiful garden.   It was here she used
to entertain the *élite* of London society with magnificent *fêtes*, *bals champêtres*, and public breakfasts.
After one of those *fêtes*, I called one morning to pay
my respects ; and, on ringing the bell, the servant
ushered me into the conservatory, where I found
Lady Harrington, the celebrated cantatrice Mrs.
Billington, and the Duke of Sussex ; who was said
to be very much *épris* with the English " Catalani,"
as she was called.

Mrs. Billington was extremely beautiful, though
it was absurd to compare her to Catalani as a singer ;
but she was the favourite of the Duke of Sussex,
which made her many friends.   During my visit,
chocolate and tea-cakes were served to our party,
when Lady Harrington related a curious anecdote
about those cakes.   She said her friend Madame de
Narbonne, during the emigration, determined not to
live upon the bounty of foreigners, found means to
amass money enough to enable her to open a shop

in Chelsea, not far from the then fashionable balls of Ranelagh.

It had been the custom in France, before the Revolution, for young ladies in some noble families to learn the art of making preserves and pastry; accordingly, Madame de Narbonne commenced her operations under the auspices of some of her ac- quaintances; and all those who went to Ranelagh made a point of stopping and buying some of her cakes. Their fame spread like lightning through- out the West End, and orders were given to have them sent for breakfast and tea in many great houses in the neighbourhood of St. James's. Madamé de Narbonne employed a Scotch maid-servant to execute her orders. The name of this woman was "Sally Lunn," and ever since a particular kind of tea-cake has gone by that name.

Madame de Narbonne, not speaking English, re- plied to her customers (when they inquired the name of her *brioches*), "bon;" hence the etymology of "bun," according to Lady Harrington: but I confess that I do not feel quite satisfied with her derivation.

PICTON'S OPINION OF OUR OFFICERS. — During my passage from Ramsgate to Ostend, with Sir Thomas Picton, *en route* to Waterloo, to which I alluded in a previous page, the general, whose demeanour was stern and rather forbidding, and of whom we all stood very much in awe, was on this occasion in great good-humour and high spirits. He talked, with his usual oaths (which the reader will pardon me if I transcribe), a good deal about the Peninsular war, and the relative merits of the

English and French armies.   He greatly praised the
soldier-like qualities and military talents of the
French officers, and said—

"If I had fifty thousand such men as I com-
manded in Spain, with French officers at their head,
I'm d——d if I wouldn't march from one end of
Europe to the other."

We were all astounded at this praise of the
French; and Chambers, very much piqued, observed—

"This is the first time we have heard, Sir Thomas,
that French officers were superior to ours."

"What!" said Picton, "never heard they were
superior to ours? why, d——n it, where is our
military education? where our military schools and
colleges? We have none: absolutely none. Our
greatest generals, Marlborough and Wellington,
learnt the art of war in France. Nine French
officers out of ten can command an army, whilst our
fellows, though as brave as lions, are totally and
utterly ignorant of their profession. D——n it,
sir, they know nothing. We are saved by our
non-commissioned officers, who are the best in the
world."

We all felt very much disgusted and humiliated
at these remarks, and considered them at the time
very unjust; but I am now certain that the general
was right, and that our officers at that time, beyond
extraordinary dash and pluck, had none of the
qualities required in those who were destined to
command the finest troops in the world.

That true soldier, General Foy, in his history of
the Peninsular war, is of the same opinion as the
gallant Picton respecting our commissioned and

non-commissioned officers; and he had many good opportunities of judging, for he was opposed to us on many a hard-fought field; but now, thank Heaven, our system is much improved. Patronage can no longer do everything, and a strict examination is necessary for all candidates for commissions in the army.

ADMIRAL NAGLE.—Admiral Nagle was a great favourite of George the Fourth, and passed much of his time with his Majesty. He was a bold, weather-beaten tar, but nevertheless a perfect gentleman, with exceedingly pleasing manners, and possessed of much good-nature and agreeability. The late Duke of Cambridge on one occasion sent his brother a cream-coloured horse, from the royal stud at Hanover, and the king gave the animal to Colonel Peters, the riding-master. Admiral Nagle ventured to express a hope, that if his Majesty received a similar present from Hanover, he would graciously make him a present of it, upon which the king replied, " Certainly, Nagle, you shall have one."

The admiral was shortly afterwards sent to Portsmouth, to superintend the building of the royal yacht, during which time Strohling, the fashionable painter of the day, was summoned, and ordered to paint over the admiral's favourite hack, to make it appear like one of the Hanoverian breed. The horse was accordingly placed in the riding-school, and, in an incredibly short period, the metamorphosis was successfully completed. In due time the admiral returned from Portsmouth, and, as usual, went to the royal stables, and was charmed to see that his Majesty had fulfilled his promise. He lost no time in going to Carlton House to return thanks, when the King said, "Well, Nagle, how do you like the horse I sent you?" "Very much," was the reply; "but I should like to try his paces before I can give your Majesty a decided opinion about him." "Well, then, let him be saddled, though it does rain, and gallop him round the park and return here, and let me know what you think of him." It rained cats and dogs; the paint was gradually washed off the horse, to the admiral's great astonishment, and he returned to Carlton House, where the King and his friends had watched his departure and arrival with the greatest delight. The admiral was welcomed with roars of laughter, which he took with great good-humour; and, about a month afterwards, the King presented him with a real Hanoverian horse of great value.

THE LATE LORD SCARBOROUGH.—Lord Lumley, the late Lord Scarborough, was living in Paris in the winter of 1816; and, notwithstanding his lameness, was one of the gayest of the gay, ever attending dinners, balls, and *fêtes*. At a *fête* given by Lady Elizabeth Stuart, Lumley was flirting with one of the beautiful Lady Harleys, when Madame de Staël inquired of Lady Oxford the name of the person who was in conversation with her daughter. Her ladyship replied, Monsieur Lumley. "*L'homme laid! quel drôle de nom! mais c'est vrai; il n'est pas joli garçon!*" Ever after, he was known in Paris by the appellation of "*L'homme laid.*"

POTAGE À LA POMPADOUR.—We are apt to talk a good deal of the wisdom of our ancestors; but in the midst of a certain amount of civilisation, much rude magnificence, and great display, those good people were completely ignorant of, and unacquainted with many of the refinements and even necessaries of life, as the following anecdote will prove.

About a hundred years ago, in the reign of Louis the Fifteenth, when his mistress, the Marquise de Pompadour, governed France with absolute power, the Duke of Norfolk was much in favour with that lady. One morning, at her toilette,—to the close of which, consisting of powdering and hair-dressing, her friends were admitted, according to the custom of that time—when the usual compliments had passed, his Grace's attention was riveted to a certain article of furniture in a distant part of the room, of a somewhat octagonal shape, which was entirely new to him. As a considerable crowd of courtiers surrounded the royal favourite, he was able to approach something closer, and to discover that the object of his curiosity was of solid gold, with the Marquise's arms richly engraved, and that it was placed upon a wooden stand.

The Duke of Norfolk took an opportunity of inquiring from one of the *femmes de chambre* for what purpose this magnificent piece of plate was used; and the reply, given without any signs of bashfulness, struck him with utter amazement and some confusion. In the course of the day, the *soubrette* communicated this incident to her mistress, as rather a good joke; and Madame de Pompadour, who was anxious that the Duke should have some souvenir of his stay in France, and of her friendship for him, gave instructions to her silversmith to make another piece of plate exactly similar to that which had so much attracted his Grace's attention. It was very richly ornamented, and had the Duke's arms engraved on one side, and those of Madame de Pompadour on the other. It was carefully packed up, and forwarded to the Duchess of Norfolk, by a messenger belonging to the French court.

Upon receiving the present from the Marquise de Pompadour, the Duchess was delighted, and said—

"How very kind of the Marquise! I never saw so beautiful a soup tureen; I suppose its shape is *la grande mode* of the day!"

A few days after the present had been received, the Duke of Norfolk arrived from Paris, and a great dinner was given at Norfolk House to celebrate his safe return. In those days *les diners à la Russe* were not invented, and the dishes, of magnificent silver gilt, were placed upon the table, and served by those who sat opposite to them.

When dinner was announced, and the guests had sat down, the Duke was perfectly aghast with horror and amazement; for there in front of him he beheld the mysterious piece of plate filled with excellent mutton broth. The present of the fair Marquise is said to be still in existence in one of the country residences of the chief of the noble family of Howard, but restored from its culinary duties to the original legitimate purpose for which it was intended. But it is only on rare occasions, such as the visits of royalty, that this heirloom is displayed; when the taste of the fair Marquise is highly admired.

BEARDING THE LION IN HIS DEN.—In 1820, a friend of mine, belonging to the same battalion of

the Guards as myself, was sent from the Tower
with a detachment to the Bank of England. On
his arrival, he informed the porter that a lady
would present herself at the door about dinner
time, and that he was to escort her to the officers'
room. The porter meanwhile communicated with
the Governor, who sent strict orders that no female
was to be admitted within the walls of the Bank.
The lady in due time arrived, but was refused
admission.

The officer having been informed by one of the
sergeants that orders had been given by the Governor not to allow the lady to enter, ejected the porter
from his lodge, with many oaths and threats, and
gave it in charge to the sergeant. The porter ran
to the Governor, stating that the officer would place
the Governor and himself, if he caught him, in the
black-hole; for he swore that he commanded at the
Bank, and no one should interfere with him or his
visitors.

The Governor kept out of the way, but sent a
clerk to the commanding officer of the regiment,
stating what had occurred, who in his turn sent a
report to the Horse Guards of the whole affair.
The Duke of York desired my friend to appear before him next day, when he was asked by his Royal
Highness for an explanation. The officer admitted
all that had been reported of him, but declared that,
as he had been entrusted with the custody and safe
keeping of the Bank of England, he regretted not
having put the Governor into the black-hole for his
interference.

The Duke of York was so amused and tickled by
the coolness and *sang froid*, and I may say impu-

dence, of my friend, that he could not help laughing; and after a slight reprimand, asked him to dinner. The Duke used frequently to mention this anecdote to his particular friends as a very good joke; but he was the kindest of men, and I am not sure whether the young officer would not have found his escapade taken up in a very different manner by most commanding officers.

A MAD FRIEND.—Mr. Adam G * * *, a gentleman of large fortune, living in Hill Street, Berkeley Square, met me one afternoon in Hyde Park, and invited me to dine with him on the same day. He informed me that he had only asked two friends to dine with him; one of whom, he observed, I saw before me. A. G * * * was accompanied by a gentleman, who appeared to be a quiet and inoffensive person; but he held in his right hand a sort of life-preserver, which seemed rather strange. But as I did not know who the man was, I thought no more about it.

At seven, the hour of dinner, I made my appearance, and found the unknown gentleman waiting in the drawing-room. Dinner was shortly afterwards announced. It was excellent, and everything passed off peaceably, until my suspicions were aroused by hearing the person whom I had seen with A. G * * * in the park, and who was seated at our Amphitryon's left, say—

" You had better not drink any more wine! "

Soon afterwards we all left for the drawing-room, where coffee was served. Politics began to be discussed, and Lord Grey's name accidentally mentioned, when A. G * * * evinced considerable irritation, burst out into vehement abuse of that noble personage, and at last showed evident symptoms of insanity. Not wishing to witness any more proofs of this poor fellow's malady, I was preparing to leave ; when he cried out—

" Don't leave me, Gronow ; for that fellow," pointing to his friend, " is going to put the strait-waistcoat on me. He has rung the bell for his assistant." I appeared to grant his request, but was determined to make my escape ; and, in the act of opening the door, I found myself in the clutches of A. G * * *, who held me with a grasp of iron ; but, luckily, the keeper came to my assistance, and, after a struggle, released me.

The following night I called to inquire after my friend, and found that he had been removed to the neighbourhood of London for change of air. At the same time I was assured, that owing to the Reform Bill, which disfranchised a borough in Cornwall, where A. G * * * had expended a fortune in purchasing houses and building others, to secure his seat as M.P., this circumstance had the effect of driving him mad; and hence his aversion to the great originator of the Reform Bill.

Lord Althorpe.— Mr. Morier, formerly our minister in Switzerland, who had been Lord Althorpe's fag at Westminster, and always remained on terms of great intimacy with him, was calling one morning in Downing Street, at the time the noble lord was Chancellor of the Exchequer, and found him at breakfast. Mr. Morier, appearing to be struck by something he saw on the table, Lord Althorpe asked him what he was thinking of, when

Mr. Morier said, " I am looking at your teapots, Althorpe, for they appear to me to be wonderfully like those I used to clean for you when I was your fag."

"They are the very same teapots," replied the Chancellor of the Exchequer. "They remind me of my happy school-days, and I like to stick to my old acquaintances."

Lord Althorpe was rather singular in his dress. Even in the dog-days, he was always buttoned up to the chin ; and I once heard O'Connell say, that no one had ever been able to discover whether his lordship wore a shirt or not, for there were no visible signs of one, either on the neck or wrists ; but that it was evident he had made " a shift " to do without one.

Lord Althorpe was a bad and tedious speaker ; his financial statements, given out as they were with endless humming and hawing, and constant hesitation, made his hearers feel quite nervous and uncomfortable ; but he was possessed of great good sense, and was so upright and honourable a man, and such a thorough gentleman, that the Reformed House of Commons—a difficult one to manage— had more confidence in him than they would have had in any one else, however eloquent and fluent he might have been.

O'CONNELL.—During the time I was in the House of Commons, I saw a good deal of O'Connell, and frequently dined at his house in Great George Street. He was nowhere seen to more advantage than presiding at his own table, in all the pride of hospitality, surrounded by a numerous body of friends

and relations. His dinners were plain but good ;
there were always large joints and plenty of wine.
His conversation was most interesting : he had a
fund of anecdote, and used to relate most curious
stories about the Union and the state of society in
Ireland when he was a young man. Though a good
hater, he could do justice to political opponents ;
and I once heard him say, in speaking of Lord
Castlereagh, the minister, "Castlereagh, with all his
faults, was a fine fellow, and as brave as Achilles."

In the House I very often sat next to him ; he
was always gay and cheerful, and sometimes very
amusing : like most Irishmen, he was at all times
ready for a joke. I remember, on a division, when
the name of Charles Tynte did not appear on the
Government side, I expressed my astonishment, and
said there must be a mistake, as I always understood he was a Liberal.

"No, no, my good friend," said O'Connell ; "you
must henceforth set him down amongst the neutral
Tyntes" (tints).

SNUFF-TAKING.— Snuff-taking became generally
the fashion in France in the early part of the reign
of Louis XV. In the unfortunate reign of Louis
XVI., the beautiful Marie-Antoinette preferred bon-
bons to snuff, and prided herself on her *bonbonnières;*
while the old ladies of her court carried snuff-boxes
of immense dimensions, with the miniatures of their
lovers and children on the lid.

In England, Queen Charlotte, the grandmother
of our gracious Queen, was so fond of snuff, that
she was the principal cause of making it fashionable.
I recollect having seen her Majesty on the terrace

at Windsor walking with the King, George III., when, to the great delight of the Eton boys, she applied her finger and thumb to her gold box, out of which her Majesty appeared to have fished a considerable quantity, for the royal nose was covered with snuff both within and without.

All the old ladies in London took a prodigious quantity. I once called upon the old Duchess of Manchester in Berkeley Square, when she did me the honour to offer me a pinch of her best snuff. I was then young, but nevertheless accepted the Duchess's offer, and snuffled up a decent quantity; which made me sneeze for at least an hour afterwards, creating much mirth in the drawing-room, where many persons were assembled. The Duchess observed how happy she would be if snuff could have the same effect upon her nose as it had upon mine.

George IV. always carried a snuff-box; but it appeared to me as if his Majesty took snuff for fashion's sake. He would take the box in his left hand, and, opening it with his right thumb and fore-finger, introduce them into this costly reservoir of snuff, and with a consequential air convey the same to the nose; but never suffered any to enter; indeed, those who were well acquainted with his Majesty frequently told me he took snuff for effect, but never liked it, and allowed all of it to escape from his finger and thumb before it reached the nose.

I should say that the majority of men of fashion at the period I am speaking of carried snuff-boxes. If you knew a man intimately, he would offer you a pinch out of his own box; but if others, not so well acquainted, wished for a pinch, it was actually refused. In those days of snuff-taking, at the tables of great people, and the messes of regiments, snuff-boxes of large proportions followed the bottle, and everybody was at liberty to help himself.

It was reported that Brummell, who was cele-brated for the beauty of his snuff-boxes and the quality of his snuff, was once dining at the Pavilion with the Prince, and incurred his master's heavy displeasure in the following manner. The then Bishop of Winchester perceiving Brummell's snuff-box within his reach, very naturally took it up and supplied himself with a pinch; upon which Brum-mell told his servant, who was standing behind his chair, to throw the rest of the snuff into the fire or on the floor. The Prince all the while looked daggers: he gave Master Brummell a good wigging the following day, and never forgot the insult offered to the Bishop. Brummell was then apparently in great favour, but the Prince from that period began to show his dislike for the Beau on several occa-sions; and shortly afterwards quarrelled with him, and kept him at arm's length for the remainder of his life.

PETITION AGAINST MY RETURN FOR STAFFORD, AND LORD CAMPBELL.—On the assembling of the first Reformed Parliament, amongst the petitions presented was a very extraordinary one against my return for Stafford. I forget the exact wording of this precious document, but the purport of it was, that I ought to be unseated because I had not bribed the electors sufficiently. When Mr. Lee, the clerk, read out this humble petition, roars of laughter were heard from all sides of the House, and the Speaker, very much scandalised, ruled that it could not be received.

On leaving the House, I met the late Lord Campbell, then Solicitor-General, who had been M.P. for Stafford in the last Parliament. He immediately called out, "Here comes the immaculate Gronow, who did not bribe the electors of Stafford to their hearts' content." I replied that I supposed they expected me to give all the wives of electors pianofortes, as he was reported to have done; but that he had been quite right to bribe, as his election had made him Solicitor-General. Sir John Campbell laughed, and said I must not talk of bribery to one of his Majesty's principal law-officers; but added, "There is nothing like leather"—a cant expression which was, and I believe is still, used by the worthy and independent electors of Stafford, who are mostly shoemakers, and who take care to sell their leather at election time at a highly remunerative price.

THE LATE LORD DUDLEY.—The English have, as we all know, the reputation among foreigners of being *des originaux;* and I am inclined to believe that we are a queer race of people, and that there are more "characters" among us than are to be found abroad.

One of the most conspicuous of the eccentric oddities who flourished forty years ago was Lord Dudley and Ward. I need not speak of his powers of conversation, which were most brilliant when he chose to exert them, of his sarcastic wit, and cultivated intellect. These great gifts were obscured by a singular absence of mind, which he carried to such a pitch, that some persons maintained that much of this peculiarity was assumed. Rather an amusing anecdote is related of him, in which the " biter was bit ; " that is, supposing it to have been true that his " distractions " were not altogether genuine.

It happened one day that, coming out of the House of Lords, Lord Dudley's carriage was not to be found. It was late at night, and Lord Dudley, who was extremely nervous about catching cold, was in a frantic state of excitement. Lord H * * * kindly offered to set him down at Dudley House, which proposal was thankfully accepted. During the drive, Lord Dudley began, according to his usual custom, to talk to himself in an audible tone, and the burden of his song was as follows : —" A deuce of a bore ! This tiresome man has taken me home, and will expect me to ask him to dinner. I suppose I must do so, but it is a horrid nuisance."

Lord H * * * closed his eyes, and, assuming the same sleepy monotonous voice, muttered forth, " What a dreadful bore ! This good-natured fellow Dudley will think himself obliged to invite me to dinner, and I shall be forced to go. I hope he won't ask me, for he gives d——d bad dinners."

Lord Dudley started, looked very much confused, but said nothing. He, however, never forgave his friend ; for he prided himself upon being a good hater.

Another time, when dining with Lord W * * *, who particularly piqued himself upon his dinners, he began apologising to the company for the badness of the *entrées*, and excused himself for their

execrable quality on account of the illness of his
cook.

He was once paying a morning visit to the
beautiful Lady M * * *.   He sat an unconscionably
long time, and the lady, after giving him some
friendly hints, took up her work and tried to make
conversation.   Lord Dudley broke a long fit of
silence by muttering, " A very pretty woman this
Lady M * * *! She stays a devilish long time—I
wish she'd go."   He thought Lady M * * * was
paying him a visit in his own house.

At a dinner some thirty years ago at Sir George
Warrender's, Lord Dudley took out a beautiful
young married lady, who was extremely shy.   Sir
George was a singular mixture of extravagance and
economy, and though (for he was a renowned epicure, and commonly known by the name of Sir
George Provender) he fed his guests plentifully, the
warming department was neglected, and the atmosphere of the dining-room resembled that of Nova
Zembla.

Lord Dudley asked the young lady where she
would like to sit, and, out of pure shyness, she
pointed to the nearest chair, which happened to be
in the corner furthest from the fire.   After they
had sat down, she could hear Lord Dudley muttering angry sentences, in which she could almost
fancy she heard herself consigned to the depths of
an unmentionable place.   But what was her horror,
when, after shivering and shaking for some time
without speaking a word except to himself, Lord
Dudley turned round, and in an angry voice asked
for his cloak.   It was one of that large sort of
cloaks such as coachmen sometimes wore in Eng-

land, with a gradation of capes; and in this he wrapped himself, and remained during the whole of dinner without speaking a word to his fair neighbour.

Lord Dudley was for a short time Secretary of State for Foreign Affairs, but became more and more eccentric, and, not very long after his resignation, was obliged to be placed under restraint. He eventually, I believe, entirely lost his reason, and died in 1833.

INDEX.

———

THE END.

LIST OF SUBSCRIBERS UP TO 15th SEPTEMBER, 1984

A
Michael J. Abberton
J.S. Abbott
Vice-Admiral Sir
Conolly Abel Smith
Major J.W. Aggleton
M.B.E.
S.C. Alexander
J.A. Allen
J.H. Allen
James Allen
Sir Richard Allen
KCMG
J.R. Allt
Mrs M.R. Ambrose
Miss Diane Andrews
A.W. Anstey
Lt Col R.M. Arnold
D.A. Ashley
P.R. Ashley
P. Attenborough

B
Mrs R.W.S. Baker
Mrs W.T. Ballantyne
G.W. Barber
C.F.R. Barclay
John Barker
Lt Col B.A.S. Barnes
C.G. Barnett
F.J. Barratt
A.G.S. Barstow
W.G. Bate
E.T. Baxter
Paul Beale
J.R. Beaumont JP
DL
Walter Bee
Alan Beecham
Gp Capt R.E. Beeny,
OBE
Captain G.C. Belbin
RM (Ret)
N.J. Belcher
C.L.G. Bell
William Bell
Mark Bennett
D.V.B. Bennett

Sigi R. Bergmann
The Hon Sir Anthony
Berry
M.F. Berry
Mrs G. de V.
Beveridge
J.R. Bickford Smith
P.J. Bickford-Smith
Roger Bickley
Major K.R. McK
Biggs
Lavinia Jane
Bingham
Drayton Bird
R.J. Bird
B.R. Bird
Lt Col A.L. Birt
L.H. Stuart Black
A.J. Blackett-Ord
Peter Blacklock
Lt Col Sir Simon
Bland
B.H. Bliss
Otis Skinner Blodget
W.P. Blyth
A.H. Boddy
C.H.A. Bott
A.F. Boucher-Giles
G. Bourne-May
Dr J.R. Bowers
James T. Bowie
John G. Bowler
J.F. Boydell
Viscount Boyne
Captain A.J.
Bradshaw
Hon P.E. Brassey
G.W. Brazendale
CMG
Dr O.B. Brears CMG
S. Bridge
Mrs Richard Bridges
J.L. Bridges
Dr D.A. Brigg
Mrs M. Briggs
D.C. Bright
Frank Brightman
G.C.V. Brittain

Sir Ronald Brockman
D.H.V. Brogan
K.C. Brookes
P.M. Brown
Miss C. Brown
The Hon James Bruce
Sir Arthur Buchanan-
Jardine
T.F.J. Burland
Lieut A.G. Burns RN
T. Burrill
D.V.S. Burroughs
Sir Richard Butler
Dermot S.L. Butler

C
G.A. Calver
J.L. Campbell
L.R. Campfield
R.J. Canning
Robert Carew
A.M. Carr-Gomm
Major F.W.L.
Carslaw
Major J.S. Carter
A.G. Casewell
Mrs E.L. Catto
Sir Charles Cave Bt
The Earl Cawdor
Mrs E. Cawkwell
Gordon Cawthorne
Mrs A. Cazenove
Lord Charles Cecil
Major J.P. Chadwick
W.T. Chaffer
G.W.D. Chamier
P.M. Charles
Rosemary Cheetham
Mrs B. Chetwynd-
Stapylton
E.F. Choppen
Mrs J.B.W. Christie
J.R. Clack
D.L. Clarke
F. Clegg
R.H. Close-Smith
H.L. Coatalen
Tom Cochrane

J.W.G. Cocke
Robert Coggins
R.H. Collard
Lt Gen Sir G.
Collingwood KBE
Edwin Collins
Mrs S.P. Conan-
Davies
Capt I.S.M. Condie
M.L. Congdon
F.A. Connelly
J.C. Conner
Mrs C. Conway
Terence Cooke
J.M.C. Cooper
W.H. Cooper
Anthony Cooper
John Cope MP
Michael F. Corbett
M.H. Couchman
P. Roylance Court
B.R. Couzens
Mrs J. Cox
T.J.L. Cox
H.P. Craig
J.E. Craig
Col J.F. Cramphorn
TD DL
John Crawford
J. Creek
M.G. Cripps
J.P.O. Crowe
G. Cuttle

D
T.L.A. Daintith
J.C.P. Dalton
J.R. Dalton
N.B. Dance
M.E.T. Davies
Mrs J.A. Davis
Simon Daw
E.G.J. Dawe
Peter A.J. Day
C.V.W. de Falbe
Miss S. de Laya
G.R. Deacon
Mrs A.D. Deacon
Martyn J. Dearden
E. Dearing
Rowland P. Dell

Lord Denham
John Devaux
Mrs Peter Dixon
M.F. Dobbs
R.C.T. Dorsett
Viscount Downe
P.J. Downs
Dr J.J. Drever
Anthony Drewe
H.I. Duck
R.H. Dudley
C.D. Dunstan
P.G. Durrans
Daniel J. Dwyer

E
Sir George Earle Bt
A.C. Eaton
A.F. Eden
Major F.M. Edwards
K.C. Elkins
J.D. Ellis
F. Ellis
Mrs G. Elwes
Mrs R.P.S. Erskine-
Tulloch
M.G. Esther
M.R. Etherton
J.H. Etherton
C.A. Eugster
E.J. Evans

F
Dr J. Hamilton
Fairley
J. Fareham
T.C. Farmbrough
Y. Farrar
Major A. Farrant
Rev Matthew Farrell
CC
James Farrer
T.M. Fawcett
D.W.L. Fellowes
R.F.R. Fenwick-
Owen
Major R.S. Ferguson
S.A. Ferris
R.A.J. Finn
Mrs M.Y. Fisk
J.M. Fison

A.R. Fleming
Mrs E.C. Foden
Mrs S. Ford-Hunter
Dr C.A. Foster
Mrs D.J. Foster
Charles Fox
K.M. Fox
Mrs R. Fremantle
James A. Fresson
J.C. Fuller
Dr M.J.P. Furniss

G
R. de V. Gaisford
O. Gardener
Mrs Audrey Gardham
W.J. Garforth
A.F. Garnett
N.A. Gatrell
Ivan Gault
His Hon Judge S.S.
Gill
Sir William Gladstone
Bt
A.H. Goddard
Captain W.E.B.
Godsal RN
Major D.H. Godsal
RN
Mrs Bronwen
Goldsmid
His Hon Judge A.C.
Goodall
G.B. Graham
R.E. Greenwood
Capt J.S. Greenwood
J.S. Griffith
Brig E.L.G. Griffith-
Williams
Gordon Griffiths
His Hon Judge B.
Griffiths
J.D. Grossart
A.D. Gunner
P.L. Guy MH

H
Darby Haddon
Mrs P.R. Hadfield
J. Hafok
A.D.A.S. Hall

Mrs A.B. Hall
J.R. Hall
M.W. Hallaran
G.H. Hamilton Mack
Col J.G. Hamilton-
Russell
G.W. Hamlyn CBE
D.T.C. Hanbury
Guy Hannen MC
E.C.R. Hanquart
Donald R. Hanson
Mrs G.St J. Hardy
Lady E.M. Hardy-
Roberts
G.I. Harley
Mrs Rita F. Harris
C.E. Harrison
Philip J. Harrison
Mrs Patricia Harrison
Dr Nicholas Hart
Alan Hartnell
Count J. Havenaar
Kazimirski
Joseph Hawes
Dr P.W. Hawkes
Nicholas S. Hawksley
Sir Claude Hayes
KCMG
I.S. Haynes MFH
Sir Francis Head Bt
John Heald
S/Leader N.V.O.P.
Healey
James Heneage
Timothy Heneage
J.M. Henty
R.A. Herries
Christian Lady
Hesketh
M.D. Hewison
B.C. Heywood
E.C. Hicks
Brian Hicks
P.M. Higgins
S. de Premorel
Higgons
Peter Hiley
F.B. Hill
J.A. de C. Hill
G.E.D. Hiller
J.R. Hinchliffe

M.R. Hoare
Lady C. Hoare
A.R.A. Hobson
T. Hodson
Ivan Hoffe MRCVS
Sir Guy Holland Bt
David C. Hollis
Mr & Mrs R.W.J.
Hopkins
G.W. Hopkinson
H.L. Hoppe
J.M. Horsfall
Capt M.A. Houghton
Mr & Mrs M.J.
Howard
D. Howcroft
F.G. Howell
Dr M. Hughes
P.B. Hunter
James Hunter Blair
T.F. Hutchinson
Geoffrey Hutton

I
G.W. Iredell
C. Kenneth Irvine
J.G. Irving
H.B. Ismay Cheape

J
Mrs J.M. Jachim
L.A. Jackson
R.H. James
David Jeffcoat
C.P. Jenner MH
Mrs P.A. Jerram
The Earl of Jersey
B.J. Johnson
J.P. Johnson
L.E. Johnson
Cdr & Mrs D.M.
Johnson
W.S. Johnston
Arthur E. Jones
Timothy Jones
H.L. Jukes

K
L.S. Kale
Mrs E. Kay

C.A.G. Keeling
J.E. Kelly
Francis Kelly
J. Kenneth
F.C. Kent
Dr D.F. Kerr
Alistair W.J. Kerr
T.W. Killick
T. Kimber
Jonathan G.N. King
Dr Mary Ellen Kitler
D.A. Knight
S.J. Knowles
M.S. Kochanski
J.M. Kolbert
H.P. Kos

L
L.P.F. L'Estrange
OBE FRSA
Dr F.B. Lake
Miss H. Lambert
Col F. Lane Fox
Mrs V.A. Langridge
R.J.O. Lascelles
The Hon Hugh
Lawson-Johnston
Clare Le Vay
Simon Lebus
M.S. Ledger
D.A. Lee
G.D. Lees
His Honour Judge
C.N. Lees
Frank Lehmann
Mrs E.M. Lethbridge
J.W.P. Lewis
Sir Anthony Lincoln
KCMG CVO
Dr Charles Lipp
William Lister
Maj Gen R.E. Lloyd
Surgeon Captain
J.A.N. Lock
T. Longuet-Higgins
John Lonnen
C.L. Loyd MC JP
The Hon Mrs
Anthony Luard
Dr S.B. Lucas
P.H. Lucas

P.M. Luttman-Johnson

M

R.A. Macdonald
Lt Col C.H.T. Macfetridge
R.D. Mackay
The Rev Hugh Mackay
S.C.R. Mackean
J.H.M. Mackenzie
J.A.H.M. Mackenzie
D. Mackessack
Lt Col G.J.H. Mackie
N.G. Mackinley
Macleod
I.S. Mackinney
K.M. Macleod DSC
J.J. Macnamara
R.N. Alington Maguire
Joan Mahony
Capt Dugald Malcolm
Mrs C.G. Malfroy
D.C. Mansel Lewis
A. Marchant
Major H.D.G. Martindale
Peter I. Maslen
R.J. Mason
Alan Mason
Brig P.H.M. May
H. Maynard
John McCaig
J.N. McClean
Peter O. McDougall
Dr Ewen McEwen
D.J. McGlynn
W.A. McIntosh
Colin McIntyre
Stuart McKeever
Mrs Sheila McKinley
Mrs Christine McLean
M.D. McMillan
J. McMullen
M.A. Meacham
C.J. Mears
W.J. Melrose
T.J. Mercer
R.G.C. Messervy

John C. Michaelson
The Lord Middleton
Col D.A.N.C. Miers
A. Mildmay-White
H. Raoul Millais
A.P. Millen
C.H. Millin
D. Mitchell
G. Money-Coutts
E.G.H. Moody
R. More O'Ferrall
David J. Morgan
I.J. Morgan
G.S. Morgan-Grenville
G.E. Morris
Mrs G.F. Morris
Maxwell Morris
Sir William Mount Bt
J.W. Munn
John Murray QC

N

M. Nairn
Mrs S.J. Nash
P. Naylor
John Wynne Naylor
David Negus FRCS
C.S.W. Newbury
Major C.L.D. Newell
M.W. Newton
M.T. Nicholson
A.T.R. Nicholson
Mrs R.A.B. Nicolle
R. Le N. Noble
W.R. Norman
A.H.W.P. Norton
D.H.L. Nugent

O

Edward P. O'Doherty
C.P. O'Donoghue
D. O'Halloran
Roseanne O'Reilly
James A. Ogilvie
J.M.Y. Oliver CC
Sir Ronald Orr-Ewing Bt

P

Sir Julian Paget Bt
N.H. Pakenham Mahon

Michael W. Parrish
E.B. Park
Anthony V. Parker
H.M. Parker
Jonathan Pearson
R.T. Pearson
Mervyn R.C. Peckham
R.S.L. Penn
R.W. Perceval
D.J. Peters
V.M. Pettifer
A.N. Phillips
Dr A.J.B. Phillips MB BS
C.N. Phipps
Sir Charles Pickthorn Bt
W.L. Pilkington
A.H. Pincis
F.S. Pitt
Mrs L. Plank
David J. Pollard
Mrs Pooley
Dr Vincent Powell-Smith
Philip J.M. Prain
J.S. Prescot
Col R.F. Preston
J. Maurice Price QC
C.H. Priestley
Mr & Mrs John Pringle
Timothy Proctor
Mrs F.E.M. Puxon

Q

John Quayle

R

M.F. Race
Maj Gen Sir Digby Raeburn
R.W.R. Rainsford Hannay
R.S.C. Ralli
J.H. Ratcliff
Major J.C. Ratcliffe
Major D.W. Rayner
Peter Read

P.F. Rednall
P.J.D. Regester
Dr Robert Reid
N.J. Reid
Mrs E.J. Reid
Dr R.E. Rewell
Colonel J. Richards
Sir Charles Richmond
Brown
C.W. Richmond-
Watson
Andrew W.G. Rickett
Capt N.J. Ridout
Mrs Margaret Ritchie
T.J. Roberts
W.I. Roberts
J.C. Robertson CBE
Wg/Cdr S. Robinson
RAF (Rtd)
M.L.R. Romer
D.R. Rosevear
C.M. Ross
The Lord Rothermere
Pamela Rowe
The Rev A.G.B.
Rowe
R.A. Russell
Dr E. Barbara A.W.
Russell
J.F. Rutherford

S
Simon Sainsbury
R.P.A. Sale
Captain G.E.
Sampson RN
Anthony Sanford
F.W. Saunders
Henry J. Saunders
John N. Savory
Anthony A. Scott
J.D. Scouller
Dr J.P. Scrivener
Gerald E. Seager
Alan Sears
J.C. Sedgwick
William Seymour
A. Seymour-Jones
M.M. Shannon
M.E. Sharp
Julian B.C.W. Sharp

V.K. Sharpington
Dr M.E. Sheard
A.J. Shears
Mrs W.E. Sherston
Mrs M.N.H. Short
Stuart Sillars
Miss Sarah Sills
C.A.G. Simkins
M.K.O. Simpson-
Orlebar
Henry G. Skinner
Harold Smith
N.L.H. Smith
Robert S. Smith
S.T. Smyth
Mrs Maureen Smyth
L.E. Snellgrove
Mrs I.J. Barclay Sole
Peter A. Spanoghe
Sir John Sparrow
R.G.T. Speer
The Hon Mrs Stacey
H.J.A. Stanford
W.K. Stead
E.W. Stearn
Mrs S.R. Stebbing
T.F.G. Stevens
J.R. Strong FRCS
D.B. Sumpter
P.A. Surtees
Dr R.N.P. Sutton
A. Symonds

T
E. Talbot Rice
Alec I. Taylor
Maurice Taylor
Mrs C.A. Taylor
Miss Bridget Temple
E.H. Thomas
M.R.C. Thomas
Peter C. Thomas
Hugh R. Thomas
Donald Thompson
MP
Edward Thompson
Ray Thompson
M.G. Thomson
Brig M.C. Thursby
Pelham
E.H. Tindall

Bruce Todd
Maj Gen D.A.H.
Toler
H.W. Townsend
J.J. Trapp
D.W. Tudor-Pole
T.S. Turnbull
M.T. Turnbull
R.C. Tyrrell

U
R.J. Unstead

V
D.B. Vale
S. van Praet
D'Amerloo
Mrs Susan
Verberkmoes
Major The Hon N.H.
Villiers

W
Michael Wace
T. Wainwright
Dr Peter Wakely
Richard Walduck
J.H. Walker
Major P.J.R. Waller
MBE DL
B.J. Wallis
W.J.F. Ward
Miss Jean Wardrop
W.A. Warre
A.T. Warwick CEng
MIEE
R.K. Watson
M.R. Watson
C.M. Watt
I.H. Wear
Mrs H.D. Webb
Dr Paul Wellings
C.R. Wells
R.G. Wells
Lady Wells
E. Davan Wetton,
CBE
William R.G. West
G. Westall
Col L.H.M. Westropp
George A. Wheatley

G.H.H. Wheler
M. Whitaker
Humphrey Whitbread
C.R. White
Edmund H. White
Mrs S.K. White
R.H. White
A.P. Whitehead
F.R. Whitmarsh
J.C.A. Whitworth
H.H. Wicks
F.N.H. Widdrington
J.G.S. Wilkinson

W.H.G. Wilks
J.P. Williams MChir
John Williams
Major General
E.A.W. Williams
Lt Col G.T.G.
Williams
John Winch
R. Windsor-Clive
Barone R. Winspeare
John Winter
Harry Wolton
Douglas J. Wood

Major M.G.
Woodhams
F.A. Woods
W.D. Wright
Mrs David Wright
Dr R.F. Wyatt
C.P. Wykeham-
Martin

Y
John H. Yarroll
N.W.S. Yonge

PUBLICATIONS OF
THE R.S. SURTEES SOCIETY

SOME EXPERIENCES

and

FURTHER EXPERIENCES OF AN IRISH R.M.

by E. Œ. Somerville and Martin Ross

Some Experiences and *Further Experiences* each contain twelve episodes in which Major Sinclair Yeates recounts, with sober dignity, humour and tolerance, his social, sporting and professional discomfitures as a Resident Magistrate in south-west Ireland at the turn of the century. The rhetoric and deceit of the natives provide the wit and drama. Circumstances make Major Yeates a connoisseur of whole-hearted insincerity.

The R.S. Surtees Society's editions of *Some Experiences* and *Further Experiences* are as nearly as practicable facsimiles of the first editions, of 1899 and 1908 respectively. They include the black and white illustrations by **Miss Somerville** from the first editions (30 in *Some Experiences* and 35 in *Further Experiences*) and an Introduction by **Molly Keane** who wrote the best-seller *Good Behaviour* and has lived most of her life in Southern Ireland.

Price **£7.95,** in each case, packing and postage included. Instructions for ordering are on page 363.

R.S. SURTEES

Mr. Sponge's Sporting Tour. Facsimile of 1853 edition. 13 full-page coloured plates and 90 engravings by **John Leach.** Introduction by **Auberon Waugh.**

Mr. Facey Romford's Hounds, 24 plates by **Leach** and **'Phiz'.** 50 engravings. Introduction by **Enoch Powell.**

"Ask Mamma". Facsimile of 1858 edition, 13 plates and 70 engravings by **Leach.** Introduction by **Rebecca West.**

Handley Cross; or, **Mr. Jorrocks' Hunt.** Facsimile of 1854 edition. 17 plates and 100 engravings by **Leach.** Introduction by **Raymond Carr.**

Jorrocks' Jaunts and Jollities. Facsimile of 1874 edition. 31 plates by **Henry Alken, 'Phiz'** and **W. Heath.** Introduction by **Michael Wharton** ('Peter Simple').

Price £14.95 in each case, post free. Prices for separate sets of coloured plates are *Sponge* £5, *Romford* £8, *"Ask Mamma"* £5, *Handley Cross* £6 and *Jaunts and Jollities* £8.

The Horseman's Manual: being a treatise on Soundness, the Law of Warranty and generally on the Laws relating to Horses. Surtees' first book, published in 1831. Hugh Davidson has published a numbered facsimile edition of 600 copies, of which 180 remain.
Price £10.50, packing and postage included.

Special Offer. **Mr. Facey Romford's Hounds,** with uncut pages (which some members prefer and of which 70 copies remain) is offered at £12.20.

Further R.S. Surtees novels After *Hillingdon Hall,* to be available at the end of March 1985, (see advertisement at the beginning of this book) it is the intention of the Society to publish **Plain or Ringlets?** and **Hawbuck Grange** at yearly intervals. As in the case of the earlier publications they will be facsimiles of the best of the earlier editions. With their republication the Society will have republished all eight of R.S. Surtees' completed novels.

Captain Gronow

Further copies of this volume of Gronow's Reminiscences are available at £14.95, packing and postage included.

For the second volume the pre-publication prices are, until 31st May, 1985, £11.50 for books which are collected and £13.50 for books which are posted.

For full information, see the advertisement at the beginning of this book.

Illustrations available separately

Complete sets of the full-page plates which appear in the Society's publications are offered at the following prices, which include packing and postage.

Mr. Sponge's Sporting Tour. 13 coloured plates by John Leech. Price £5.

Mr. Facey Romford's Hounds. 24 coloured plates, 14 by Leech and 10 by 'Phiz'. Price £8.

"Ask Mamma". 13 coloured plates by Leech. Price £5.

Handley Cross. 17 coloured plates by Leech. Price £6.

Jaunts and Jollities. 31 plates of which 21 (coloured) are by Henry Alken, 1 (coloured) by W. Heath and 9 (uncoloured) by 'Phiz'. Price £8.

The Reminiscences of Captain Gronow. 17 coloured plates. Price £6.

Ordering

Send your order to **the Hon. Mrs. Robert Pomeroy, R.S. Surtees Society, Rockfield House, Nunney, Nr. Frome, Somerset.** Please show your requirement, name and address clearly. Your order should be accompanied by a cheque for the appropriate amount, made payable to the R.S. Surtees Society. If you are ordering more than one item, it would be helpful if you would include a note showing how the sum on your cheque is made up.

Books to be collected

Pre-publication subscribers for *Hillingdon Hall* and/or *The Reminiscences of Captain Gronow II* who choose to collect their books must collect them from J.A. Allen & Co. Ltd., 1 Grosvenor Place, Buckingham Palace Road, London, S.W.1. They will be notified when their books are ready for collection.

J. A. ALLEN & CO. (THE HORSEMAN'S BOOKSHOP) LTD.

1 LOWER GROSVENOR PLACE, LONDON, SW1

(Adjacent to Royal Mews, Buckingham Palace).

**For Over Half a Century we have
Specialised in Books Old & Modern
On Hunting and all Equine and
Equestrian Sports**

Catalogues Issued

Telephone 834/5606 (3 lines)